WITHDRAWN

P.65

Computer Monographs
GENERAL EDITOR: Stanley Gill, M.A., Ph.D., Chairman, Software Sciences
  Holdings Ltd, London

ASSOCIATE EDITOR: J. J. Florentin, Ph.D., Imperial College, London

Quick COBOL

Quick COBOL

L. Coddington

Macdonald · London and
American Elsevier Inc. · New York

Sole distributors for the British Isles and Commonwealth
Macdonald & Co. (Publishers) Ltd.
49–50 Poland Street, London W.1

Sole distributors for the United States and Dependencies
American Elsevier Publishing Company, Inc.
52 Vanderbilt Avenue New York N.Y. 10017

All remaining areas
Elsevier Publishing Company
P.O. Box 211, Jan van Galenstraat 335, Amsterdam, The Netherlands

British SBN 356 03899 8
American ISBN 0 444 19587 4
Library of Congress Catalog Card No. 71 164899

Made and printed in Great Britain by
Balding & Mansell Ltd., London and Wisbech

Contents

COBOL A definition . . .

The name COBOL stands for COmmon Business Oriented Language. It is a system for writing computer programs, particularly for commercial and non-scientific applications, in a language that is not too far removed from ordinary English. This makes it very easy to learn, and it is particularly suited to people without computer training: it is possible to write useful and efficient programs after only a short study. COBOL is not, however, a language specially designed for beginners: COBOL programs can be written in a fraction of the time needed for writing programs in 'low-level' languages, and they can be much more easily amended and understood. For this reason, thousands of programs have been written in COBOL—it is probably the most widely used programming language. No computer worthy of the name is put on the market without a 'compiler', a program that will take COBOL programs written in the language described in this book, and convert them into computer-language programs.

... and an acknowledgement

COBOL is an industry language and is not the property of any company or group of companies, or of any organisation or group of organisations.

No warranty, expressed or implied, is made by any contributor or by the COBOL Committee as to the accuracy and functioning of the programming system and language. Moreover, no responsibility is assumed by any contributor, or by the Committee, in connection therewith.

Procedures have been established for the maintenance of COBOL. Inquiries concerning the procedures for proposing changes should be directed to the Executive Committee of the Conference on Data Systems Languages.

The authors and copyright holders of the copyrighted material used herein (FLOW-MATIC (Trademark of Sperry Rand Corporation), Programming for the UNIVAC © R I and II, Data Automation Systems copyrighted 1958, 1959, by Sperry Rand Corporation; IBM Commercial Translator Form No. F28–8013, copyrighted 1959 by IBM; FACT, DSI 27A5260–2760, copyrighted 1960 by Minneapolis-Honeywell) have specifically authorised the use of this material in whole or in part, in the COBOL specifications. Such authorisation extends to the reproduction and use of COBOL specifications in programming manuals or similar publications.

Macdonald acknowledges the permission of International Computers Limited to reproduce the copyright form on page 236.

Introduction

1.1 About this book

1.1.1 The aim of the book

This book is intended to be useful to two classes of people.

It is addressed primarily to *users* of computers—the department head or line manager, the production controller, the accountant, the auditor, the doctor, or bank manager, or solicitor, or student who is involved, or who is about to be involved, with computers, either as an occasional customer or as one who finds that the major portion of his work is to be done by computer, or as the man who is ultimately responsible for the use of the computer in the firm.

The second class of people is computer personnel, who want an easier introduction to COBOL than is normally provided in the manufacturer's handbooks.

There is no need to explain how the book will be useful to this second class. They can read it straight through (starting at Chapter 2 if they are familiar with basic programming concepts) and start writing their COBOL programs.

The utility of the book for the first class is more open to controversy. Some managers and executives don't want to know about computers—they want to use them, they say, and don't want to know their workings any more than they do the workings of the telephone. It would be interesting to explore how far this attitude is responsible for the frequent failure of management to get full value out of their computers; but all we need say here is that the book is not for them. On the other hand, many managers do get interested in computers, and it is to them that this book is addressed. Some of them may write programs themselves; many will feel that it is a good thing to know more about computers, without worrying too much about whether they 'need to know' or not. The knowledge they acquire from this book will do something to enable them to work better with computer people, to explain what they want the computer to do, to understand the limitations of computers, to set and accept realistic deadlines for programming. It may well prove to be a useful introduction to programming in general, as well as to the COBOL language in particular, but it is not primarily a book on 'Computers for the

1

Manager'—there are already many excellent ones—much less a book on computer fundamentals, or programming techniques as such, or the principles of data handling and electronic data processing. Of course it has to touch on broader questions from time to time, but it is essentially a book covering a restricted field with a restricted aim: to fill in just *one* of the gaps between the manager and his computer.

The book is, I hope, readable: it is not as easy as a novel—its readers are, after all, expected to be prepared to put in some concentration and effort; but it is probably not as difficult as a textbook on chess or bridge (programming is not unlike a skilled game, say one of the sophisticated forms of patience). But it is meant to be *read*, in a bus or train or car or aeroplane, perhaps, and for this reason (and others) there are no exercises, though the reader is sometimes invited to complete or vary an example, or to ring the changes on the examples he has been given. What is *much more* important than exercises is that the reader should think constantly about his own applications, and ask himself 'How would I use this routine in my own work? What are the "data-names" I would assign if I were programming my own records?' This is really the only way to apply computer knowledge to your own requirements; set-pieces on particular applications are of no interest to those who do not use that application, inadequate to those who do—and, in a way, they obscure the idea of *general purpose* computers and languages.

1.1.2 Your technical knowledge

One can write a program with only a minimal knowledge of how a computer works (the difficulty is to convince learners that this is true). It seems reasonable to expect that anyone who starts on a book on programming has at least that minimal knowledge; all that you need can be gained from a one day 'appreciation' course, or the most elementary introduction. As long as you understand that:

—'information' can be entered ('input') into the computer by means of cards or paper tapes which have patterns of holes punched in them to represent letters and digits;

—that these cards or tapes produce patterns of electrical pulses, six or eight for each character of information;

—that these electrical patterns can be stored and remembered in specific 'locations' in the computer's store (sometimes called its 'memory' or 'core store' or simply 'core', because it is composed of magnetic rings or 'cores') and can be manipulated and retrieved ('output') from it as necessary, for example, by printing;

then you will not find any portion of this book incomprehensible by reason of a lack of understanding of the working of computers. In particular, it is not necessary to know anything at all about binary arithmetic, octal or hexadecimal coding, or other such topics; you can think entirely in terms of letters, digits, words, and other familiar concepts. It *is* desirable to know some of the characteristics of punched cards, tape, printers, and other 'peripherals' of the computer, because they represent the means by which the computer communicates with the outside world.

1.3 The scope of the book

The criterion I have tried to apply all through this book is: Is this the sort of thing the beginner will need to know? or will understand? or will want to use? Or, on the other hand, should it be omitted because it will confuse him at this stage—better to leave it, because he will learn it the more easily later on when he is more familiar with the language; or is such a facility likely to be too dependent on the particular computer you happen to have, or on the implementation that you are using? Sometimes, too, I have had to deal more briefly than I would have liked with programming techniques that are not, strictly speaking, part of COBOL. This is essentially a subjective judgement, reflecting my own experience and practice, and I cannot expect everyone to agree with it. I can only hope that any experienced programmer who happens to look through the book will not condemn it if it omits his own favourite programming tricks, or attempts to explain, in simple terms, something which he knows to be in fact much more complicated. It is, after all, one man's book, not the product of a committee.

One type of decision that has been particularly hard arises from the number of different COBOL implementations that are in use. This book corresponds by and large with the lowest level of the American National Standards Institute's COBOL, though I have departed from that (infrequently) where it seemed that learners might benefit, for example, in the use of commas and semicolons. A history of COBOL, and a more detailed account of the extent to which this book describes ANSI COBOL, will be found in Chapter 4 and Appendix 1.

However, a number of implementations now widely used were written before the ANSI standard was published, and one certainly cannot criticise them for not conforming to it (in some respects nonstandard implementations may fairly claim to be better than the standard). It would be an almost impossible task, and certainly beyond the scope of an elementary book, to indicate every point at which some implementation may differ from that described here. I have adopted the compromise of indicating the likeliest points at which the programmer should check whether his COBOL is peculiar. The learner should not be put off by this; possibly the expert will be more concerned about these divergences than the tyro will be! Nor should he think that the expression 'the lowest level of COBOL' implies that he is getting a somehow inferior brand; the lowest level of COBOL is completely self-contained as a programming language, and in fact many experienced programmers find it quite adequate for writing practical and efficient programs, and do not bother to learn, or use, the more advanced and difficult features—which often do little more than provide more concise methods for doing what can be done at the lowest level.

1.1.4   The plan of the book

Chapter 1 is for absolute beginners, who have the minimum of computer knowledge. It describes how a simple process that we carry out without thinking about can be described in a slightly more formal style that approximates to computer languages. This simple example is used to illustrate looping and decision-making.

Anyone with any experience at all of programming can start with Chapter 2. Here the simple process described in Chapter 1 is written as a COBOL procedure, and the elements of the Procedure Division are explained, to give a quick preview of the elements of COBOL; after which we embark on 'six easy lessons' each illustrating, by means of a COBOL program, some features of the Data and Procedure Divisions.

In Chapter 3 we deal with more advanced COBOL facilities that are more easily and economically dealt with by a systematic exposition, in narrative form, than by illustrative programs.

There is, inevitably, some ground covered more than once in Chapters 1, 2, and 3 but this method has the advantage that the reader gets an early introduction to a 'working' COBOL that will enable him to write operational programs by the end of Chapter 2 if not before; and in any case the parts that are reiterated are the important and basic ones, and are none the worse for being repeated from different aspects!

Finally, Chapter 4 illustrates the use of COBOL, not by a single set-piece for some specific application, but by describing applications routines that are the 'building blocks' of all programs; here, the manager should begin to see the relevance of COBOL to the work he wants his computer to do. Chapter 4 also contains practical hints on the writing of programs, and other information that will be of use to the budding programmer.

1.2 About programs

2.1 A model program

A simple arithmetical routine will do very well to illustrate the concept and construction of a program. Let us suppose that we have a list of numbers, in pairs:

$$123 \quad 145$$
$$234 \quad 701$$
$$321 \quad 543$$
$$\dots \quad \dots \quad \text{and so on;}$$

and we wish to add together the numbers in each pair, and, when we have added together all the pairs, print out the highest total found. If the list consisted merely of the three pairs shown above, the 'output' would be 935, the sum of 234 and 701.

Do not be misled by the simplicity of this program into thinking that it is trivial. As we shall show, it embodies the fundamental features of a computer program and the basic principles that make the computer such a useful tool.

5

The main difficulty that most people have in converting such a process into computer terms is that we have all been so well trained (or 'programmed') in our early years to do this sort of thing, that we do it without giving any thought at all to the actual steps involved. It may help if we think of the task being done with the help of a desk adding machine, with a keyboard and 'register' in which the results appear—a cash register would do. Then we read a pair of numbers, enter them into the machine by pressing the appropriate keys and an Add key; and then make a note on a piece of paper of the result. We repeat the operation with the second pair; we do not need to write the result if it is *less* that the previous one; if it is not less, we cross out the first total and substitute the second, which is now the 'Last Highest Total'. We may describe this process rather more formally:

1. Read (the next) pair of numbers.
2. Add them.
3. If the total of this pair is smaller than the Last Highest Total, ignore the current total and go back to instruction 1. Otherwise—
4. Copy the current total in place of the 'Last Highest Total'; then go back to instruction 1.

And when there are no more numbers, stop.

Two points may be bothering the attentive reader:

1. When the first pair of numbers is added, there is no 'Last Highest Total' to compare them with; so we assume that at that point the 'Last Highest Total' is zero, which means that after the first comparison the first sum is entered there. When we have finished all the pairs, the number in Last Highest Total is the answer.

2. The case where a current total is equal to the Last Highest Total already recorded is implicitly provided for: we replace the last highest total unless the current total is smaller. This means that if they are equal, the current total replaces the last highest total; this, of course, makes no difference.

With present-day facilities, at least, it is not sufficient to define a job for the computer as laconically as one would for a human, for example, 'Add up these pairs of numbers and tell me the highest'. The computer needs to have the job defined in terms much closer to the built-in repertoire of instructions that it can execute, and it is the function of COBOL (and other languages) to enable the programmer to write 'instructions' in a language not too far removed from natural expressions, which can nevertheless be converted by the computer into its own language. This, you will find, can be done for an immense variety of jobs, with a remarkably limited vocabulary. The art of programming is to break down such problems as

'Add up these numbers and find the highest total',

or 'Evaluate the slopes and intercepts of the regression lines of the following set of points',

or 'Print out all outstanding hire-purchase charges and calculate the interest',

or 'Put the spacecraft into orbit',

into sequences of instructions such as the above; in other words to reformulate the requirement in computer language.

2.2 Reiteration: Loops

The addition of pairs of numbers, as in our example, will seem trivial as a specification for a computer program, if we think of it on the scale on which we would carry it out by hand—at most a hundred or so pairs. But if we think in terms of thousands of pairs, a requirement which can easily arise in modern data processing, it is well worth while to convert it to instructions as shown, because we can, once these instructions are written, use them to deal with as many pairs as we please, to a number far beyond the capacity of a human. This is because we have separated 'instructions' and 'data'. We don't say, 'Add 123 and 145', 'Compare 166 with 000': we say 'Add a pair of numbers', 'Compare the result with the last highest total', and so on. We repeat the same sequence of instructions over and over again, for as many pairs as there are in the list; but the actual value of the numbers represented in general terms by 'a pair of numbers', 'current result', 'last highest result' may be variable, or different, at each 'pass', that is, each time we go through the sequence. This is one of the fundamental features of computers. If you cannot define a task as the reiteration of the same set of *instructions* on constantly changing *data*, then it is not a lot of use writing a computer program for it. Fortunately most routine scientific computations, and commercial data-handling processes, at least at the lower levels, can be so defined; and such definition is now being extended to some of the operations

7

of management and government that were previously thought to be the exclusive province of humans.

The reiterative nature of the process can be seen from its layout in the form of a *flow-chart* (Fig. 1.1) to which we have added a routine to detect the end of the data, which is explained in the next paragraph. The arrowed lines form a *loop*, starting at Read, going through the instructions, then 'looping back', from 1, to the first instruction. The effect is to read in a pair of numbers, 'process' them, and then return to read in the next pair. The idea, and the word, loop, are basic in computer programming. All programs, because of their reiterative nature, consist of a loop (the 'main loop'); and, in varying degrees, of interlocking loops, or loops 'nested' in other loops, sometimes in baffling complexity. We might say that loops are as essential to programs as the circulation of the blood is to the human: in the human the blood is refreshed at each cycle, and in the loop the same procedures are carried out on constantly changing data.

1.2.3 Getting out of the loop

An important point about loops is that you must be able to get out of them, otherwise the computer will continue endlessly (until the operator stops it), carrying out the same sequence of instructions when it has run out of data—a quite useless activity. So for every loop we have to provide an exit or escape, to tell the computer when to leave the loop and go to the next step, which in our case is to stop—something you would not expect to have to tell a human! We do this by specifying a *condition* which the computer can test each time it goes through the loop, and if it finds that the condition is fulfilled, or *satisfied*, it takes a step which brings it out of the loop. There are various ways of doing this which we will discuss in detail later; in our example, in order to provide a simple condition, we will make the assumption that none of the numbers read in can exceed say 700—they might for example be distances between major towns in Great Britain; if a number greater than 700 is read in, that indicates that the list is finished. So we put in, as the last item on the list, a number higher than 700, say 777. How this works should be obvious from the flow-chart and full sequence of instructions, in Fig. 1.1.

1. Read a pair of numbers.
2. Is the first of the pair equal to 777?
   If so, go to instruction 7.
   If not, go to the next instruction.
3. Add the two numbers.
4. Is the total greater than the Last Highest Total?
   If not, go to instruction 1.
   If so, go to the next instruction.
5. Copy the current total in place of the Last Highest Total.
6. Go back to instruction 1.
7. Write out the number in Last Highest Total (it is the answer).
8. Stop.

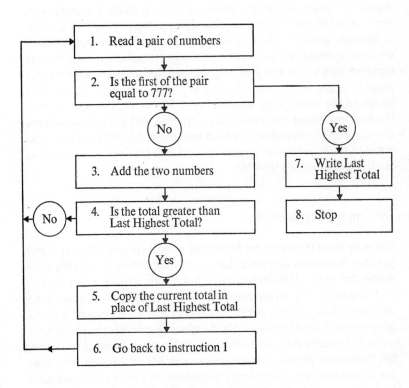

Fig. 1.1. Finding the highest total

9

1.2.4 Decisions

The process by which we look for the number 777 and *branch* to one instruction or another (for example, to stop or add), according to whether or not we find it, is called a *conditional jump*, or sometimes simply *Test and Branch*: we jump, or branch, out of the sequence of instructions according to the result of a test. In the flow-chart, there is another conditional jump, following the test 'Is the last total higher . . .'. Here the test is used not to jump out of the loop, but to determine which of two paths is to be taken, both of which eventually lead us back to the beginning of the loop in readiness for another pass. The final Go back is an *unconditional jump*: no matter what happened at the comparison, at this point we go back to square one.

It is by means of such conditional jumps that the computer 'makes decisions': according to the result of some tests the program takes *one or other* of two alternative paths through the instructions and this is the *only* sort of decision a computer can make. We shall see later on how to string together such tests so as to make tests of whatever complexity we like, but basically the decision rests on whether one number is greater than another, or is positive or negative, or, what comes to the same thing, whether some 'binary digit' is 0 or 1. Even the most advanced and powerful computers, and the most vital programs, depend, ultimately, on such tests; and the ability of the computer to follow alternative paths as a result of the test is what makes modern computation possible.

1.2.5 Storing the instructions

Not only must the computer follow the same sequence of instructions possibly thousands or even millions of times, before it finds the condition that allows it to leave a loop; but it must also be able to jump, on leaving the loop, to an instruction which is behind or ahead of the one that it has reached. All the instructions to which any part of the program may need to jump must therefore be stored in the computer's memory; usually this means that the whole program must be stored, but there are sophisticated techniques to get round this when the number of instructions is very large. Moreover, in our example, we need each pair of numbers only long enough to do the addition; but it may sometimes be necessary to store data, as well as instructions, so as to have access to it over and over again, at electronic speeds—for example, on consulting a table of prices for each invoice read in, or sorting a file into order. Ordinarily, and as far as this section is concerned, we store the whole program, and the program calls in ('Read') such data as it wants, when it wants it.

2.6 A program to retrieve information

The reader may feel that a program such as the one illustrated, which we think of as an arithmetical process, is really different in nature from

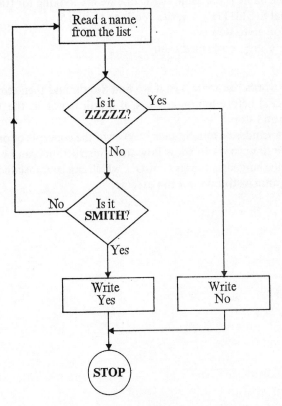

Fig. 1.2. Flow-chart for section 1.2.6

11

the operations of data processing in the commercial field, in which the data consists of words and names as well as numbers. This is not so; exactly the same type of instructions can be used for non-mathematical work, on alphabetical lists for example. If we have a list of names, in random order, and we want to find out if the name SMITH appears among them, we are carrying out the very simplest form of file-search, or data retrieval. To point the analogy with the pair-summing example, we will mark the end of the list with ZZZZZ, as 777 did. Now the sequence of operations is:

1. Read the next name from the list;
2. If the name is ZZZZZ go to step 4.
   If not, go to the next instruction.
3. If the name is the same as the one we are looking for (that is, 'is equal to SMITH')— Write 'Yes'; go to step 5.
   If not, go to step 1.
4. Write 'No'; go to next step.
5. Stop.

In other words, we write Yes if we find Smith, and then stop; if we find ZZZZZ before Smith—that is, if Smith is not in the list—we write No and stop.

This concludes our preliminary survey of the concepts of programming. We now go on to show how these instructions can be written in a specific language, that is COBOL, which can be translated, by the machine, into instructions it can execute.

Beginning COBOL

2.1 The elements of COBOL

1.1 Introducing COBOL

In Chapter 1 we described how the process of adding pairs of numbers to find the highest total was broken down into simple statements. In order to signal the end of the list of numbers to be added, 777 was entered as the last number; it is known that 777 can only occur as the 'end' signal, and not as one of the numbers to be added.

If you read the following you will find that it has a familiar ring about it:

```
PROCEDURE DIVISION.
BEGINNING.
   READ NUMBER-PAIRS.
   IF FIRST-OF-PAIR EQUAL TO 777 GO TO FINISH.
   ADD    FIRST-OF-PAIR,    SECOND-OF-PAIR,    GIVING
      CURRENT-TOTAL.
   IF CURRENT-TOTAL GREATER THAN LAST-HIGHEST-
      TOTAL, MOVE CURRENT-TOTAL TO LAST-HIGHEST-
      TOTAL.
   GO TO BEGINNING.
FINISH.
   MOVE LAST-HIGHEST-TOTAL TO ANSWER.
   WRITE ANSWER-RECORD.
   STOP RUN.
```

This is, of course, the COBOL version of the Number-Pairs example. If you compare the COBOL 'statements' with the breakdown of the processes, and the flow-chart, in Fig. 1.1 (p. 9) you will see that the COBOL statements correspond very closely with the 'natural language' expressions such as 'Read a pair of numbers', 'If the first number is equal to 777 . . . '. The only other clue you need at this stage is that if the test in an **IF** expression has the answer 'No', you ignore the rest of the statement (up to the full stop) and carry on with the next instruction in sequence. The two statements following **FINISH** merely mean 'Write out the Last Highest Total'.

A similar problem described in Chapter 1 was to find out if the name SMITH appeared in a list of names; the end of the list was indicated by ZZZZZ. A COBOL version of this is:

PROCEDURE DIVISION.
STARTIT.
    READ NAME-LIST.
    IF NAME EQUAL TO 'ZZZZZ' GO TO NOT-THERE.
    IF NAME EQUAL TO 'SMITH' GO TO FOUNDIT.
    GO TO STARTIT.
FOUNDIT.
    MOVE 'YES' TO ANSWER.
    GO TO ENDIT.
NOT-THERE.
    MOVE 'NO' TO ANSWER.
ENDIT.
    WRITE ANSWER-RECORD.
    STOP RUN.

The expressions **MOVE 'YES' TO ANSWER, WRITE ANSWER-RECORD** mean: Write 'Yes'. Similarly for **MOVE 'NO' TO ANSWER.**

This program is a little more complex, but if you remember the rule just stated about **IF**s you should be able to follow the logic, Fig. 1.2 (p. 11). Don't bother, at this stage, about such grammatical niceties such as why **ZZZZZ** and **SMITH** are in quotes, and **777** was not. The sequence is: If the name just read in from the list is **ZZZZZ**, then we have finished the list—and we have not found **SMITH**, so we write **NO**. If it is **SMITH**, we write **YES** and stop the run, without doing any more processing on the rest of the list. If the name read in is neither, we go back to **STARTIT** and read another name.

2.1.1.1   The vocabulary of COBOL programs

The only words in these programs that are actually part of the COBOL language are:

PROCEDURE DIVISION.
READ
IF ... EQUAL TO ...

ADD ... GIVING ...
MOVE ... TO ...
GO TO
WRITE
STOP RUN.

The Procedure Division is the name of the part of the COBOL program which contains the actual instructions that are to be carried out. All the other words, with the exception of **IF ... EQUAL TO ...** are imperative verbs, or verbal phrases: the **IF**s can also conveniently be thought of as imperatives, implying 'COMPARE ... ; **IF** they are **EQUAL ...** ' followed by another imperative statement.

All other words in the programs are *made up by the programmer;* in fact COBOL is a language in which all the verbs are imperative and you make up the nouns as you go along! These other words fall into three classes:

Procedure names (**STARTIT, FINISH, BEGINNING, ENDIT, FOUNDIT, NOT-THERE**). They mainly represent points to which we 'jump' or 'branch' by means of a **GO TO**, like 'instruction 1' or 'step 4' in earlier examples. **GO TO STARTIT** means leave the present sequence of instructions and carry on with those following the name **STARTIT**.

Data-names (**NUMBER-PAIRS, CURRENT-TOTAL, NAME, ANSWER,** and many others). These are made up by the programmer to designate *locations of store which hold the current values* to be used in the program. Thus **FIRST-OF-PAIR** and **SECOND-OF-PAIR** are locations in store that hold the first and second, respectively, of the pair of numbers that has just been read in; and **ADD FIRST-OF-PAIR, SECOND-OF-PAIR GIVING CURRENT-TOTAL** means: Add the contents of the location with the name **FIRST-OF-PAIR** to the contents of the location with the name **SECOND-OF-PAIR**, and put the result in the location named **CURRENT-TOTAL**. And **MOVE CURRENT-TOTAL TO LAST-HIGHEST-TOTAL** means: Copy the contents of location **CURRENT-TOTAL** into location **LAST-HIGHEST-TOTAL** (so that the contents of **LAST-HIGHEST-TOTAL** are the same as those of **CURRENT-TOTAL**, the previous contents of **LAST-HIGHEST-TOTAL** being automatically erased).

15

Literals are: **777**, which is a *numeric* literal, consisting of digits only; and *alphanumeric* literals (**YES, NO, SMITH, ZZZZZ**) which consist of letters (they can also contain digits, which is why they are called alphanumeric). They are not true data-names: **'SMITH'** is not only the name of a location in store, but the contents of that location. The numeric literals should need no explanation; they are just common sense.

2.1.1.2   The structure of the COBOL programs

Each program consists of a number of *statements*, each terminated by a full stop. Most statements are imperative in form, and consist of a verb followed by an object or *operand*. The operand is a data-name, or literal, except in the case of **GO TO** where it is a procedure-name. An **IF** expression is always followed by an imperative expression.

Strictly speaking, a sequence of words followed by a full stop is a *sentence*, and a sentence may consist of *one or more* statements. But in Chapter 2 we shall use sentences consisting of only one statement (or an **IF** test and an imperative) so that statement and sentence may be taken to be synonymous.

Statements, or sentences, are grouped into *paragraphs*, each of which has a procedure name (or paragraph name). Within a paragraph, the instructions are executed in the order in which they are written: the procedure names are used in altering the sequence of instructions, since they are the points named to **GO TO** statements. They are like bus stops where you can get on or off or change buses, which you must not do anywhere else; and as at bus stops you can stay on if you want to.

Paragraphs, again, may be grouped into *sections*, which have names like procedure names, followed by **SECTION**. They are mainly useful in more advanced COBOL, where you may decide not to hold the whole program in core at the same time.

Though they are not allowed in ANSI COBOL Level 1, we have used commas and semicolons anywhere in this book where they appear to give greater clarity; they have no effect on the programs (but full stops do!).

16

.1.3 Variations on the Number-Pairs theme

This simple program suggests itself as the framework for programs to give such information as:

What is the *smallest* total in the number-pairs?
What is the largest first number (not counting 777)?
What is the sum of the first numbers in the pairs? or the second numbers? or all of the numbers?
Are there any first numbers less than 100?
If you are told that the first number is always less than the second (for example, the first number is year of birth and the second is year of death) can you check that this is true?

All the COBOL you need for such inquiries can be found in the Number-Pairs program. You can probably see at once how the first two questions, for example, could be put in COBOL; while you may be able to see the outline of answers for the others, the actual COBOL grammar will be explained in the Six Easy Lessons which follow; COBOL programs which perform the above functions are given at the end of Chapter 2.

These examples have been put in to show you the sort of thing that can be done even with the little COBOL you have learnt so far, and to give you confidence by enabling you to 'juggle' with COBOL to produce new results; you may very well think up additional examples. If, however, you feel you would like something more than this quick review of COBOL before you try them, leave them till you get to the end of Chapter 2. They are not like the usual end-of-chapter exercises; if you skip them now, this will not impair your understanding of what comes later.

.1.2 Preparing the program

These examples give a pretty good idea of the sort of thing a programmer actually has to write in a COBOL program. We will emphasise again that these instructions are not merely typical of elementary programs; the most sophisticated applications are written in language like this.

17

The programmer has to write sets of statements for the four 'Divisions' of COBOL:

The Identification Division,
The Environment Division,
The Data Division,
The Procedure Division,

and the four Divisions, in that order, form the complete COBOL program. The Data Division will be described next, and the main features of the Data Division and Procedure Division will be illustrated in the programs of Chapter 2. The first two Divisions, which are more stereotyped and will, generally, be of less interest to the beginner, are described at the end of Chapter 2. It will, however, simplify the explanation of the working of the program if at this stage we describe what happens between the completion of the program by the programmer and its application in the computer to supply the required results.

When the programmer has written and checked his program (a process described in more detail in Chapter 4, 'Practical Programming'), it is punched on cards or tape: typically, the lines of program, for example,

MOVE 'YES' TO ANSWER.
READ NUMBER-PAIRS.

are punched one per card or paper tape record. The cards are assembled as in Fig. 2.1, in which, for completeness and conformity with modern practice, we have shown them preceded by 'control' or 'steering' cards required by the operating system of the computer.

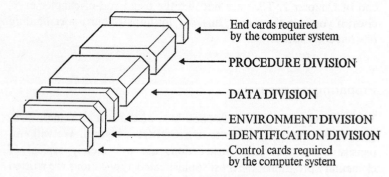

End cards required
by the computer system
PROCEDURE DIVISION
DATA DIVISION
ENVIRONMENT DIVISION
IDENTIFICATION DIVISION
Control cards required
by the computer system

Fig. 2.1. Layout of a COBOL source deck

These are not part of COBOL and depend entirely on your installation, so we will say no more about them.

.2.1 Compilation

When the programmer is satisfied that his program, and its punched version, are correct, he passes it to the computer for *compilation*. Compilation is the process of turning the *source* (that is, COBOL) program, with its quasi-English statements, into a form which can be executed by the computer, that is, a form in machine code. This is done by the *compiler*, which is a very large and complex program almost always supplied by the computer manufacturer. The compiler is 'loaded' into the computer; it accepts the source program as its data, and converts the source program into machine-language, checking at the same time that the source program conforms to the formal rules of the language. The compiler's output, the machine-language program (known as the *object* program) is written out on to a machine-readable medium such as magnetic tape. The programmer will probably never see this object program, except as a reel of tape, and may have no idea what the coding looks like.

In due course, at 'run time', the object program is loaded into the computer, this time to function as a program; it calls in the data for the job—for example, the pairs of numbers—and carries out its task. The two processes 'compile' and 'run' are illustrated in Fig. 2.2. Once compiled, the object program can be run as often as required.

2.1.3 The Data Division

In the examples on the Procedure Division, we used data-names, made up by the programmer, to designate locations in the store which held the current value of the data. It is now time to explain how each item of data, for example, each pair of numbers, finds its way to the designated area so that it can be used in the program.

(a) Compilation

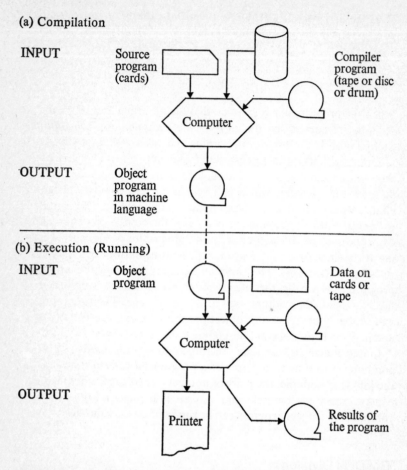

Not all of the possible permutations of input and output devices are shown. Once compiled, the program can be executed as often as required, with different data, without recompilation.

Fig. 2.2. (a) Compilation
(b) Execution (running)

3.1 Records

The input in the Number-Pairs program consisted of two data items, the first number and the second number. They were always read in together; this we would expect, if they were, for example, both punched on the same card. After each **READ** order, a new pair of numbers was presented to the program.

Any set of data that is handled by a single **READ** (or **WRITE**), as the numbers pairs were, is called a *record*. In practice, in this book, we shall take a record to be the information on a single punched card (or a corresponding section of paper tape, demarcated by some special character), or a line of print, or a small stretch of magnetic tape.

.3.2 Record descriptions

In the Find-Smith program, the record consisted of a single name; each time a **READ** order was given, the next name was 'made available' to the program. More commonly, however, the record contains several items of data, arranged, on each record, in a similar way: each data item will occupy a *field* of the card. The programmer writes a Record Description to describe the arrangement of the fields in a record, on card or tape or printline: he does this by stating how many characters there are in each field (starting from the left), whether they are digits or 'alphanumeric' or alphabetic; and sometimes other information is given. This information, for each field, is called the **PICTURE** of the field, and is conveyed in a clause beginning 'PICTURE IS...'.

For example, for each of the numbers in Number-Pairs we want three columns of card (or tape) since no number can exceed three digits; and it would be reasonable to punch these at the extreme left of the card—the first number in columns 1–3, the second in 4–6. We might then write a Record Description:

01 NUMPAIRS.
02 FIRST-OF-PAIR, PICTURE IS 999.
02 SECOND-OF-PAIR, PICTURE IS 999.

The record-name, chosen by the programmer like any other data-

21

name, is **NUMPAIRS**; it is assigned a *level-number* **01** which is used exclusively for record names. The fields of the record can be designated by *lower* level numbers, **02, 03,** etc. In Chapter 2 we shall use levels **01** and **02** only.

In a **PICTURE** clause, '**9**' stands for 'any digit' (including **9** itself); '**999**' means that the number consists of three digits, or, rather, that three columns are allotted to it in the record; it may, of course, consist of less than three digits, in which case the significant digits will be preceded by spaces or zeros (it is not usually necessary to punch preceding zeros).

Since we start counting columns from the left of the card or tape record, the **PICTURE** indicates where the fields are placed in the record. This applies not only to the input record, where the **PICTURE**s tell the program where to find the data-items, but also to the output record, where the **PICTURE**s give a 'plan' of the layout of the print-line.

The Find-Smith Record Description might be:

01 LIST-OF-NAMES.
02 SURNAMES PICTURE IS XXXXX.

or, since there is only one data-field in the record, we could write

01 LIST-OF-NAMES PICTURE IS XXXXX.

'**X**' stands for 'any character', including **X** and also including all digits and punctuation marks, etc., allowed for on the computer. This **PICTURE** tells us that the name on each card occupies the first five columns, and that in fact no name is longer than five letters (or, to be strictly accurate, that we are not going to take any notice of more than the first five letters of any name). Much more elaborate formats will be illustrated later on.

The programmer has to write a Record Description for each type of record structure that he is going to use in his program—almost certainly there will be at least two, one for the input record and one for the output, and there may be more; whether there is only one data record of a given type, or many thousands, each record type must have a Record Description, with a 'record name' at level **01**, and every record read in or printed must conform to one of these Record Descriptions.

The concept of levels is dealt with in more detail in Chapter 3, but there is nothing difficult about the idea. The Record Description is rather like the Contents page of a book. If we take the **01** level to represent a chapter, the **02** levels represent section-headings, and the **03** levels subsection headings, in the book, and so on for as many levels as we need or are allowed. But though the chapters, say, have their own headings, they do not exist independently of their subordinate parts; nor does **LIST-OF-NAMES** exist independently of its constituent names. On the other hand we can refer to chapters as a whole, or to their subheadings individually, as long as they have names. The analogy with the COBOL level system is very close.

3.3 The records in core

How then do these data-items get into the allocated areas of core? The Record Description gives the position of each data-item on the card—in effect it provides a map of the record. But it does more than this; the Record Description is also an instruction to the compiler to set aside a portion of core store, of the size specified in the **PICTURE**, and to note, for future reference, that the record- and data-names that we have used correspond to these portions of core. Then, at run time, the program for Number-Pairs will read a card and copy the digits in the first three columns into the store area called **FIRST-OF-PAIR**, and the contents of columns 4–6 into the area labelled **SECOND-OF-PAIR**. (In this case it will ignore the rest of the card, whether blank or not, since we have not defined any data in it.) From then on, whenever we mention either of these data-names (or, in appropriate circumstances, the record-name) the instruction, whatever it is, will be carried out on the current contents of these locations. When another card is read in, the previous contents of the locations are overwritten by the new values, and lost. Fig. 2.3 illustrates this process.

3.4 Files

The Data Division is subdivided into two sections, the **FILE SECTION** and the **WORKING-STORAGE SECTION**. The **FILE SECTION** deals with the descriptions of the data that is read into

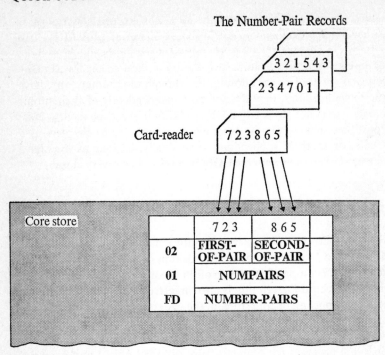

Fig. 2.3. Reading in and storing the Number-Pair records

and out of the computer by *peripheral devices* such as card readers and printers, whereas the **WORKING-STORAGE SECTION** deals with data elements that are dealt with only in store; this section is described in Programs EASY and FOX. For the moment we will confine ourselves to the File Section.

A file is nothing more than a collection of records. A file may contain just one record, or thousands, each record consisting of one card, or one segment of tape, or one line of print—but all conforming to the record-description we have given: the number-pairs file, for example, may consist of hundreds or thousands of cards (or just one), each carrying two numbers, in the same position on each. A file can contain any number of record-descriptions, so that there can, in fact, be many different types of record in a file; but in Chapter 2 we shall have only one record-description in each file, for the sake of simplicity, and leave the discussion of multi-record files to Chapter 3. Moreover, in Chapter 2 we shall have only two files in each program, a file of cards, or paper tape records, for input, and a print-file for output.

3.5 The function of files

The programmer gives a name to each of his files; in the Data Division it is preceded by the letters **FD** for File Description, and followed by a full stop. The importance of the File-name is that it can be used to link the record descriptions with the peripheral devices— card readers, printers—on which the records corresponding to these descriptions are to be found. In the Environment Division, each of the file-names used in the Data Division is *assigned* to one or other of these peripherals. Thus we have a link between the individual data-item and the 'outside world':

Data-item	Belongs to Record-name	Which belongs to File-name	Which will be found on peripheral
FIRST-OF-PAIR	**NUMPAIRS**	**NUMBER-PAIRS**	Card-reader
SURNAMES	**LIST-OF-NAMES**	**NAME-LIST**	Card-reader
ANSWER	**ANSWER-RECORD**	**OUTFILE**	Printer

3.6 Making up names

We have said that the programmer makes up his own names for data-items and procedure-names, and also the program-name. He may have to observe certain rules laid down by his own installation manager or chief programmer, to avoid duplication of program-names or to ensure that data-sets and files used in more than one program have consistent names (some users find that it pays to carry standardisation to considerable lengths); but as far as COBOL is concerned he has a large degree of freedom. A data-name must contain at least one letter (procedure names can be digital). The names must not contain more than 30 characters, and these characters may be letters (A–Z), digits (∅–9), or hyphen (-). The hyphen must not be the first or last character, and spaces are not allowed. Thus **CARD RECORD** is not a data-name, but **CARD-RECORD** is.

An important restriction is that the programmer must not use COBOL *reserved words* except in the sense in which they are used in the COBOL language. Reserved words are the active vocabulary of COBOL; they are those which have a special meaning, such as the 'verbs' **MOVE, ADD, OPEN**; and 'nouns' such as **FILE, INPUT**. A list is given in Appendix 2. Note particularly that **DATA** is a reserved word!

The slightest change in a data-name is sufficient to turn it into a new one, as far as the program is concerned. If you define **LABOUR-CHARGES** in the Data Division, and then refer in the Procedure Division to **LABOURCHARGES** or **LABOR-CHARGES**, the computer will tell you that it doesn't know what you are talking about. Note also that some implementations recognise only the first six or eight characters, so that names must be unique on these.

2.2 Six easy lessons

2.2.1 Program ALPHA

This is the first of 'six easy lessons' illustrating the cardinal features of the COBOL language. We have already seen examples of the Procedure Division, in the Number-Pairs and Find-Smith programs. Program ALPHA and some of the others that follow are indeed rather simpler in logical construction than these two, which were meant to show in broad outline how COBOL works and what it looks like; the programs which follow are intended to define the COBOL vocabulary more precisely and to teach you to write the 'grammatical' COBOL that the compilers demand.

All that Program ALPHA does is read in 80-column cards and print out the contents of each card on a printer, with a margin of 20 spaces on each side of the 80 characters copied from the card (some or all of which may themselves, of course, be spaces). The name ALPHA has been chosen by the programmer and will appear in the Identification Division; the Data Division and the Procedure Division of the source program (as it would look if the program-cards, as punched, were printed out) are shown in Fig. 2.4.

Simple as it is, the program ALPHA, if supplied with an Identification Division, and Environment Division, and any control cards that the particular system might require, would run on any machine that has a COBOL compiler; and might well be a useful 'service' program in the computer installation, for example, for finding out what was on a pack of cards that had lost their label.

The review of the Data Division and Procedure Division elements that follows fills in and formalises the information you already have.

```
DATA DIVISION.
FILE SECTION.
FD INFILE.
01 CARD-RECORD PICTURE IS X(80).

FD OUTFILE.
01  PRINTLINE.
    02 FILLER PICTURE IS X(20).
    02 PRINT-RECORD PICTURE IS X(80).
    02 FILLER PICTURE IS X(20).

PROCEDURE DIVISION.
INITIAL-ACTION.
    OPEN INPUT INFILE.
    OPEN OUTPUT OUTFILE.

MAIN-LOOP.
    READ INFILE AT END GO TO FINISH.
    MOVE CARD-RECORD TO PRINT-RECORD.
    WRITE PRINTLINE AFTER 1.
    GO TO MAIN-LOOP.

FINISH.
    CLOSE INPUT INFILE.
    CLOSE OUTPUT OUTFILE.
    STOP RUN.
```

Fig. 2.4. (a) Program ALPHA

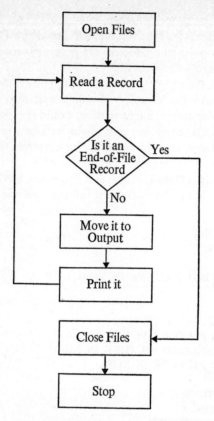

Fig. 2.4. (b) Program ALPHA: flow-chart

This may seem tedious; but the compensation is that when you understand this program and the elements in it, you are more than half-way to an operational command of the language!

2.2.1.1 Data Division

The **FILE SECTION** contains two files, for which the programmer has chosen the names **INFILE** and **OUTFILE.** They are preceded by the letters **FD** and followed by full stops (all full stops shown in these programs *must* be there, and full stops must not be used anywhere else; commas and semicolons are optional; no other punctuation signs can be used).

Each file has one type of record in it: these have the names **CARD-RECORD** for input, and **PRINTLINE** for output. **CARD-RECORD** has a **PICTURE 'X(80)'**; X, you already know, stands for 'any character'; X(80) is a shorthand way of writing 80 Xs. **PICTURE IS** can be, and in future will be, abbreviated to **PIC**.

CARD-RECORD is known as an *elementary item* because it is not divided into subordinate fields defining individual items within the record; the record is to be dealt with always as a whole unit of 80 characters. Elementary items *must* have **PICTURES**; and they are the only items that can. The output record, **PRINTLINE**, is divided into three fields, each with level **02**, which shows that they are part of the record whose name precedes them with level **01**; **PRINTLINE** is therefore a *group* item, whose elementary items are the three fields **FILLER**, **PRINT-RECORD**, and **FILLER**, each of which has a **PICTURE**. **FILLER** is a COBOL reserved word, and for the moment we can take the entries **FILLER PIC X(20)** to mean '20 blank spaces'. Thus the first **FILLER** puts a margin of 20 blanks to the left of **PRINT-RECORD**; it positions it at the centre of the page. **PRINT-RECORD** itself occupies 80 characters, leaving (on a 120-character printer) 20 characters on the right, which are taken care of by the second **FILLER PIC X(20)**.

2.1.2 Procedure Division

This is divided into three paragraphs:

INITIAL-ACTION, which 'opens' the input and output files; in this case, it is merely a formality required by COBOL grammar.

MAIN-LOOP does the main work of the program. It reads in a record from an input device, and tests it to see if it is an End-of-File type of record; if so, it branches to the **FINISH** routine; if not, it copies the record from the input area to the output area, and then writes it. This operation processes only *one* record, so after writing that record the program returns to the beginning of **MAIN-LOOP** to repeat it on another record.

29

FINISH. When the End-of-File signal is found, indicating that there are no more cards to be read, the files are closed—a formality complementary to opening—and the job is finished.

We will now examine the COBOL verbs in more detail. They are:

OPEN, CLOSE
READ, WRITE
MOVE, GO TO, STOP.

Each of these has a very precisely defined meaning.

OPEN, CLOSE. These instructions open and close the files; that is, they carry out certain 'housekeeping' functions which are important in magnetic tape and disc handling, where they save the programmer a lot of work, but as far as card handling and printing are concerned they are a formality. **OPEN INPUT INFILE** and **OPEN OUTPUT OUTFILE** could be written in a single statement, viz.:

OPEN INPUT INFILE, OUTPUT OUTFILE

and we shall so write them in future.

READ followed by a *file-name* gives the program the next record from that file (which, of course, is got from the input device to which the file is assigned), and copies its contents into the named input area in core, thereby erasing what was originally in the input area.

WRITE followed by a *record-name* will copy data from the output area for printing (or for writing on magnetic tape). The file to which the record belongs determines the peripheral to be used for output.

WRITE may destroy the contents of the output area; you cannot, without special provision, **WRITE** the same record more than once.

Note that you **READ** a file-name, but **WRITE** a record-name:

READ INFILE (not **CARD-RECORD**); but—
WRITE PRINTLINE (not **OUTFILE**).

This is an important distinction which you must remember. It is not capricious: the reason is that in any file you can have several different types of record (as we have already said) with different names at **01** level; and in the actual input file the records belonging to the different record-types may be mixed up together, so that you may not know what type of record comes next until you have actually got it, by means of a **READ**, and examined it. Thus you say 'Get me a record from file **INFILE**' without specifying what the record name is. In a **WRITE**, however, it is assumed, reasonably enough, that you know what type of record you want to write, so you give the record name rather than the file name.

AT END GO TO . . . is really a conditional branch meaning: If (after the **READ**) the record is found to be an End-of-File record, go to . . . The End-of-File is a type of record (the exact form depends on the type of machine you have) which indicates that all the records in the file have been read. It is like the **999** or **ZZZZZ** we used in the earlier programs, but it is of more general application, and is recognised by the program without any specific definition. Assume, generally, that each **READ** must be followed by this conditional clause.

AFTER 1 means 'after moving to a new line'. It is strictly unnecessary in standard COBOL, since this has a 'default option' (that is, a standard procedure that is used if no other instruction is given) which moves the printer to a new line on a **WRITE**. You can also say **AFTER 2**, to get double spacing.

MOVE is a very important verb, which has *two* operands. It is used to *copy* the contents of the first location named to the second:

MOVE CARD-RECORD TO PRINT-RECORD.

means: copy the contents of the area called **CARD-RECORD** into the area called **PRINT-RECORD**. The original contents of the area **CARD-RECORD** are unaltered; unlike **WRITE**, **MOVE** can be used to move a record as often as we like without altering it. The previous contents of the 'receiving' field, however, are *completely* erased by the **MOVE**: as we shall see, if we **MOVE** a record consisting of a single letter to an 80-character field, the other 79 characters will be wiped out (in fact replaced by spaces). **MOVE** is one of the most frequently used verbs in COBOL.

STOP is a pretty obvious verb. **STOP RUN** tells the computer: when you come to this instruction in the program the job is complete and you can go on to another one.

GO TO is another very common verb. Its operand is a procedure-name, not a data-name. It is a *sequence-control* verb, and signifies that the next instruction to be carried out is the first one of the paragraph named as the operand. It thus breaks the normal sequence of opera-

31

tions, which is from one to the next as written, skipping over paragraph-names. You can jump to any point in the **PROCEDURE DIVISION**, 'forward' as in **GO TO FINISH** or 'backward' as in **GO TO MAIN-LOOP**, as long as the point to which you want to jump has a label, that is a procedure-name. That is the main point of dividing the Procedure Division into paragraphs; the procedure-name immediately following **PROCEDURE DIVISION** (here, **INITIAL-ACTION**) is mandatory and must be there even if you do not jump to it, but the other two paragraph-names are in fact jumped to—they appear as the operands of **GO TO**s. There is no harm in putting in procedure-names even if you do not jump to them—they may make the program clearer, or they may be standard routines that you use in more than one program (and can thus transfer as a whole) or you need them to mark the end of the previous procedure. In themselves they make no difference to the sequence of instructions: if the last instruction of a procedure is not a jump, or is a condition that is not satisfied, you go on to the first instruction of the next procedure just as if the procedure name were not there. It is very common to jump to a procedure at some point in the program, and at another just enter it from the preceding instructions. A simple example of this is in ALPHA, where on the 'first pass' we enter **MAIN-LOOP** directly from the last instruction of **INITIAL-ACTION**, and thereafter jump to it from the end of **MAIN-LOOP**.

2.2.1.3 How the Data and Procedure Divisions work together

Fig. 2.5 is a diagram of the 'progress' of a record through the computer, in program ALPHA. An input area of 80 characters is set up, by the **PIC X(80)** in the Data Division, and an output area of 120 characters, which is the *sum* of the **PICTURE**s in the output record, is also set up. The **READ** copies the card contents into the program's input area, the **MOVE** copies the contents of the input area to the output area, and the **WRITE** copies the contents of the output area to the printer.

The **FILLER**s and the **PRINT-RECORD** all have the level **02**, because they are all fields subordinate to the Record **PRINTLINE**. You can have a record, at **01** level, without subdivisions, in which case it will be an elementary item and will have a **PICTURE**; but you

32

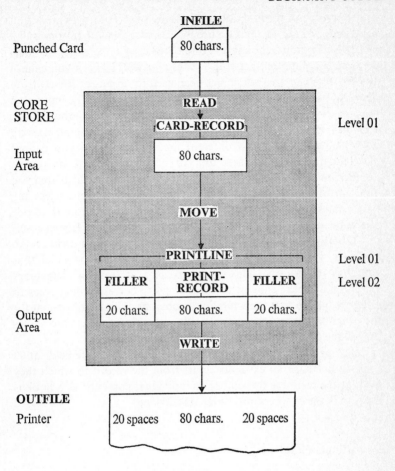

Fig. 2.5. A storage diagram for ALPHA

cannot have lower levels (**02, 03**, etc.) without subordinating them to an **01** entry. Every data item in the File Section must be defined ultimately (perhaps through a whole hierarchy of levels) as part of a record at **01** level. The Record Description in turn must be allotted to a File Description, and this again must be assigned to some piece of hardware in the Environment Division. Only thus can we set up the 'chain of command' which brings data into store.

33

The process of reading into an input area, **MOVE**ing to an output area, and writing from the output area, is common to almost all COBOL programs, though there may, of course, be pages of intermediate computation, between **READ** and **WRITE**; but you cannot **WRITE** from an area which has been used for input (or **READ** from an output area, though you are less likely to try this). The input area belongs to the input file, and the output area belongs to the output file, and they must therefore have different names. In general, naming each file-name reserves a different area of core, and you cannot allow a data-item in one area to have the same name as an item in another area—if you do, the computer will not know which area you are referring to, and to avoid this it will, at compile time, reject any data names that appear in the Data Division under more than one file-name, unless 'qualified' in the Procedure Division. (Higher levels of COBOL allow you to use the same name in different areas and to *qualify* it by naming a higher level to which it belongs and which thus identifies it uniquely. This is unnecessary at least in elementary COBOL: it is easy enough to allot names to corresponding areas in different files so that their relation is obvious. This is convenient for the programmer and the computer doesn't care how alike the names are as long as they are different).

This diagram makes it clear, too, that the subordinate fields at **02** level do not have an existence apart from the record to which they belong; the record is the sum of its individual parts just as a book is the sum of the chapters into which it is divided.

2.2.2 Program BINGO

2.2.2.1 Fields, spaces, and fillers.

Program ALPHA could be compiled and could be of use in the computer room. It is not very elegant, since the material will be printed as it was punched on cards, where the usual practice is not to leave spaces between fields, and it will not therefore be very easy to read. If we don't know how the material is split into fields, we have to put up with that, but if we do know we can produce a much more intelligible output, though the program will be of less general use.

The input of program BINGO (Fig. 2.6) is a card, for example, a stock card, which is divided into four fields; a part-number of seven columns, called **PARTNO**; a part-description, called **DESCR**, for which 20 columns are allowed; a price in new pence called **PRICE**, of 3 columns; and a stock reserve number, **RESNO**, of 5 columns. **PARTNO** and **RESNO** will be alphanumeric, that is, may contain both letters and digits, so they have the descriptor X. **PRICE** and **RESNO** will never contain anything but digits, so instead of X we use the descriptor 9, meaning any of the digits 0–9. It is always better

PROGRAM BINGO

DATA DIVISION.
FILE SECTION.

FD CARDFILE.
01 CARDREC.
    02 PARTNO   PIC X(7).
    02 DESCR   PIC X(20).
    02 PRICE   PIC 999.
    02 RESNO   PIC 9(5).

FD PRINTFILE.
01 PRINTLINE.
    02   FILLER PIC X(20).
    02 PRPARTNO   PIC X(7).
    02   FILLER PIC X(5).
    02 PRDESCR   PIC X(20).
    02   FILLER PIC X(5).
    02 PRPRICE   PIC 999.
    02   FILLER PIC X(5).
    02 PRRESNO   PIC 99999.
    02   FILLER PIC X(50).

(The **PRINTLINE** format shows how spacing and insetting can be used to improve the appearance and clarify the structure of a Record Description. It would be equally legal, however, to write the **FILLER**s immediately after the level number, like the data-names, and the **PIC**s immediately after them.)

Fig. 2.6. (a) Program BINGO: Data division

PROCEDURE DIVISION.

INITRUN.
   OPEN INPUT CARDFILE, OUTPUT PRINTFILE.
   MOVE SPACE TO PRINTLINE.

PROCESSIT.
   READ CARDFILE AT END GO TO FINISH.
   MOVE PARTNO TO PRPARTNO.
   MOVE PRICE TO PRPRICE.
   MOVE DESCR TO PRDESCR.
   MOVE RESNO TO PRRESNO.
   WRITE PRINTLINE AFTER 1.
   GO TO PROCESSIT.

FINISH.
   CLOSE CARDFILE, PRINTFILE.
   STOP RUN.

Fig. 2.6. (b) Program BINGO: procedure division

to use '9' for fields which we know are always going to contain digits, especially if we are going to do arithmetic with them. Here X would do as well, since we are not doing arithmetic, but it is a good convention to follow.

The input record will look like this:

   Column

1	8	28	31	35

ABC1234CUPHOOKS, LARGE 21100100

You will see that in the Data Division I have described the card only as far as column 35. The rest of the card may be blank, or it may contain material I don't want for this program; so I have not specified its make-up, which means that no storage space will be reserved for it and the program will ignore columns 36–80 on reading a card. There would be no harm in putting the other fields in—it would save rewriting the Data Division if I did at some time want to use them. If I only wanted the first five characters, say, I could write

01 CARDRECORD PIC XXXXX.

36

But remember that on a printer output one should account for all columns.

I will assume that in the printout it will be sufficient to have 20 spaces on the left of the print and 5 spaces between each field. This leaves 50 spaces (5 inches) as a right-hand margin. Of course these spacings can be adjusted to suit the customer, as long as they add up to 120. So the printed data will be of the form:

(20 sp.) **ABC1234   CUPHOOKS, LARGE   211 00100** (50 sp.)

Each item in the output fields is given a distinct name; I have chosen to use the name of the corresponding input field with **PR** (for **PRINT**) prefixed to it. These formats illustrate a general rule with which you will become very familiar: any data which you wish to handle as an individual item—even a single character—must be given its own data-name and **PICTURE** in the Data Division. Here we have to **MOVE** the input fields separately to output, because they have to go into fields split up by the **FILLER**s in the output record. Moving the input record as a whole—**MOVE CARDREC TO PRINTLINE**—would put the 35 characters of **CARDREC** into the *first 35* print positions, which is not what we want at all.

The moving is done by four individual **MOVE**s in the Procedure Division. These are preceded, in **INITRUN**, by the order **MOVE SPACE TO PRINTLINE**. This is an order which should have appeared in Program ALPHA, but which I omitted for the sake of simplicity. The effect is to 'clear' the print-line area; if I give a **WRITE** immediately after **MOVE SPACE**, I would get a blank line printed. I have to do this **MOVE** in order to ensure that the **FILLER** areas are in fact filled with spaces—that they don't, for example, contain characters left over from previous programs. It is a rule in COBOL that you cannot use **FILLER** as an address, that is, you cannot say **MOVE SPACE TO FILLER**. I have to clear the whole area containing **FILLER**s; the data areas such as **PRPARTNO** will, of course, be filled up with data at a later stage, but the **FILLER**s will remain blank.

FILLER can be used in input as well as output; in input its meaning is 'ignore, or skip over, the number of columns named as **FILLER**'. It is used where there are blank columns, or columns whose contents we are not interested in, in the input record (unless all such areas are to the right of the area we do want, in which we have the situation in

37

this program, and don't need to have a **FILLER**). If in this program we had, for example, a card number or other wanted data in column 80, we would have to write:

. . . .
  02 RESNO PIC 9(5).
  02 FILLER PIC X(44).
  02 CARDNUMBER PIC 9.

The **FILLER** of 44 characters covers the columns 36–79. It is usual to give **FILLER**s a **PICTURE** of type X, but it doesn't matter much.

    SPACE is not the name of a data-area, like **PARTNO**, etc., and it is not defined in the Data Division. It is a special COBOL word, a reserved word, and is called a *figurative constant*. All it means is 'as many spaces as there are positions in the receiving field'. You can use it as a 'sending address', but not as a receiving address: you can **MOVE SPACE TO PARTNO**, which fills the whole of the **PARTNO** field with spaces, but you can't say **MOVE PARTNO TO SPACE**. **ZERO** is another figurative constant we shall use a lot: it means 'as many zeros as there are digit positions in the receiving field'. ANSI COBOL Level 1 allows only these two forms, but most implementations allow **SPACE** or **SPACES**, **ZERO**, **ZEROS**, and **ZEROES**.

    You can juggle with program BINGO without having to learn anything new. For example, suppose I wanted to print the Part Number at the extreme right of the line, to make it easier for reference:

  02 FILLER PIC X(32).
  02 PRDESCR PIC X(20).
. . . .
  02 PRRESNO PIC (5).
  02 FILLER PIC X(43).
  02 PRPARTNO PIC X(7).

PRPARTNO will now appear in print positions 114–120. If I wanted to print it at *both* ends of the line, I would leave the format as in the program except for the concluding **FILLER**, which would be X(43) instead of X(50), and this would be followed by **PRPARTNO-2 PIC X(7)**. I have to give the second **PRPARTNO** a new name to distinguish it from the first one, and I shall need two **MOVEs** in the Procedure Division:

MOVE PARTNO TO PRPARTNO.
MOVE PARTNO TO PRPARTNO-2.

It doesn't matter what order the **MOVEs** are done in, since the **WRITE** does not take place until all the **MOVEs** are completed.

I can alter the order of the fields, for example, I can print **DESCR** to the right of **PRICE**, by changing their positions in the **PRINT-LINE** format—again the order of the **MOVEs** doesn't matter. But note that I can't fiddle with the *input* format in this way: the input format describes, and must follow, the design of the card. But we can juggle to our heart's content with the output record, as long as the total of characters remains at 120. Try out some transformations for yourself.

.3 Program CHARLIE

.1 Comparisons and decisions

In this program every input record contains a commodity number, of six characters, followed by five blank columns; and then ten fields of four digits each, giving the price of the commodity, in pence, in each of the years 1960–9.

We require to read in the cards and on each card *compare* the 1960 price (in field **PRICE60**: see Fig. 2.7) with the price in 1969 (field **PRICE69**). If we find any commodity whose price is the same in both years, we print out the commodity number, leaving the rest of the printline blank.

This is an illustration of a fundamental function of the computer, sometimes called *decision making*. The program compares two locations in core, and takes different actions according to the result of the comparison—almost always the action involves a branch to different parts of the program, according to the result.

Program CHARLIE.

DATA DIVISION.
FILE SECTION.

FD CARDFILE.
01 TABLEREC.

02 COMMOD-NO	PIC X(6).	
02 FILLER	PIC X(5).	
02 PRICE60	PIC 9999.	
02 PRICE61	PIC 9999.	
02 PRICE62	PIC 9999.	
02 PRICE63	PIC 9999.	
02 PRICE64	PIC 9999.	
02 PRICE65	PIC 9999.	
02 PRICE66	PIC 9999.	
02 PRICE67	PIC 9999.	
02 PRICE68	PIC 9999.	
02 PRICE69	PIC 9999.	

FD PRINTFILE.
01 PRINTLINE.

02 COMMODITY	PIC X(6).
02 FILLER	PIC X(114).

Fig. 2.7. (a) Program CHARLIE: data division

The comparison is, basically, the question
Is A equal to, greater than, or less than B?
or Is A *not* equal to, not greater than, not less than B?
(where A and B are, respectively, the contents of locations A and B).
The answer will be Yes or No; for example, if A is *less* than B

Is A less than B?	is answered Yes;
Is A equal to B?	No;
Is A greater than B?	No;
Is A not less than B?	No;
is A not equal to B?	Yes;
Is A not greater than B?	Yes.

```
PROCEDURE DIVISION.
INITRUN.
    OPEN INPUT CARDFILE, OUTPUT PRINTFILE.
    MOVE SPACES TO PRINTLINE.

PROCESSING.
    READ CARDFILE, AT END GO TO FINISH.
    IF PRICE60 EQUAL TO PRICE69, GO TO PRINTIT.
    GO TO PROCESSING.

PRINTIT.
    MOVE COMMOD-NO TO COMMODITY.
    WRITE PRINTLINE AFTER 1.
    GO TO PROCESSING.

FINISH.
    CLOSE CARDFILE, PRINTFILE.
    STOP RUN.
```

Fig. 2.7. (b) Program CHARLIE: procedure division

In COBOL the comparison is done by the *conditional* or **IF** statements:

IF A IS EQUAL TO B . . .
IF A IS NOT GREATER THAN B . . .

and so on (**IS** and **THAN** may be omitted).

The conditional expression is followed, as part of the same statement, by a *consequent* which describes an action to be carried out if the condition is *satisfied*, that is, if the answer to the **IF** is **YES**. If it is not satisfied, the consequent is ignored, and the program continues with the next sentence, that is, after the first full stop following the **IF** statement. The consequent may be a series of statements, forming a complete sentence (with no full stop before the end), but in Chapter 2 we shall restrict it to one statement, nearly always a **GO TO**.

In program CHARLIE the comparison is done in **IF PRICE60 EQUAL TO PRICE69** and the consequent is **GO TO PRINTIT**. If they are *not* equal, the consequent is ignored and the next statement, **GO TO PROCESSING**, is carried out. The effect of this is, of course,

41

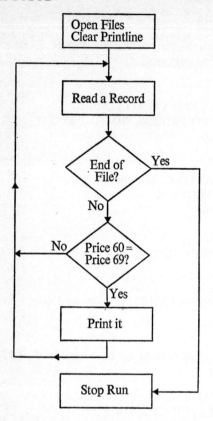

Fig. 2.7. (c) Program CHARLIE: flow-chart

that if the two prices are not equal the record is ignored and the next one read in. It is possible, and often necessary, to build up elaborate and complicated series of **IF**s, but in Chapter 2 we will confine ourselves to the simpler cases, without trying to achieve either elegance or economy.

42

.2.4 Program DOG

.4.1 Literals

Program DOG gives more examples of decision making, and also shows a new way of getting data into the computer. It uses the same data as Program CHARLIE, except that **COMMOD-NO** is broken down into two parts, a 'class indicator' of two letters, and an index number of four digits; the object of the program is to list all commodities of class **BM** whose price in 1969 was the same as in 1960. So we have to compare **ALPHPART** with the letters **BM**; if 'ALPHPART** is not equal to **BM**' we ignore the record, without bothering to go on to compare the prices; if it is equal, then we have to make the further test on the two prices, and if this is satisfied we print the commodity number.

What is new here is how to get the letters **BM** into the program. The simplest way is as shown:

IF ALPHPART NOT EQUAL TO 'BM' GO TO PROCESSING.

Anything enclosed in quotes is called a *literal*, or more precisely a *non-numeric literal*, or *alphanumeric literal*. It can include digits and any other symbols allowed on the computer, as well as letters and spaces (though not quotes); and it can be up to 120 characters long.

The quotes which enclose the literal are necessary because if I wrote

IF ALPHPART NOT EQUAL TO BM GO TO PROCESSING

the compiler would look for an area of storage to which the name **BM** is assigned, and defined, like **ALPHPART** etc., in the Data Division; and, not finding it, would print out a note complaining about it. The quotes, in other words, distinguish non-numeric literals from data names.

Numeric literals, which are dealt with more fully in the next program, do *not* have quotes:

IF NUMPART EQUAL TO 249 GO TO ...

Since they consist of digits they cannot be taken for data-names, so the quotes are unnecessary. So to put in an actual numerical value, just write it in the statement without quotes.

```
Program DOG
DATA DIVISION.
FILE SECTION.
FD CARDFILE.
01 TABLEREC.
   02 ALPHPART   PIC XX.
   02 NUMPART    PIC 9999.
   02 FILLER     PIC X(5).
   02 PRICE60    PIC 9999.
(and so on as in Program CHARLIE)
FD PRINTFILE.
01 PRINTLINE.
   02 PRINTALPH  PIC XX.
   02 PRINTNUM   PIC 9999.
   02 FILLER     PIC X(114).


PROCEDURE DIVISION.
INITRUN.
   OPEN INPUT CARDFILE, OUTPUT PRINTFILE.
   MOVE SPACES TO PRINTLINE.


PROCESSING.
   READ CARDFILE AT END GO TO FINISH.
   IF ALPHPART NOT EQUAL TO 'BM' GO TO PROCESSING.
   IF PRICE60 EQUAL TO PRICE69 GO TO PRINTIT.
   GO TO PROCESSING.


PRINTIT.
   MOVE ALPHPART TO PRINTALPH.
   MOVE NUMPART TO PRINTNUM.
   WRITE PRINTLINE AFTER 1.
   GO TO PROCESSING.


FINISH.
   CLOSE CARDFILE, PRINTLINE.
   STOP RUN.
```

Fig. 2.8. (a) Program DOG

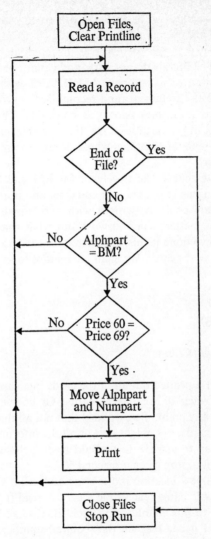

Fig. 2.8. (b) Program DOG: flow-chart

45

All the data-names we have dealt with so far are the names of *variables*; they are the names, or addresses, of areas of store whose contents will vary as records are read in, computations are done, and so forth. The literals do not vary, and cannot be changed in the program: if I wanted to compare **ALPHPART** with '**CZ**' I would have to rewrite the statement (and recompile the program). That is why literals are sometimes known as constants. They are not the addresses of storage locations, like the variable names, but are, rather, the contents of locations whose addresses are not known to the programmer.

You will note that in the two tests, for **BM** and for equality of prices, I have in one case used 'not equal to' and in the other 'equal to'. The program could be written with two 'equals', or two 'not equals' for that matter; can you work out what changes would be necessary? I have done it this way merely to save an instruction or two and to make it neater. We shall have more to say about this in Chapter 3.

2.2.5 Program EASY

2.2.5.1 Working-Storage: Counters

Program ALPHA printed out all of the cards in a card file; the program stopped when it ran out of cards. Of course the operator could stop it at any point, if we decided that not all the cards were to be printed—50 cards, say, might give us all the information we need. But the best way to achieve this would be to get the computer to count the cards and stop when it reached 50.

We can set aside a location in the store and call it **COUNTER** or some such suitable name; each time a card is read (or printed, perhaps) we add 1 to this counter; and each time we add 1 we test the counter to see if it has reached the required number. If it has, we branch to the end of the program.

We know by now that in order to set aside storage for any particular data item, we must name it in the Data Division; but every entry in the Data Division, at least in the File Section which is all we have had so far, must be related to a record name and ultimately to a File Description: how are we to set aside storage for a counter which will appear neither in input nor output? It is not read in with the input, nor printed in the output: it is entirely an internal affair, used to control the program. For this type of storage, the **WORKING-STORAGE SECTION** is provided in the Data Division, in addition to the **FILE SECTION**. Note the hyphen in **WORKING-STORAGE**: it must be there.

In Program EASY, the Working-Storage Section contains the entry:

77 COUNTER PIC 99 VALUE IS ZERO.

ZERO is a figurative constant, used for numeric fields exactly as **SPACES** is used for non-numeric; it should not need further explanation. We say that **VALUE IS ZERO** *zeroises* the counter, or *initialises* it, that is, gives it an initial value, which may be changed in the program.

The level number is 77: this number appears only in Working-Storage Section data descriptions. Items with level 77 cannot be part of a larger file structure; in particular they are not related to an **01** record-name, nor an FD, because they are not part of a file or record and are not assigned to any input/output equipment. Nor can they have subordinate fields. For these reasons they are called *independent* items. They must have a **PICTURE** because they are, necessarily, elementary items. They should also have a **VALUE** clause, otherwise their initial value is 'indeterminate' (if you didn't have a **VALUE** clause, you would have to see that in **PROCEDURE** you **MOVE** a value to them before using them). The **VALUE** can be a figurative constant, as here, or a literal, numeric or non-numeric. **VALUE** can *only* be used in the Working-Storage Section. Its effect, here, is the same as **MOVE ZERO TO COUNTER** in the Procedure Division.

Arithmetic instructions have been left to Chapter 3, but **ADD 1 TO COUNTER** needs little explanation. After it has been executed the contents of **COUNTER** are one more than they were before—contrast **MOVE 1 TO COUNTER**, which makes the content of **COUNTER** equal to 1; if we used this, the counter would never reach 50 and the program would be 'in a loop'.

The first card is read and printed with **COUNTER** equal to zero; it is then 'incremented' and tested, when it will have the value 1. Thus the 50th card will be read with **COUNTER** equal to 49; it will then be incremented and on testing will be found equal to 50; and since

47

```
Program EASY.
DATA DIVISION.
FILE SECTION.

FD  CARDFILE.
01  CARDRECORD PIC X(80).

FD  PRINTFILE.
01  PRINTLINE.
      02 FILLER PIC X(20).
      02 CARD-DATA PIC X(80).
      02 FILLER PIC X(20).

WORKING-STORAGE SECTION.
77 COUNTER PIC 99 VALUE IS ZERO.

PROCEDURE DIVISION.
INITRUN.
   OPEN INPUT CARDFILE, OUTPUT PRINTFILE.
   MOVE SPACES TO PRINTLINE.

READEM.
   READ CARDFILE AT END GO TO FINISH.
   MOVE CARD-RECORD TO CARD-DATA.
   WRITE PRINTLINE AFTER 1.
   ADD 1 TO COUNTER.
   IF COUNTER LESS THAN 50 GO TO READEM.

FINISH.
   CLOSE CARDFILE, PRINTFILE.
   STOP RUN.
```

Fig. 2.9. (a) Program EASY

we have read 50 cards we 'jump out' when the **COUNTER** is equal to 50. As long as it is *less than* 50 we want to read another card. We could write

> **IF COUNTER EQUAL TO 50 GO TO FINISH.**
> **GO TO READEM.**

but the version shown saves us a **GO TO**.

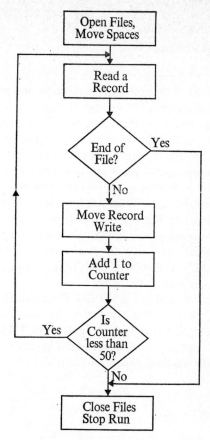

Fig. 2.9. (b) Program EASY: flow-chart

This is a model of a 'loop' which you will have to write innumerable times in the course of programming. It has the four elements initialise, increment, process, and test, which can be carried out in many different orders. For instance you could write:

MOVE ZERO TO COUNTER   – Initialise
READEM.
   ADD 1 TO COUNTER.   – Increment

49

IF COUNTER EQUAL TO . . . GO TO FINISH. – Test
READ . . . (Move, Write)   – Process
GO TO READEM.

Here we shall read the first record with the counter at 1, and process it with the counter at that value; we shall read and process the 50th record with the counter at 50; so when the counter is equal to 51 we jump out. You should try the effect, with little play-throughs and flow-charts, of putting the 'increment' and the 'test' at different points in the loop. The manipulation of counters in this fashion is an art learnt with practice: if you want to count up to N you have to make sure that you don't stop at N – 1 or carry on to N+1 or more, or fail to get beyond zero. When you have some experience you will find that the chart in Fig. 4.11 will help you. The only other point we will make here is that it is sometimes more efficient to decrement the counter, initialising it with the *final* value and subtracting 1 each time (**SUBTRACT 1 FROM COUNTER**), testing for 1 or zero according to the layout of the loop.

You still have to have **AT END GO TO FINISH**, in the **READ**, although you are providing for a stop by 'dropping through' to **FINISH** when **COUNTER** is no longer **LESS THAN 50**. The **AT END** clause is required by COBOL, and it is justified, because after all there might be less than 50 cards in the pack!

2.2.6 Program FOX

2.2.6.1 Working-Storage: Temporary storage

77-level entries, as well as providing for storage and data which is not represented in files, are used to allot storage for temporary or intermediate results, which are arrived at in the course of the program but which are not printed out until the end of the program. This is illustrated in Program FOX, which is very like the simple program described in Chapter 1. The program reads, from successive cards, a field called **TONS**, which occupies the first four columns (the rest of the record is of no interest in this program and is therefore not described). At the end of the program it prints out the highest value it has found for **TONS**. To do this, we set up a temporary store called

TEMP. Each time a card is read in, the value of **TONS** on that card is compared with the current value of **TEMP**. If **TEMP** is larger we ignore that card; if **TONS** is larger (or equal) we MOVE **TONS TO TEMP**. Thus when we have read in all the cards, **TEMP** will contain the highest value found for **TONS**, or at least the last occurrence of that value. **TEMP** is set initially to zero; at the end of the program, we have to **MOVE** it to its place in the output record—we can't write from Working-Storage.

```
Program FOX.
DATA DIVISION.
FILE SECTION.
FD CARDFILE.
01   CARDREC.
       02 TONS PIC 9999.
FD PRINTFILE.
01   PRINTLINE.
       02 FILLER PIC X(20).
       02 HIGHTONS PIC 9999.
       02 FILLER PIC X(96).
WORKING-STORAGE SECTION.
77 TEMP PIC 9999 VALUE IS ZERO.

PROCEDURE DIVISION.
INITRUN.
     OPEN INPUT CARDFILE OUTPUT PRINTFILE.
     MOVE SPACE TO PRINTLINE.
READIT.
     READ CARDFILE AT END GO TO FINISH.
     IF TONS LESS THAN TEMP GO TO READIT.
     MOVE TONS TO TEMP.
     GO TO READIT.
FINISH.
     MOVE TEMP TO HIGHTONS.
     WRITE PRINTLINE AFTER 1.
     CLOSE CARDFILE, PRINTFILE.
STOP RUN.
```

Fig. 2.10. Program FOX

51

There is no particular reason in this case why I should not have used the print location, **HIGHTONS**, itself, to act as a temporary store for the intermediate results, since this record is not printed out until the end of the program. This would have saved setting up a Working-Storage location and would have avoided the **MOVE** to output at the end of the run. But in general it is better to use a specific store: if there had been some intermediate printing, for example, if I had printed out a record each time I found a higher value, the contents of **HIGHTONS** would have been lost and would therefore have been useless for comparison, since a **WRITE** destroys the information in the output area. Moreover, this is a very simple program; in a more complex one, you might later introduce amendments and improvements which involved intermediate printing, and you might forget that **HIGHTONS** was in use as a temporary store, as well as for output.

In addition to 77-entries, you can have entries in Record-Format in the Working-Storage, that is, a Record name with **01** level, and subordinate fields with their own level numbers, exactly as in the File Section; but they do not have an **FD** entry because they do not belong to an input/output file. This usage is illustrated in Chapter 3.

2.3 Variations on the Number-Pairs theme: Solutions

At the beginning of Chapter 2, it was pointed out that the basic program could serve as a framework for many variations, The logical basic program itself has been illustrated, with a Data Division and a Procedure Division, in Program FOX; as a recapitulation for Chapter 2 we will suggest COBOL solutions for the variations.

1. What is the smallest total in the number-pairs?

It is easy enough to see that you write **IF CURRENT-TOTAL LESS THAN LAST-SMALLEST-TOTAL . . .**; perhaps what you did not spot was that in the Data Division you must give **LAST-SMALLEST-TOTAL** the highest possible initial value—if it has a **PIC 9999** you should give it a **VALUE** of **9999**. If you left it at zero then you would never find **CURRENT-TOTAL LESS THAN LAST-SMALLEST-TOTAL** (unless you allow negative values for the number-pairs, which we have not dealt with yet) and the Smallest Total printed out would be zero, which may not be true. You have to give it the highest possible value so as to ensure that it is replaced by a 'real' value as soon as possible in the run.

2. What is the largest first number, not counting 777 (the end-of-data signal)?

Of course you omit the addition instruction, in fact you ignore the second number altogether. Test for 777 before comparing the input number with **LAST-HIGHEST-NUMBER**: if you write

> **IF FIRST-OF-PAIR GREATER THAN LAST-HIGHEST-**
> **NUMBER MOVE FIRST-OF-PAIR TO LAST-HIGHEST-**
> **NUMBER.**
> **IF FIRST-OF-PAIR EQUAL TO 777 GO TO FINISH.**

then when 777 comes up it will be taken as a 'data' number and (since we have postulated that there is no data number greater than 776) will be printed out as the highest number found, in the data.

3. What is the sum of the first numbers in the pairs; or the second numbers; or of all the numbers?

What you will realise now, which you probably would not have done at the beginning of this part, is that all three totals can be computed in the same run:

> **IF FIRST-OF-PAIR EQUAL TO 777 GO TO FINISH.**
> **ADD FIRST-OF-PAIR TO FIRST-TOTAL.**
> **ADD SECOND-OF-PAIR TO SECOND-TOTAL.**
> **ADD FIRST-OF-PAIR TO GRAND-TOTAL.**
> **ADD SECOND-OF-PAIR TO GRAND-TOTAL.**
> **GO TO BEGINNING.**

The four **ADD**s, moreover, can be done in any order. **FIRST-TOTAL**, **SECOND-TOTAL**, and **GRAND-TOTAL** must be defined in the Data Division, with sufficiently large **PICTURES** (this point is dealt with in more detail in Chapter 3).

4. Are there any first numbers less than **100**?

Let us assume that we write **YES** if we find a number less than **100**, and **NO** if we reach the End-of-Data card without finding such a number.

> **IF FIRST OF PAIR EQUAL TO 777 GO TO FINISH-2.**
> **IF FIRST-OF-PAIR LESS THAN 100 GO TO FINISH.**
> **GO TO BEGINNING.**

FINISH.
  MOVE 'YES' TO ANSWER.
  WRITE ANSWER-RECORD.
FINISH-2.
  MOVE 'NO' TO ANSWER.
  WRITE ANSWER-RECORD.
  CLOSE files.
  STOP RUN.

Did you spot the error? We shall write **YES** and then 'drop through' to **FINISH-2**; so if a number less than **100** is found we shall find **YES** on one line and **NO** on the next. You need a **GO TO** at the end of **FINISH**—to a paragraph consisting of the **CLOSE** and **STOP** orders. You would drop through to these, quite correctly, without a **GO TO**, from **FINISH-2**. In Chapter 3 you will learn about the **PERFORM** which will help you to avoid *bêtises* such as that shown in the program.

And you might as well count how many such numbers there are, instead of stopping as soon as you find one; then you will think of printing out the position in the data (for example, the number of the card) at which such numbers appear, and so on and so on. . . . All this is at your finger-tips now.

5. If you are told that the first number is always less than the second, can you check that this is true?

The structure of this program is practically the same as the preceding one: we write **YES** if the condition is satisfied (that is, we read the whole file without finding a first number which is not less than the second) and **NO** if the condition is violated; and in the latter case, stop. For a change, let us write

  IF FIRST-OF-PAIR EQUAL TO 777 GO TO FINISH-2.
  IF FIRST-OF-PAIR NOT LESS THAN SECOND-OF-PAIR GO
    TO FINISH.
  GO TO BEGINNING.

If these numbers are, in fact, years of birth and death, would you be quite satisfied with the above—bearing in mind that a child can die in the year it is born? How would you allow for such cases?

2.4 The Identification and Environment Divisions

Both of these Divisions must be present, and they must precede the Data and Procedure Divisions (see Fig. 2.1). In that figure, control cards giving instructions to the operating system of the computer are shown preceding and following the pack of COBOL cards; these will be required by most installations nowadays. They are not a part of COBOL and it is not possible here to give any guidance on their use; you must adopt the practice of your own installation. Probably you will find that there is a library of standard sets which you can use without alteration.

The Identification Division is very simple. Only one entry, the Program name, is compulsory; this is written on the line following the Division header:

IDENTIFICATION DIVISION.
PROGRAM-ID. BINGO.

if **BINGO** is the name you have chosen. Consult the computer manager about possible restrictions on program names: generally, they will have to conform to the rules for procedure names and only part of the name (for example, the first 8 letters) may actually be recognised by the operating system, so it must be unique on those. You are also allowed entries for:

AUTHOR.
INSTALLATION.
DATE-WRITTEN.
SECURITY.
REMARKS.

The Environment Division describes the computer configuration on which the program is to be compiled and run (they may be different), and gives information to the compiler about the allocation of input/output hardware (readers, printers, tapes, etc.) It is therefore particularly dependent upon the actual computer and the manufacturer's conventions and implementation of COBOL, and you must find out what terminology is employed in your own installation. The Division consists of two Sections, the **CONFIGURATION SECTION** and the **INPUT-OUTPUT SECTION,** both of which must appear.

55

The Configuration Section has two subheads, **SOURCE-COM-PUTER** (on which the program is to be compiled) and **OBJECT-COMPUTER** (on which it is to be run). The actual nature of these entries, and of other entries which allow the assignment of various mnemonic names and switches (**SPECIAL-NAMES**) is so machine-dependent that we shall not attempt to deal further with them.

The Input-Output Section can be omitted if no files are being used in the program (unlikely, but it can happen). If there are files, there is one obligatory heading, **FILE-CONTROL**; there is also **I-O-CONTROL** (note the hyphens) which can be omitted and should only be used by the beginner with the advice of an expert.

Under **FILE-CONTROL**, we have the **SELECT** clauses, which for Program **CHARLIE** might read:

INPUT-OUTPUT SECTION.
FILE-CONTROL.
    SELECT CARDFILE ASSIGN CARD-READER.
    SELECT PRINTFILE ASSIGN PRINTER.

—in other words, each **FD** name in the program is *assigned* to a specific device, and must be so assigned once and once only. The device-names (**CARD-READER, PRINTER**) will differ in different implementations.

You have now 'broken the back' of the COBOL language; you have learnt enough to be able to write useful programs. Chapter 3 provides a recapitulation and amplification of Chapter 2. Almost any computer procedures are, in theory, possible with what has been described in Chapter 2, but they might in some cases be extraordinarily tedious and roundabout, and Chapter 3 shows how the work of the programmer may be made easier.

More advanced COBOL

3.1 Introduction

Chapter 3 completes the study of the COBOL facilities appropriate to an elementary book. Advanced topics such as segmentation, library usage, control of storage and peripherals in the Environment Division, as well as the subtler ramifications and implications of the elementary COBOL features, are omitted; not only are they unsuitable for beginners or for those who merely want to know what a programming language looks like, but they are too often dependent on the characteristics of particular computers, implementations, operating systems, and installations. The reader who finishes Chapter 2 will find that he still has a good deal to learn about full COBOL—which, it is hoped, will be the easier to learn thanks to the presentation of the elementary material in this book; but, even at this point, without learning any more, he should be able to write efficient and effective COBOL programs, perhaps not up to professional standards, but good enough to be acceptable in any computer installation.

3.2 Data structure and storage

.2.1 Levels and group items

Though none of the programs in Chapter 2 used more than two levels in the record descriptions, it was mentioned that we are allowed more than that. In fact we can have levels 03, 04, . . . up to level **10** (in COBOL level 1) or 49 (in COBOL Level 2); level **77** is used for independent items in Working-Storage, and **66** and **88** for special data types not dealt with in this book. Thus we could combine the Commodity Number descriptions of Programs CHARLIE and DOG:

01 TABLEREC.
   02 COMMOD-NO.

> 03 ALPHPART PIC XX.
> 03 NUMPART PIC 9999.
> 02 PRICE60   etc.

Then we can either process **COMMOD-NO** as a whole, as in CHARLIE, or as its component parts, as in DOG. Note that the **PICTURE**s have moved from level **02** to the new elementary level, **03**. It is fairly obvious commonsense that a level-number 'governs' all subsequent entries until an equal or higher level number is encountered—higher, that is, in the hierarchy of levels, which means numerically smaller: **01** is higher than **02**. So all entries following **02 COMMOD-NO** are part of that field until we reach another **02**, (or an **01**).

As already stated, any item which you want to process separately must have its own data-name—that is why we had to break down **COMMOD-NO** into **ALPHPART** and **NUMPART**. Once you have broken down a record into elementary items, corresponding to the separate items of data, you can group them (in the same sequence) for your own convenience. If you are always going to handle them as individual items, like the **PRICE** entries in the above example, the only grouping you need is at the **01** level, to give the whole record a name. In fact we shall nearly always find it convenient to group elementary items into groups below **01** level; we could always achieve the results we want by separate handling of the items, like **ALPH-PART** and **NUMPART**, but definition as a group item will save us two **MOVE**s, two definitions in the ouput area, where we may not need separate definitions; and so on. If you have a sequence of fields of the same structure, (that is, the same meaning and size, like the **PRICE** items) it is a good rule to group them. If you did not, then at some later stage you may perhaps find that you want to do so because grouping will save you writing a lot of program; and to insert a group name you will have to rewrite all the lower-level items in order to give them a lower level number. You can avoid this by making use of the fact that the level numbers need not be consecutive: you can (and must) use **01** for the record level, and then you can use **03, 05, 07**, etc., so that any group names inserted later can use **02, 04,** etc. It is usual, though not necessary, to inset lower level groups at intervals of four places.

The power and flexibility of the COBOL record-description

```
01 PERSONNEL-RECORD.
   03 FULLNAME.
      05 SURNAME        PIC X(20).
      05 FIRSTNAME.
         07 INITIALFN   PIC X.
         07 RESTFN      PIC X(9).
      05 SECONDNAME.
         07 INITIALSN   PIC X.
         07 RESTSN      PIC X(9).
   03 DOB.
      05 DAY            PIC 99.
      05 MONTH          PIC XXX.
      05 YEAR           PIC 9999.
   03 SEX               PIC X.
   03 MARSTATUS         PIC X.
   03 WORKS-NO          PIC 9999.
```

ALLOCATION OF STORAGE BY CHARACTERS

Level

01	PERSONNEL-RECORD								
03	FULLNAME			DOB			S	M	Wks No.
05	SURNAME	1st NAME	2nd NAME	D	M	Y			
07		I	REST	I	REST					

SMITH	A	RTHUR	G	EORGE	29	AUG	1929	M	D	2371

Fig. 3.1. Personnel-record
   (a) COBOL data division format
   (b) Store Layout

59

method will be amply illustrated in the following pages. We will conclude this section with a fairly elaborate and realistic data description, a personnel record which is punched to the following design:

		Cols.
Surname	20 chs. maximum; punched to left of field, if fewer:	1–20
First name	10 chs. maximum; punched to left of field, if fewer:	21–30
Second name	10 chs. maximum; punched to left of field, if fewer:	31–40
Date of Birth	9 chs. (day, month, year)	41–49
Sex	1 character (M or F)	50
Marital status	1 character (M, S, D, W)	51
Works Number	4 digits	52–55

The programmer understands that it may sometimes be desirable to list only the initials of the forenames, and that we may need separate runs on year of birth only. A suggested record description, and a picture of the store layout, is given in Fig. 3.1.

Because the data under the record name **PERSONNEL-RECORD** may be called for either as a single block, or as individual items, or as groups of individual items in variety of combinations, the data is stored in *contiguous* store locations, occupying a single block equivalent to 55 characters. No matter how much we subdivide it, the record takes up no more than the sum of its elementary items; in fact the length of a record is defined as the sum of its **PICTURES**. Another point to notice is that any grouping must be over *consecutive* fields: it is not possible, for example, to define a group field consisting of **SURNAME** and initials only.

3.2.2 Multirecord files

With card usage, at least, we are limited to 80 card columns in a record, and many of the records used in a computer cannot be limited to 80 columns; a library catalogue, for example, will need a large number of characters for author, classification, title, publisher, accession number, and date, etc. Obviously we need more than one card per book for all this information; and these cards will not only carry different types of information but will have to be of different formats, though they are all in the same file, that is, they come under the same **FD** and are assigned to the same peripheral—the card reader—in the Environment Division.

COBOL allows us to have more than one record name, each with an **01** level, in the same **FD**. We give a **READ** for the File-name, as usual; having got a record into store we carry out some test to see what sort of record it is. Thus we can not only have sets of cards which belong, logically, to the same category of information, such as different parts of the library 'record', but we can have completely different types of record: if we have only one card-reader, for example, *all* card records used in the program must go under the same **FD**.

```
FD MAIN-CATALOGUE.
01  AUTHOR-CARD.
        03 ACCESSION-NO        PIC X(10).
        03 FULLNAME.
            05 SURNAME         PIC X(40).
            05 FORENAMES.
                07 FIRST-NAME.
                    09 INITIAL-FN  PIC X.
                    09 REST-FN     PIC X(10).
(etc.; to whatever depth is necessary, up to col. 79)
    03 CODE PIC 9.
01  TITLE-CARD.
    03 ACCESSION-NO  PIC X(10).
    03 TITLE         PIC X(69).
    03 CODE          PIC 9.
01  TITLE-CONTD.
    03 ACCESSION-NO  PIC X(10).
    03 TITLE-2       PIC X(69).
    03 CODE          PIC 9.
01  CLASSIFICATION.
    03 ACCESSION-NO. PIC X(10).
    03 CLASS-NO      PIC X(20).
    03 PUBLISHER     PIC X(30).
    03 YEAR-PUB      PIC XXXX.
    03 OTHER-INF     PIC X(15).
    03 CODE          PIC 9.
```

Fig. 3.2. File description, MAIN CATALOGUE

61

An outline File Description is given in Fig. 3.2. There are either three or four cards for each book; one is for the author's name; there are one, or two, for the title, depending on its length; and one for other information about the book. A real catalogue might have even more; there is no limit, in principle, to the possible number of record-names within a file. However, where the records form part of a larger logical set (here, the complete catalogue entry for each book) it is usual to have in each record an entry common to all records in the set. This is useful in card-handling (for example, in order to put the records in order again if the file is disarranged) and in computer handling: we can read in card-records and make them into a simple record on tape, of about 200 characters, by using the common entry (here, the accession number) to link the records of each set (see 4.2.3).

We also have a *code* to distinguish one type of record from another. This is one digit, and we will assume it to be 1 on the author card, 2 on the Title card, 3 on the Title-continuation card, and 4 on the Classification card.

The following bit of program illustrates the use of the code. We want to count how many books in the library were published by the Oxford University Press, which is always punched as **OUP**. This will, of course, be on the card with code 4, in columns 31–33. We set up a counter called **PUB-COUNTER** at level **77** in Working-Storage. Then

```
READ-A-CARD.
    READ MAIN-CATALOGUE AT END GO TO DONEIT.
    IF CODE NOT EQUAL TO 4 GO TO READ-A-CARD.
    IF PUBLISHER EQUAL TO 'OUP' ADD 1 TO PUB-COUNTER.
    GO TO READ-A-CARD.
```

If we didn't test the code number, we would be looking for **OUP** in 31–34 of *every* record, and so books entitled

RECIPES FOR TOMATO SOUPS
or **AUTOMATIC CARRIAGE COUPLINGS**

would contribute to the over-all **OUP** count. Similarly, in routines too long to illustrate here, we might use characteristics involving two or more records in the same catalogue entry, for example, the number of books published by a given author in a given year. In that case we would not only look for the codes 1 and 4, but having found them we would check that they had the same accession number, that is, that they referred to the same book.

To print the book catalogue, we would have multiple print-formats as record-names under **FD PRINT-FILE,** for example, **PRINTLINE-1, PRINTLINE-2, PRINTLINE-3, PRINTLINE-4,** because the characters must be distributed differently, in different fields, for different codes (though 2 and 3 could, in this case, be the same); we might want different line spacing or insets for each type, and so on. Having identified each type of record by its code we would need a **MOVE** for each type of record-name.

It must be emphasised that there is only one **FD** for all of these records, because they are all in the same File on the same peripheral, the card-reader or the printer in this case. And just as there cannot be more than one **FD** for any peripheral, so there is just one input area for each **FD**. This means that each input record enters the *same* input area; the record descriptions *implicitly redefine* the fields of the input area. Thus according to which type of record is in the input area, character 31 of that area is part of the surname; part of the title; or the first character of the publisher field. On the other hand, we know that whatever record is in the input area, character 80 is a code which will tell us how the fields are distributed in the input area. If we could be sure that the records were always going to appear in the input area in a given rotation, we could dispense with the code; we would merely keep a count of the records being read and we would know for example that every fourth one is the same. But this is not the case here—because sometimes an entry has three cards, sometimes four—and in any case it is unsafe to rely on strict rotation since the accidental omission or duplication of a card could make nonsense of all subsequent work. If all types of record are mixed up in any order, we shall certainly need some field on each which is unique for each type, for testing as a code or identifier. On the other hand, no code or identifier will be necessary where the different types of record are segregated, for example, where we are reading in two lots of data, one after the other, for the same program. A common example of this is reading in cards carrying some details, for example, of prices, which we store; then we read in 'transaction-cards' of a quite different design, using the stored prices to complete the transaction-cards. As long as we can detect the end of the price-cards there is no need for special identifiers, nor for testing each card to see what it is, although they will be under the same **FD** exactly as before.

The use of a code to distinguish between records of different formats is one of the ways in which we can relax the strict standards of uniformity which had to be imposed in the early days of data-processing (and still are, by unimaginative or hidebound programmers). If we have two or more sources of data, such as customers who send in orders, we can allow each source to prepare and lay out its data in whatever way best suits it, as long as the record contains all the information we want, and also contains some unique feature or characteristic field which we can use as a code to tell us what the source, and therefore what the format, is. We may want to punch accounts or returns from customers or other authorities over whom we have no control, and who might flatly refuse to accept our 'standard' format—after all they might be dealing with a lot of other people who have their own 'standards'! The multiple record facility gives us a reasonable latitude in dealing with variable input.

We have said that each record description 'implicitly redefines' the input area, at **01** level. We can also redefine items at lower levels, that is, within records, by the use of the **REDEFINES** verb (which must *not* be used at **01** level in the File Section). It can be used to economise storage space, and also to avoid tedious repetition of record descriptions that differ only in minor particulars. Neither of these is of first importance to the beginner, and we will postpone further discussion of this verb until we come to discuss the construction of tables. Used with the **OCCURS** verb, the **REDEFINES** offers some powerful facilities.

3.2.3 Working-Storage

Working-Storage is the maid of all work of the computer store. All data-names that are not part of input or output files must be defined here, down to the least important counter (it is very easy to invent on the spot a data-name for a 'switch' or counter in the white heat of programming the Procedure Division, and forget to legitimise it in the Data Division; your program will be thrown out at compilation).

The entries in the Working-Storage can be classified as Independent or Record-Format. The Independent entries must be given first: these have the level number 77. They cannot have subfields or be part of a hierarchical structure like the Record-Format.

The Record-Format entries are exactly like the entries in the File Section, and can have the same sort of structure. But they cannot have a File Description (**FD**) entry, because all **FD** entries must be assigned (in the Environment Division) to a peripheral device, and Working-Storage entries are not associated with any peripheral. Record-Formats are sometimes known as contiguous storage, since the fields are grouped, in contrast to the 'independent' 77 entries.

All Working-Storage entries should, as a matter of good practice, be given an initial **VALUE,** They can of course be modified by arithmetic, or **MOVE**s, in the Procedure Division; but it is illegal to use them as the operands of **READ** or **WRITE** verbs. If you want to read data into them (either to give them an initial value, or to modify the value in the program) you must first of all read it into a File Section input area and then **MOVE** it to Working-Storage. Similarly, if you try to **WRITE** a Working-Storage area, the compiler will reject it. You must first **MOVE** it to an output area.

There will be a good deal more to be said about Record-Formats in Working-Storage when we come to deal with Table-Handling. We may say here, however, that one of the principal uses of Record-Format is to provide a 'siding' or 'holding area' for records read in. In the programs we have had so far, we have always handled records in the sequence read-write-read-write, completing our dealings with one record (either writing it out or overwriting it by reading in another record) at a time. But we may need to compare two records before we can decide which to write out first (rather as in Program FOX, but at record level); many similar cases will be illustrated in Chapter 4. In such cases we would set up a Record-Format in Working-Storage to act as a holding area, though it might not need to be as elaborately structured as for general file handling.

Another use of Record-Format is to restructure an input record, where the format used for punching, and reflected in the input area set-up, is not the most convenient for internal handling. One thing we cannot do with the COBOL record description format is make groups of fields that are not contiguous in the record—in the example in Fig. 3.2, we could not group surnames and initials because rest-of-first-name intervened. But we can set up a Working-Storage record:

01 WNAME.
    03 WSURNAME PIC X (20).
    03 WINITIAL-1 PIC X.
    03 WINITIAL-2 PIC X.

We **MOVE SURNAME, INITIALFN, AND INITIALSN,** and then we can handle surname and initials as a single group, **WNAME.**

3.2.4 Elementary items

So far we have used only two symbols in **PICTURE**s, **X** and **9**. A third symbol, **A**, is available for data which is purely alphabetic, that is contains only the letters A-Z and space. This is not much used nowadays; there may be some situations where it is worth using, but in most cases there is no disadvantage, and some advantage, in using X, even if the item is purely alphabetic.

Two other types of symbol can be used in the **PICTURE**: these are the *editing symbols*, which are the subject of this section; and the *operational* symbols, which are dealt with in the next section.

3.2.4.1 Editing symbols

Editing is a means of improving the appearance of the output for the reader, by replacing, or inserting characters. Most editing conventions are applicable to numeric items only, but some alphanumeric editing is allowed. Editing symbols can be used in any data description, but in this book we shall use them only in connection with *output formats for printing*, and you are strongly advised, on account of the limitations on the use of edited fields, to restrict your use in this way.

Editing is actually carried out by a **MOVE** (or other form of data transfer, for example, **ADD**) of data to an *edited field*, that is a field whose **PICTURE** contains editing symbols. A *numeric edited* field consists of the symbol **9** with one or more editing symbols

$$Z + - , . * £ B 0$$

and an alphanumeric edited field consists of combinations of **X**, and possibly **9** and **A**, with **B** or **0**. We will now describe the function of these symbols.

The **Z** symbol

This is perhaps the most commonly used of the editing symbols. It is used to suppress leading zeros and replace them with spaces. We always have to allow enough digits (that is, **9**s) in a **PICTURE** to cope with the largest possible value that may be given to that field. When we print out the field, any number which has fewer digits than the maximum will be printed out with leading zeros, for example, with a **PICTURE 99999**, (allowing for a value up to 99999) the value 1 will be printed out as 00001. This may be inelegant and confusing to the reader, so we write the **PICTURE** as **ZZZZ9** (or **Z(4)9**). Now all leading zeros, that is, all zeros to the left of the first significant digit, will be replaced by blanks, so that we shall no longer get 00001 but simply   **1**, where the one is actually preceded by four blanks. With this **PICTURE**, the last digit will always be printed, even if it is zero. If we write **ZZZZZ**, or **Z(5)**, then if the answer is zero five blanks will be printed. (In fact a special entry is provided in the data description, **BLANK WHEN ZERO**, which has the same effect.) The Z symbol is useful, for example, when laying out material in tabular form where some of the 'cells' of the table may have zero entries. Since the blanks *replace* zeros, the alignment is not affected; for example, with **PIC ZZZZZ9**,

000012 is printed as	**12**
007428	**7428**
000000	**0**
100034	**100034**

with column alignment as shown.

So if the Working-Storage location **WS-PAGE-NO**, with **PIC 9999**, contains **0034**, then the statement **MOVE WS-PAGE-NO TO PRINT-PAGE-NO** (with **PIC ZZZ9**) will 'edit' the item and print **34**.

A similar function is performed by the 'cheque protection character', the asterisk, illustrated in the next section. **Z** and ***** are called *replacement* symbols.

Floating symbols: **£ + −**

If we have a **PIC 999999** for an input or Working-Storage item which represents pounds sterling, we can give it an output **PICTURE £££££9** (note that there are *six* £s, making a total of seven characters, though there are only six 9s in the original **PICTURE**). With this **PICTURE,**

000329 will be printed as   **£329**
123456   **£123456**

The second example makes it clear why we have the extra **£** symbol in the **PICTURE**. This is, of course, a protection against fraud. The replacement symbol * is an alternative. **PIC £*****9** will edit **000329** into **£***329**, thus making it difficult to enter digits before the true sum. If we have asked for **BLANK WHEN ZERO,** a zero answer will be printed as all asterisks, not all blanks—a useful device for the auditor.

The **£** sign is called a floating symbol because its position 'floats' in the output item, as it can appear in any of the positions occupied by a **£** sign in the **PICTURE**. The other floating symbols are + and − (the representation of plus and minus in internal storage and input is dealt with in the next section). If we write a series of + in a **PICTURE** then in the output the number will be preceded (immediately) by a + if it is positive, by − if it is negative. If I write a series of −, then the number will be preceded by − if negative, and by blank if positive:

++++++9 will cause (+)004528 to be printed **+4528**
and   (−)004528   **−4528**
−−−−−−9 will cause (+)004528   **4528**
(−)004528   **−4528**

Note the additional symbol, as in the case of the **£**.

Insertion symbols **. , B 0**

The period, '.' is called a Special Insertion character; ℵ is used to represent the decimal point for alignment purposes in an output **PICTURE**. Thus if we have a number in storage, say **4523**, which is a number of pounds (without pence), and move it to an output **PICTURE** which represents pounds and pence, **£££££9.99,** the number will be printed as **£4523.00.** We shall have more to say on decimal points when we deal with the operational symbols.

A comma can be used, for decoration: **PIC ZZZ,ZZZ,ZZ9** will print **001234567** as **1,234,567; 000000032** as **32**. Continental users are allowed to use the comma as a decimal point, and the period as a separator symbol, by an entry in a part of the Environment Division called **SPECIAL-NAMES**.

The symbols **B** and **0** (zero) can be used with either **X** or **9**. **B** inserts a blank; **0** inserts a zero. Thus if we have an item (representing degrees, minutes, and seconds) **0342314** we can **MOVE** it to an output **PICTURE ZZ9B99B99**, so that it is printed as **34 23 14**. This is obviously less trouble than putting in **FILLER**s.

0 is used to insert zeros, but is less common.

2.4.2   JUSTIFIED

B and **0** are the only two editing symbols that can be used with **X** and **A** data. However, a form of editing is providing by the **JUSTIFIED RIGHT** clause. When a field is described as **X** or **A**, any item that contains less than the specified number of characters is placed at the *left* of the field, and spaces are inserted, as required, to fill up the field on the right. Thus (where _ means space): with a data description **CITY-NAME PIC X(15)**, the name **LONDON** will be stored in the form:

| LONDON _ _ _ _ _ _ _ _ _ |

with nine spaces to the right. Another way of saying this is that implicit justification for alphabetic and alphanumeric fields is to the left. But if I write

CITY-NAME PIC X(15) JUSTIFIED RIGHT

the storage will be

| _ _ _ _ _ _ _ _ _ LONDON |

This facility may be useful in lining up output records. It must not be used with numeric data, which is implicitly justified right anyway, on the decimal point. **JUSTIFIED RIGHT** can be abbreviated to **JUST RIGHT**. **JUSTIFIED** may be described as a form of editing, but a **JUSTIFIED** field is not, technically, edited, and is not subject to the restrictions on edited fields.

General rules for editing symbols.

The symbols **A X 9 0 Z * B + − £** can be used with a repeat indicator in brackets: **£(6)9** stands for **££££££9**.

In the Data Division, you must not assign a **VALUE** to an edited field. This rule will cause you no difficulty if you use editing only in output record, since they cannot be given a **VALUE** anyway, being in the File Section.

The rules for combining editing symbols (and operational symbols) in the same **PICTURE**, the sequence in which they may appear, and the **MOVE**ing of edited fields and their use in arithmetical work, are complicated and subtle, and you should postpone the study of these rules (which you will find in your implementor's manual) until you are thoroughly at home with COBOL. However, if you always treat the edited field as the *receiving* field, in other words use it only in output formats in the File Section, you should have no trouble.

A **PICTURE** with editing symbols is to all intents and purposes alphanumeric, even though it contains nothing but 9s and numeric editing symbols. Because it is alphanumeric it cannot be used as an operand in arithmetic statements, except as the operand of **GIVING** (see 3.3.1).

Operational symbols **V, P, S**

The operational symbols are:

V which represents a decimal point, and thus permits us to handle fractions;

P which is a 'scaling' symbol and implies multiplication (or division) by multiples of 10;

S which represents a sign (plus or minus) and thus provides for positive and negative numbers.

By their nature, these symbols must be used only in numeric fields; if they are used in **PICTURE**s containing **X** or **A** they are invalid. These characters do not occupy any space in the stored representation of the number; they do not count in determining the size of the data item; **V** and **S** do not count towards the maximum number of characters allowed in a **PICTURE** (that is, 18) though **P** does.

The representation of numbers in the computer is closely dependent upon the design of the machine, and different compilers may differ in their handling of operational symbols. For our purposes, it is enough to say that they should be reserved for data specifications for input and internal storage; they are thus distinct from the editing symbols which are reserved for output. In this section, I have tried to give rules which are generally applicable and to avoid subtleties which will confuse the beginner.

The symbol V

This is an 'implied' or 'assumed' decimal point. If we write a **PICTURE** with a **V** in it, all operations with that item in the program will be carried out as if there were a decimal point where the **V** is. Thus if a value **314159** is read in from card or tape, or **MOVE**d to an item described as **PIE PIC 9V99999**, the number will be treated as if it were 3·14159. (We make no assumption, since COBOL does not, about the way a number containing a decimal point is punched on card or tape.)

Items in input or store will be automatically lined up on their decimal point:

CALC-1	**PIC 999V99** (value read in: **2305**)	23·05
CALC-2	**PIC 9V999** (. . . . . . **1965**)	1·965
CALCSUM	**PIC 999V999**	result	25·015

The addition of **CALC-1** and **CALC-2** gives the right answer in **CALCSUM**.

The **V** also serves to align the decimal point in the output. If we **MOVE PIE TO OUTPIE**, where **OUTPIE** has the **PICTURE 9·99999**, then the stored item **314159** will be printed as 3·14159. If **OUTPIE** had **PIC 999999**, then the digit 3 would be printed out (because the **PIC** implies a decimal point after the rightmost 9); **OUTPIE PIC 999·999** would give 003·141.

In giving a **VALUE** with a decimal point to an item in Working-Storage, you write the decimal point in the literal, thus:

77 PIE PIC 9V99999 VALUE IS 3·14159.

The decimal point is not an editing symbol because the literal is not itself a **PICTURE**.

The symbol P

The symbol **P** is similar to **V**, but you will probably find that you have less use for it. While **V** is used to indicate the position of a decimal point within, or to the extreme left of, a **PICTURE**, the **P** indicates a decimal point *outside* the item. If the item is stored as 1234 then:

PP9999 means that is is to be read as ·001234
9999PPP   1234000

P is called a scaling factor. A **P** to the left of a **PICTURE** means 'Divide the number, as read in or stored, by 10' and by 100 if there are two **P**s, and so on; similarly **P**s to the right of a **PICTURE** denote multiplication by factors of 10.

It is useful in saving space in input, as on cards. The number 1234 can be punched in four columns of the card; read in with **PIC 9999PPPPP** it will be treated as **123400000**, which is quite a saving in card columns. If 1234 were punched in a six-column field, with blanks to the left, it would be read as 001234 and with a **PICTURE PP9999** would be treated as ·000012.

P can appear either to the right or left of an item, but not both. It can be preceded (but not followed) by **V**: this is in any case unnecessary since **P** implies a decimal point. It can combine with various editing symbols but we will leave these minutiae for you to investigate if ever you need to use them.

The S Symbol

This is used to indicate that the item has a sign, plus or minus. An item that is unsigned is always taken to be positive; there is never any need to punch, or write, a plus sign to show this. The **S** is only necessary if we know that the number, in input or in calculation in the store, may take on a negative value. In Working-Storage data descriptions the sign is added if the value is negative:

77 OPERATOR PIC S9 VALUE IS −1.

In input, the minus sign will be punched according to the conventions of the equipment you are using. In card coding, a minus sign is generally represented as an overpunch over one of the digits, so that a field with **PIC S999** will represent only three columns on the card.

In output, you have to specify the editing symbols plus or minus, as explained in the previous section. Thus if we have a storage location.

03 TEMPERATURE PIC S99.

we can output it as

03 OUTTEMP PIC +99.
or **03 OUTTEMP PIC −99.**

In the first case all output will have a sign, either plus or minus; in the second only the minus will be printed.

Only **P, V,** and **9** can appear in a **PICTURE** with **S**; only one **S** is allowed; no symbol except **P** can appear to the left of **S**.

4.3 The **USAGE** clause.

The two forms of **USAGE, DISPLAY** and **COMPUTATIONAL** (abbreviated to **COMP**) provide an easy way of improving the performance of the program.

Only numeric fields can be described as **COMPUTATIONAL**, for example,

03 HEIGHT PIC S9999V99 USAGE IS COMP.

The **COMP** entry is a notification to the compiler that this field is to be used predominantly for arithmetic calculation. The compiler will then convert and store the item in a form, for example, binary, which is much more efficient for computation, and the program does not have to keep converting to this form. On the other hand, **DISPLAY** means that the item is to be used chiefly in character form, for printing, sorting, comparisons, etc. If no **USAGE** is stated, an item is stored in **DISPLAY** form (this is known as a 'default option'), and has to be converted if it is used for computation. So you needn't write **USAGE IS DISPLAY** if that is what you want.

Notifying a field as **DISPLAY** or **COMP** does not, however, place any restriction on your use of the field; if you want to use a **DISPLAY** item in computation, or vice versa, all necessary conversion is done automatically. The **HEIGHT** item given above could be **MOVED** to output with an edited **PICTURE**:

03 PRINT-HEIGHT PIC −ZZZZZ. 99.

But you must not describe an edited field as **COMP**, which you are unlikely to do if you use editing only in output format.

Don't confuse this Data Division attribute with the **DISPLAY** *verb*, used in the Procedure Division, which we describe later (3.3.3).

3.2.5 Literals and **VALUE**

Values can be assigned to locations by reading in the values as data; by derivation from other locations (by a **MOVE** or arithmetic); and by explicitly assigning values.

The simplest form of explicit assignment is of course the *literal*, in which instead of naming a location whose contents are to be used in the procedure, we name the contents themselves:

> **MULTIPLY NUMBER-OF-WEEKS BY 7 GIVING NUMBER-OF-DAYS.**
> **MOVE 'ANNUAL REPORT' TO PRINT-LINE-CENTRE.**

Such literals cannot be changed without rewriting the statement and recompiling the program, so you only use them when you are pretty certain they are *not* going to be changed. They are, in the true sense, *constants*.

An alphanumeric constant may consist entirely of digits:

> **MOVE '1969' TO YEAR-SLOT.**

and it cannot be used in computations. **MOVE 1969 TO YEAR-SLOT**, using **1969** as a numeric constant, would have the same effect, and this **1969** could also, if we wished, be used in arithmetic, if **YEAR-SLOT** has a **PICTURE 9999**:

> **DIVIDE YEAR-SLOT BY 4.**

It is a good rule to use numeric literals (which can also contain a sign and a decimal point) only in comparisons or calculations with, or **MOVE**s to, fields that have been defined with **9**s.

Literals cannot be used as addresses. It is legal to write

> **MOVE CHEESE TO MOUSETRAP.**

where **CHEESE** (and **MOUSETRAP**) have been defined as datanames in the Data Division;

> **MOVE 'CHEESE' TO MOUSETRAP.**

where **'CHEESE'** is a literal and has not been defined in the Data Division is also legal. In the first place the contents of the location **CHEESE** are copied to the location **MOUSETRAP**; in the second

74

case, after the **MOVE** the location **MOUSETRAP** will contain the letters **C,H,E,E,S,E**. But you cannot **MOVE MOUSETRAP TO 'CHEESE'** because **'CHEESE'** is not an address.

Rather than use a literal form in Procedure, we may prefer to assign the literal value to a variable (data-name) in Working-Storage:

77 PIE PIC 9V99999 VALUE IS 3·14159.
77 TEN PIC 99 VALUE IS 10.
77 HEADER PIC X(13) VALUE IS 'ANNUAL REPORT'.
77 COUNTER PIC 9(5) VALUE IS ZERO.
77 BLANKLINE PIC (X120) VALUE IS SPACES.

There are two advantages in this. The first is that naming a constant in this way will normally generate less object program than naming it as a literal in the Procedure Division; though we are not concerned in this book with considerations of 'efficiency' which may save a few milliseconds here and there, this may be worth while if you use the constant frequently. Thus

ADD ONE TO COUNTER.

is more efficient than

ADD 1 TO COUNTER.

provided you have an entry in the Data Division:

77 ONE PIC 9 VALUE IS 1.

(It's very easy to forget it!)

Secondly, this is a way of giving an initial value to ('initialising') variables in the program. It is not safe to use variable names from Working-Storage until you have given them an initial value. Often, of course, the first thing you do is to **MOVE** something to these locations, as you do with File Section data-areas (which can't be initialised with a **VALUE**); but even so it is often wiser to 'clear' these stores. For example, you may have a set of counters which are going to count different types of record coming in, with

ADD ONE TO COUNTER-A.

when an A-type record is read in, and so on. But it may happen that in some run there are *no* records of a given type; then what would be moved to output at the end of the run would not necessarily be zero but whatever happened to be the contents of the store at the beginning of the run; which might be very misleading indeed.

VALUE, as we have just said, cannot be used in File Section. If you want to ensure that a File Section area has a specified initial value, you can MOVE that value to it; the literal moved must be of the same type as the receiving field (for example, alphanumeric, or SPACE, for X fields; numeric, or ZERO, for 9 fields). Where you want to clear a group item which may contain both numeric and alphanumeric fields, for example, a PRINTLINE, you can do a group MOVE which is in effect a MOVE from one alphanumeric field to another: MOVE SPACE TO PRINTLINE will put spaces in both types of field. For further information see the section on MOVEs (3.3.2).

VALUE must not be used, even in Working-Storage, with certain types of data. These are edited items, and data items with an OCCURS or REDEFINES, which are described in Section 3.5. VALUE can be used in Record-Format in Working-Storage, as well as in 77 entries. If you give a VALUE to a group-field, you must not give a VALUE to individual entries subordinate to that group-name. The commonest use of the group-value is to assign figurative constants:

> **01 WRECORD VALUE IS ZERO.**
> **03 WFLD-1 PIC 9999.**
> **03 WFLD-2 PIC 99.**
> or **01 WRECORD VALUE IS SPACE.**
> **03 WFLD-1 PIC XXXXX.**

and so on. If the record contains both numeric and alphanumeric fields, it is best to give them their VALUES individually. Some implementations may not allow the Group VALUEs shown above.

3.3 Data manipulation

We have described the various ways in which data can be put into the computer—reading it in from peripherals, assigning an initial value in Working-Storage, giving it an invariable value as a constant in the Procedure Division. But the really important and effective part of computation is done by combining two or more data fields

76

so as to produce 'new' items of information which are the results we require, or can be used in further combinations to arrive at the results. Without such data manipulation—which includes the rearrangement of the data, as in sorting—there would not be much use in computing. We take the term in its widest sense, to include:

1. Arithmetic. The verbs (of which we have already had some simple and self-explanatory samples) use two or more fields as the operands of addition, subtraction, multiplication, and division.

2. Moves. The effect of the Move on the sending and receiving fields is explained. Moves can be used to alter the order of the data between input and output.

3. Comparisons. What fields can be compared, and what are the rules for doing so. The result of the comparison determines the sequence of instructions to be followed; this is the subject of the next section in this chapter, which will complete the survey of the main aspects of computing—input/output, data manipulation, and sequence control.

3.1 Arithmetic

The general form of the **ADD** verb is

ADD A TO B.

where **A** is either a numeric literal or a data-name, and **B** is a data-name. The contents of **A** are added to **B**, and **B** now contains the sum of **A** and **B**, while **A** remains unchanged. We can have multiple addends:

ADD X, Y, Z TO B.

If we want to preserve the contents of **B**, we can write:

ADD A, B GIVING C.

Now **A** and **B** are unaltered and can be used again; **C** contains their sum. Do *not* write **ADD A *TO* B GIVING C**; it is not allowed. **GIVING** is in a way equivalent to a **MOVE**: the contents of **C**, if any, are erased and replaced by the sum of **A** and **B**.

The rules about the **ADD** are simple. They apply, as appropriate, to the other arithmetic verbs, and we will not repeat them:

77

All the items must be numeric, and must be defined in the Data Division (except literals: any of the addends (the 'sending' fields) can be a literal, and in fact they can all be literals, but such a calculation would be more suited to a desk adding machine than a computer!). The receiving field must *not* be a literal, which is fairly obvious. The operand of the **GIVING** (C, above) can be edited (but not if it is to be used in further computation); the addends must be unedited.

There is an upper limit of 18 digits on any operand, that is, its **PICTURE** must not contain more than 18 **9**s or editing symbols: **9(9).9(9)** is illegal, but **9(9)V9(9)** isn't. The operand fields need not be of the same size, or even the same **USAGE**: the COBOL compiler generates code to do the necessary conversion, as well as the automatic alignment of decimal points. But, obviously, the receiving field must be large enough to hold the sum of the addends. If **A** and **B** both have **PIC 999**, then **ADD A TO B** will be all right as long as the *sum* does not exceed three digits; but if **A**, say, is 750 and **B** is 251, it is impossible to say what the contents of **B** will be after the addition—it is unlikely that they will be right! If we knew that neither **A** nor **B** could exceed three digits, then we could give **B** a **PICTURE 9999**, and we would be safe (similarly for **ADD A, B GIVING C**).

But it is not always easy to see what the size of the result is going to be, especially if the calculation is complicated or if **A** and **B** are themselves the result of previous calculations. In that case you must make a generous allowance; and in every calculation you should add the conditional clause **ON SIZE ERROR** which is followed by an imperative statement which tells the program what to do if the result does actually exceed the allotted space. This imperative statement will generally be **GO TO SIZE-ERROR-ROUTINE** or something similar, for which see 4.7.8. If you don't put this in, the result is unpredictable (though the addends and any intermediate results will be correct); and if the error is allowed to go through without notification the results will almost certainly be wrong. If the receiving field contains *more* digit positions than the result, then the left-hand end of the receiving field will be filled with zeros. No harm is done—in fact this is an error on the right side.

If, in the receiving field, you allow too few places after the decimal point, the result will be truncated, that is, excess digits to the right will simply be lost (this is more likely to happen with multiplication, because the number of decimal places in the product is the sum of the number of decimal places in the factors). This may not matter, but you get the best results by adding the word **ROUNDED**. If **A** and **B** both have the **PICTURE 99V999,** the product of **A** times **B** will have six decimal places. You may be content, for the purposes of your program, to have the result accurate to three decimal places; then you can write

MULTIPLY A BY B GIVING C ROUNDED.

with **C** having a **PICTURE 9999V999.** Now if the fourth decimal place of result (after rounding from the right) is 5 or more, the program adds 1 to the third digit. If it is less than 5, or you do not specify **ROUNDED**, nothing is added to the third digit. In either case the fourth, fifth, and sixth digits are 'truncated'.

The other arithmetic verbs are **SUBTRACT, MULTIPLY, DIVIDE.** All can, and should, have **ROUNDED** and **SIZE ERROR** options. The forms allowed in Level 1 COBOL are:

SUBTRACT A FROM B.
SUBTRACT A, B, C, , , FROM Z.

The effect of the second form is that the sum $A+B+C+ \ldots$ is formed, and subtracted from **Z**. Each of these options can be followed by a **GIVING**.

MULTIPLY A BY B.
MULTIPLY A BY B GIVING C.

In the first, the result of the multiplication is stored in **B**, so **B** cannot be a literal: you must say **MULTIPLY 100 BY PENCE.**

DIVIDE A INTO B.
DIVIDE A INTO B GIVING C.
DIVIDE A BY B GIVING C.

Level 2 allows you to specify **GIVING C REMAINDER D.** If you haven't got this then you will have to adopt some trick such as repeated subtraction to get a remainder. An example of this is given in Check Digits, 4.2.4. Division by zero always gives a **SIZE ERROR**. This can happen in such sequences as:

SUBTRACT A FROM B GIVING C.
DIVIDE D BY C.

79

If **A** and **B** happen to take on equal values, you will get a **SIZE ERROR** on division. It is not difficult to think of real-life situations where this could happen.

COBOL is not designed for complicated arithmetic, and while such arithmetic can be done (because, after all, all mathematical computations can be broken down to simple steps, such as addition and subtraction; this is the way computers work) it will be pretty long-winded. Consider the comparatively simple algebraic expression

$$\frac{a^2 + 2ab - b^2}{3d}$$

This would, in COBOL, look somewhat as follows:

MULTIPLY A BY A GIVING ASQUARED.
MULTIPLY A BY 2 GIVING TWOA.
MULTIPLY TWOA BY B GIVING TWOAB.
MULTIPLY B BY B GIVING BSQUARED.
ADD ASQUARED TO TWOAB.
SUBTRACT BSQUARED FROM TWOAB.
MULTIPLY 3 BY D.
DIVIDE TWOAB BY D, GIVING ANSWER.

All of the data-names (**ASQUARED, TWOA, TWOAB,** etc.) must be defined in the Data Division. All steps should have **ROUNDED** and **SIZE ERROR**. Some of the steps look quite illogical when compared with the original statement (**DIVIDE TWOAB BY D,** for example); we could clean this up with more data-names.

Level 2 allows the **COMPUTE** verb followed by an arithmetic expression; with this, the above computation will look something like:

COMPUTE Z = (A*A + 2*A*B − B*B)/(D*3)

in which * means multiply; / means divide (A/B is equivalent to $A \div B$ or $\frac{A}{B}$).

3.3.2 MOVEs

The table below summarises the 'legal' position about what types of field may be moved to other types of field. You will find that in elementary programming, at least, this will mean moves of the same type and size, with or without editing. In any legal MOVE of elementary fields, all necessary conversion of USAGE and data type is automatically carried out. You can MOVE anything to an X field, except a non-integer numeric, that is a 9 field which contains a decimal point not at the extreme right. You can also MOVE X data to a 9 field, with a different USAGE, but needless to say this is not the most efficient way of programming!

Receiving Field

Sending field	Alphabetic	Alphanumeric Alphanumeric Edited	Numeric edited Numeric integer Numeric Non-integer
Alphabetic	Yes	Yes	No
Alphanumeric	Yes	Yes	Yes
Alphanumeric edited	Yes	Yes	No
Numeric integer	No	Yes	Yes
Numeric non integer	No	No	Yes
Numeric edited	No	Yes	No

Any programmer who moves data to a *smaller* field without knowing exactly what he is doing deserves all he gets. Generally speaking, alphanumeric fields will have their right-hand end chopped off and numeric fields will have digits at either end chopped off, according to the position of the decimal points.

If the receiving field is larger than the sending field, the receiving field is cleared by the MOVE and there is, after the move of the item, 'spacefill' of the unused positions on the right, for X and A fields (or on the left if the JUSTIFIED RIGHT was given for the receiving field). Thus if I MOVE an X(6) field, contents LONDON, to an X(12) field, contents NEWCASTLE, the X(12) field after the MOVE will be:

> LONDON _____

If the sending field were X(12), LONDON followed by six spaces, and the receiving field X(12), contents NEWCASTLE, the result would be the same as above.

For numeric MOVEs, there is 'zerofill' to right or left or both, as

81

appropriate, according to the decimal point. If **A** has **PIC 99V99** and contains the number 1234, and **B** has **PIC 999V999**, then after **MOVE A TO B** the contents of **B** will be **012340**, with an implied decimal point between 2 and 3.

Moving even a single character clears the whole of the receiving field, with spacefill or zero fill as appropriate.

Group moves

All of the above applies to elementary fields. Group items can also be moved, but no data or usage conversion, or editing, is done; in fact if editing is involved, that is, if a **MOVE** of any one of the elementary fields of the group would have called for editing, the **MOVE** is illegal. The group **MOVE** is best considered as a **MOVE** of a single alphanumeric field, starting from the leftmost character. No notice is taken of subordinate level structure: if we **MOVE RAW-DATA TO EDITED-DATA**, with **PICTURES** as follows:

03 RAW-DATA.	03 EDITED-DATA.
05 REFNO PIC XXX.	05 FILLER PIC X(10).
05 QUALITY PIC X(5).	05 EDREFNO PIC XXX.
05 QUANTITY PIC 99999.	05 FILLER PIC XX.
05 QUANDARY PIC X(10)	05 ED QUALITY PIC X(5).
	05 FILLER PIC XX. etc.

the three letters of **REFNO**, the five letters of **QUALITY**, and the first two digits of **QUANTITY** will go into the **FILLER** of the receiving field; the remaining three digits of **QUANTITY** will go into **EDREFNO; QUANDARY** will go into the second **FILLER** and **EDQUALITY** and so on.

One very useful group **MOVE** is **MOVE SPACES**, for example, in **MOVE SPACES TO PRINTLINE.** This substitutes spaces for all **X, A,** and **9** fields in the receiving group (some implementors do not allow this; it is such a convenient device that I have adopted it in this book).

3.3.3 ACCEPT and DISPLAY

We have assumed so far that all the information we give to the computer is either written into the program, in the form of literals, or read in from devices such as card and tape readers; and similarly that output will be on to a printer (or card or tape).

Where the amount of input and output is small, however, such devices may be too clumsy, and it is possible (if the operations chief agrees) to use the console typewriter, and sometimes other devices, for input and output where this does not exceed say 70 or 80 characters (one line).

We may want to run a program entering a control-total, which differs with each run, at some point in the program. Before that point we insert the instruction:

ACCEPT CONTROL-TOTAL.

On reaching this point the computer will stop and will print out a message to the operator telling him that it is waiting for the **CONTROL-TOTAL.** The operator will type in the control-total, supplied by the programmer or customer, and this figure will be used for **CONTROL-TOTAL** in the program. If the control total is 459 and the next instruction is

IF CONTROL-TOTAL LESS THAN 600 GO TO DEFICIENCY.

then it will **GO TO DEFICIENCY.** If we typed in 795 it would not.

DISPLAY is the output counterpart of **ACCEPT.** When the program encounters the instruction **DISPLAY** it prints out on the typewriter the current value of the data-name or names that follow it (literals and figurative constants can also appear as the operands of a **DISPLAY**). If there is more than one item you have to specify the spacing:

DISPLAY 'DAY-TOTAL' DTOT ', CREDIT: ' CRBAL '.'.

DTOT and **CRBAL** are the data names, given in the Data Division with **PIC**s ZZ9 and £££££9 respectively, for the items which we describe in the literals as **DAY-TOTAL** and **CREDIT.** If the current values of these two data-items are 45 and 1275, the console printout, when the **DISPLAY** is executed will be:

DAY-TOTAL 45, CREDIT: £1275.

In the literals we have provided a space after the name, and there is an additional space between each name and its value, in the printout, because the compiler allows as many spaces in the print as we have allocated positions in the **PICTURE**. Note the position of the comma, and the 'literal' full stop followed, in the **DISPLAY** statement, by the full stop required to end the COBOL sentence. **DISPLAY** statements can be rather confusing, especially if the data-names in the literals are the same as the data-names in the program:

DISPLAY 'DAY-TOTAL ' DAY-TOTAL ', CREDIT:'
CREDIT '.'.

It does not matter how many spaces we allow around **DTOT** and **CRBAL**, in the **DISPLAY** sentence; the compiler will allot as many spaces as have been given in the **PICTURE** and ignore these in the **DISPLAY** sentence.

In this example, the computer will print the **DISPLAY** and continue the program. You may want the operator to take some action at this point; if so you can use a **STOP** (see 3.4.7, and also Chapter 4, 4.7.7).

The operands of the **DISPLAY** (and **ACCEPT**) can be located in any part of the program (File Section or Working-Storage Section), according to ANSI COBOL.

3.3.4 Comparisons

This section deals with the legality of comparisons of items of various types and sizes (just as the previous section did for **MOVE**s). We shall go on to consider the nature of the comparisons that can be made and the logical relationships that can be used.

We all know what is meant by **A GREATER THAN B** if **A** and **B** are both numbers. COBOL does the commonsense things: for example, it takes **+000003, 003, +3, 3, 3·00** to be equal; **1** is greater than **−155**, and so is zero.

With alphanumeric fields, the situation is not so clear. By analogy with numerical order, we shall adopt the definition that a word is 'greater' than another in the sense that the 'greater' word comes later in alphabetical ('ascending') order: **LEICESTER** is greater than **LEEDS**. And spaces are 'less than' letters: **LONDON** is less than **LONDONDERRY**, and will precede it in alphabetical order. But people are not very consistent about this, and hopeless when it comes to sorting into order items containing hyphens, slashes, apostrophes, leading zeros, inset spaces, and so on.

Computers have a rigidly defined sequence for all the characters they can recognise; this is called the *collating sequence* and is based (largely) on the binary representation of the characters in the computer's internal code. This is not the same for all computers (and, in fact, representation within the same computer of the same item in 'character' and 'numeric' form may give rise to some surprises). One of the things you must look out for if you run a COBOL program on a computer it was not written for is the effect of different collating sequences: one computer may decide that one data item is equal to another, and the other that it is less, so that they will take different branches from an **IF** statement. There is generally no danger with **EQUAL TO**, and you can assume that items consisting entirely of letters, or entirely of digits, will be dealt with in the same way by all machines—manufacturers agree (reluctantly, one can't help thinking) that the digits run in the order **0123456789** and the letters in the order **ABCDEFG . . . . . . XYZ**. Otherwise they differ as much in their collating sequences as they do on the card punching for non-alphanumeric characters (the two questions are, of course, interrelated). In this book I will assume, merely for the sake of illustrations, that the ascending sequence (from lesser to greater) is space—digits—letters.

The rules for the comparison of numeric fields are simple; the comparison is done exactly as the human would do it. Where the two fields are alphanumeric, COBOL compares the two fields letter by letter, starting from the left. If two corresponding characters are the same, the pair to the right of them are then compared, and this continues until one character is found to be 'less than' the corresponding one in the other field, in which case the field containing the lesser character is the lesser field. If the **PICTURE** of item **A** specifies fewer characters than item **B**, then comparison stops when all the characters of item **A** have been compared with **B** (it will stop sooner, of course, if any differences are found between the items); item **B** is then judged to be the greater unless all the uncompared characters of **B** are spaces, in which case **A** and **B** are equal:

A PIC X(9) | C A M D E N _ _ _ |

B PIC X(12) | C A M D E N _ _ _ _ _ _ |

are equal.

It is sometimes extraordinarily difficult to set up the logic of comparison, using the collation rules, so that the program will agree that two items which a human would not think of distinguishing are in fact the same. For example, if we have a reference number written in various ways (nothing like the number of different ways humans will find of writing it!):

BG949
BG 949
BG0949
BG 0949
BG-949
BG/949
BG949

only the first and last will be accepted as identical (without some *very* subtle programming) by the computer, though the human would have no hesitation in reading them all as the same number. Again, the computer will say that 'bypass', 'by pass' and 'by-pass' are all different; and so are **ST JOHN** and **ST. JOHN.** These points must be carefully borne in mind when planning selection or retrieval programs; often the only solution is meticulous editing in data-preparation, though computer routines can be of some assistance (more is said on this in Chapter 4, 4.4.5).

To return to the rules of comparison. Edited numeric items count as alphanumeric, and follow the same rules. Other class comparisons are allowed, but the rules are difficult, and the beginner should stick to the commonsense comparisons. It is illegal to compare two literals. We can, with care, compare group items. Both groups are treated as single alphanumeric items, and the comparison is done letter by letter from left to right without any attempt to align corresponding elementary fields (cf. the group **MOVE** p. 82). You have to judge in each individual case whether a group comparison, rather than comparison of elementary items one after the other, will give you the result you want. Dates are particularly troublesome: one case where a group comparison would not do would be:

03 ESTIMATED-DATE.	03 ACTUAL-DATE.
05 ESTDAY PIC 99.	05 ACTDAY PIC 99.
05 ESTMTH PIC 99.	05 ACTMTH PIC 99.
05 ESTYR PIC 9999.	05 ACTYR PIC 9999.

with the Procedure:

IF ESTIMATED-DATE LESS THAN ACTUAL-DATE GO TO TARGET-NOT-MET.

If the Estimated Date were punched as **01061971** (1 June 1971) and the Actual Date were **22031971** (22 March 1971), the computer will say that Actual Date is greater than Estimated Date, which is not true. The comparison must be item-by-item in the order year-month-day:

IF ESTYR LESS THAN ACTYR GO TO TARGET-NOT-MET.
IF ESTYR GREATER THAN ACTYR GO TO DONE-IN-TIME.
IF ESTMTH LESS THAN ACTMTH GO TO TARGET-NOT-MET.
IF ESTMTH GREATER THAN ACTMTH GO TO DONE-IN-TIME.
IF ESTDAY LESS THAN ACTDAY GO TO TARGET-NOT-MET.
IF ESTDAY GREATER THAN ACTDAY GO TO DONE-IN-TIME.
GO TO DAMNED-CLOSE-RUN-THING.

If neither of the first two IFs is satisfied, the Estimated Year is equal to the Actual Year, so we go on to test the Months, and then the Days, in the same way. If we were merely testing whether the dates were *equal*, it would be a correct and safe use of a group comparison to write.

IF ESTIMATED-DATE EQUAL TO ACTUAL-DATE GO TO APPOINTMENT-KEPT.

If you have to do a lot of comparisons involving dates then in order to avoid doing the six comparisons shown above, you can either convert them to some single figure such as a Julian date, or you can reform them on input to Year-Month-Day (as in the BSI standard form) and put them back to Day-Month-Year (which is the form people like them in) on output:

WORKING-STORAGE SECTION.
. . . .
01 REVERSED-ESTDATE.   01 REVERSED-ACTDATE, etc.

03 REV-ESTYR PIC 9999.
03 REV-ESTMTH PIC 99.
03 REVSTDAY PIC 99.

You can now **MOVE ESTDAY, ESTMTH,** etc., on input, to the Working-Storage, and do all your comparisons on the group items **REVERSED-ESTDATE** (for example, 19710601) and **REVERSED-ACTDATE** (19710322) which will give the right answers with one or two **IF**s.

This brings us conveniently to the next topic, which is the use of such comparisons to alter the sequence of instructions.

3.4 Change of sequence

3.4.1 Introduction

The ability to take one path or another through the program, according to the result of the comparison of two data items, is one of the most important characteristics of the computer; it is this which distinguishes it from the adding machine or calculator. The ability of the programmer or analyst to specify his problem in terms of 'binary' decisions—that is, in the form of questions that can only be answered Yes or No— is correspondingly important; some would say that it is the essential part of the programmer's art, and even add that it cannot be taught: it is a faculty which distinguishes 'creative' programmers from 'coders' who merely write the coding, or computer language, for clearly specified routines. It is certainly true that the tendency is to 'modular' programming, in which a program is made up of a number of largely independent procedures, each carryout out a clearly defined function, possibly written by different programmers; these modules are linked by 'decisions' which determine which modules are to be executed, and in what sequence. COBOL is not as well adapted as some other languages for this structure, but the PERFORM verb, as we shall see, give us some facilities for modular programming.

We had an example of simple decisions in Program DOG; it is often necessary to build up much more complex 'decision trees', and they are perhaps the commonest source of error (causing a program to do what it is not meant to do) in COBOL programming. In some cases, decision tables can help, and they can even be translated by the computer into machine language. However in this section we confine ourselves to relatively simple cases.

3.4.2 The consequent

We will first consider a question of COBOL grammar. Hitherto we have generally expressed the consequent of an IF statement as a **GO TO**, and this has led to sequences like:

```
IF A EQUAL TO B GO TO FOUNDIT.
GO TO READIT.
FOUNDIT.
ADD 1 TO COUNTER.
GO TO READIT.
```

This pair of **GO TO**s could be replaced by:

```
IF A EQUAL TO B ADD 1 TO COUNTER.
GO TO READIT.
```

This is obviously tidier. But note that this construction must be used only when you want the second statement—here, **GO TO READIT** —to be carried out whatever the results of the test. If A is equal to **B** the counter is incremented and we go to **READIT**; if they are not equal, nothing is added to the counter but we still go to **READIT**. This is not the same as:

```
IF A EQUAL TO B ADD 1 TO COUNTER GO TO READIT.
```

or even

```
IF A EQUAL TO B ADD 1 TO COUNTER
GO TO READIT.
```

The omission of the full stop after **COUNTER** makes this into one sentence, equivalent to the previous one. In both cases, if A is not equal to B the statement following **GO TO READIT** will be carried out instead of the two consequent statements of the **IF**. It is a good habit in writing or checking a program to read the statement after the **IF** as the consequent of **IF A NOT EQUAL TO B**, and see if that is really what you want. The consequent, up to the next full stop, can be as long as you please; but the natural tendency is to make the shorter alternative the consequent, and if both consequents are long most programmers would feel it advisable to write two **GO TO**s, as in our first example, and make the consequents into two distinct routines. It is a question of doing what seems natural. Note that if you do have a **GO TO** in the consequent, it must be the *last* statement:

IF A EQUAL TO B GO TO EUREKA ADD 1 TO COUNTER.

is useless because the program can never get to the **ADD** instruction.

3.4.3 Multiple comparisons

In Program CHARLIE, in which the IF statement was introduced, we had a procedure which compared one field with another and took some action as a result. We may have more complex requirements, arising from the comparison of *more than one* pair of fields. We then have to use more than one **IF**. Such a case appeared in Program DOG, where we looked for records where the commodity coding was **BM** *and also* **PRICE60** was equal to **PRICE69**. This is called an **AND** relation, because both the first *and* the second condition must be satisfied. Another example of an **AND** relation can be found in a range of dates: if we want the names of people born between 1930 and 1940 (both dates inclusive) we want a **DOB** greater than 1929 *and* less than 1941. We can also have an **OR** relation, in which one at least of the conditions must be satisfied: if a factory decides to lay off all women workers and all workers over 50, the program will read:

IF SEX EQUAL TO 'F' GO TO LAYOFF.
IF DOB LESS THAN 1920 GO TO LAYOFF.
GO TO KEEP-ON-ROLL.

Note the difference between this and the **AND** condition implied if the factory wants to lay off all women over 50 (sex female *and* **DOB** less than 1920 or whatever it may be):

IF DOB LESS THAN 1920 GO TO NEXT-TEST.
GO TO KEEP-ON-ROLL.

NEXT-TEST.
    IF SEX EQUAL TO 'F' GO TO LAYOFF.
    GO TO KEEP-ON-ROLL.

Nucleus Level 2 allows the use of the logical operators **AND, OR,** so that the above expressions could be coded:

    IF DOB LESS THAN 1920 OR IF SEX EQUAL TO 'F' GO TO LAYOFF.
    IF DOB LESS THAN 1920 AND IF SEX EQUAL TO 'F' GO TO LAYOFF.

The logical operators are not necessary; the same effect can always be achieved in multiple **IF** statements, as illustrated above.

There are several ways of simplifying a chain of **IF**s, but this can give rise to many confusing variations. You could write the **AND** example as:

    IF SEX NOT EQUAL TO 'F' GO TO KEEP-ON-ROLL.
    IF DOB GREATER THAN 1919 GO TO KEEP-ON-ROLL.
    GO TO LAYOFF.

These various forms arise from the fact that 'greater than or equal to' is exactly equivalent to 'not less than'; 'not equal to' is equivalent to 'greater than or less than'; 'greater than 1919' is equivalent to 'not less than 1920'. So instead of

    IF PRICE60 EQUAL TO PRICE69 GO TO PROCESSING.
    IF PRICE60 GREATER THAN PRICE69 GO TO PROCESS-ING.

you can write the single statement

    IF PRICE60 NOT LESS THAN PRICE69 GO TO PROCESS-ING.

But the longer versions are not wrong, and it is often a waste of time to try to shorten the program after you have written it. It is a notorious foible of programmers that they will spend hours 'optimising' a program, cutting out an unnecessary statement or test, with a consequent saving of a few milliseconds or a few words of core that are of no consequence anyway. Very often, too, the first thing you write is correct, because it came 'naturally', and then you wreck it by trying to shorten it or because you have forgotten that another part of the program depends on the original version.

There is no easy way to ensure that your sequences of **IF**s are logically correct, that is, that they will do what you want them to You should certainly draw a flow-chart and 'play them through' if they are at all complicated; with practice you should be able to make a mental analysis of two or three **IF**s.

3.4.4 Other conditional statements

IF is not the only word introducing a condition test and thus permitting a branch. We have already had **AT END**, in the **READ** statement; this is nearly always followed by **GO TO**, though, as with **IF**, any imperative statement can be used. We have also had **ON SIZE ERROR**, in arithmetical statements.

The principal sequence-control verb is, of course, **GO TO**. Used by itself it is an *unconditional* branch; as the consequent of an **IF** (or **AT END**, etc.) it is a *conditional* branch. Its operand must be a paragraph name in the program. There is no harm in saying

```
    ADD 1 TO SUMMER.
    GO TO PROCNAME.
PROCNAME.
```

where the procedure name follows immediately in the program; it may be a good thing if you think the source statements, in card form, may be moved around physically as the program is written, for example, if you decide to write in another procedure immediately before **PROCNAME**; the **GO TO** is then necessary as you would not drop through to **PROCNAME** from **ADD 1 TO SUMMER**. You might also insert a **GO TO PROCNAME** where **PROCNAME** could, logically, follow straight on but you forgot to put it in, and don't want to rewrite your coding sheet and statement-numbers (4.7.2). Of course this is slovenly but everyone does it.

3.4.5 GO TO ... DEPENDING ON ...

An interesting variant of the **GO TO**, which never seems to be used as much as it ought to be, is **GO TO ... DEPENDING ON**, where the **GO TO** is followed by a set of procedure names, and the **DEPENDING ON** by a data-name with a numerical value (positive and non-zero). For example, in

GO TO AB12, BC13, WINDOW, DOOR, XYZ, DEPENDING ON STRING.

The branch is to one of the five procedures named (**AB12**, etc.) according to whether the current value of **STRING** is 1,2,3,4, or 5. In this usage, **STRING** must not have a value higher than the number of procedure-names following the **GO TO**; if it has, the whole statement is ignored and control passes to the statement following the **GO TO**.

This type of statement is useful when a condition is presented in numerical form, for example; in the Library Catalogue (3.2.2), where the code numbers 1,2,3,4 distinguished the various types of card. We could write

GO TO AUTHOR-PROC, TITLE-PROC, TITLE-PROC, CLASS-PROC DEPENDING ON CODE.

We have used **TITLE-PROC** twice; this is legal. We might have (in a non-leap year)

GO TO D31, D28, D31, D30, D31, D30, D31, D31, D30, D31, D30, D31, DEPENDING ON MONTH-NUMBER.

The branch is to one of three routines, according to the number of days in the month; **MONTH-NUMBER** 7 takes us to **D31**, for July. This form is particularly useful with rather unsystematic series like the days in month.

3.4.6 PERFORM

This verb is really a sort of return ticket version of **GO TO**. **PERFORM PROCNAME** means **GO TO** the beginning of the routine **PROCNAME**, just as an ordinary GO TO would; but at the end of **PROCNAME**—that is, at the first procedure name following **PROCNAME**—*return* to the statement immediately after the **PERFORM**.

PERFORM can be used to create a program in block structure,

93

simplifying readability and testing; (4.7.1). But even in its simpler uses, as illustrated here, it is an extremely powerful verb, which can save us a good deal of instruction writing and economise on storage space in the computer.

The **PERFORM** should be used whenever any routine is used more than once in a program. For example, we may have four items of data in a single record, and wish to write these out one item per line. This will involve four **WRITE** orders:

> **MOVE ITEM-1 TO OUTITEM.**
> **WRITE PRINTLINE AFTER 1.**
> **MOVE ITEM-2 TO OUTITEM.**
> **WRITE PRINTLINE AFTER 1.**
> etc.

The compiler will generate four **WRITE** orders. But **READ** and **WRITE** orders are among the most complex in the compiler, and generate more code than almost any other order; so four **WRITE** orders will occupy a significant amount of space.

With **PERFORM** we can do the four **WRITES** with only one **WRITE** order. We put the **WRITE** order in a paragraph (**WRITE-OUT**) on its own, either before or after the Print-Routine (as convenient) and we replace each **WRITE PRINTLINE AFTER 1** with **PERFORM WRITEOUT**:

WRITEOUT.
> **WRITE PRINTLINE AFTER 1.**
NEXT-PROC.
· · · · · · · · · · ·
> **MOVE ITEM-1 TO OUTITEM.**
> **PERFORM WRITEOUT.**
> **MOVE ITEM-2 TO OUTITEM.**
> **PERFORM WRITEOUT.**

and so on, for four items. At each **PERFORM**, there is a transfer to **WRITEOUT**; the compiler sets up a return link, that is, it remembers where it came from, and at the end of **WRITEOUT** it returns to the instruction immediately following the **PERFORM WRITEOUT**, whichever it may be. Thus after the first **PERFORM WRITEOUT** the next instruction executed is **MOVE ITEM-2 TO OUTITEM.**

A **GO TO**, instead of a **PERFORM**, would take us to **WRITE-OUT**, but we would then continue with the procedure following **WRITEOUT** (that is, **NEXT-PROC**). We could put a **GO TO** in **WRITEOUT: WRITE PRINTLINE AFTER 1, GO TO . . .** where? There are ways and means of 'remembering' where we came from, but none is as concise and easy as the **PERFORM**.

The above use of **PERFORM** doesn't save the programmer much time, although it does save store. But if instead of the simple **WRITE** we had a long and complicated routine which we wished to use more than once in the program, the saving of program time may be considerable.

There is no reason why you should not have a routine in the normal sequence, or accessed by a normal **GO TO**, and use it in another part of the program as the object of a **PERFORM**. You must remember, however, that a **PERFORM** carries out the whole paragraph; if you don't want this you have to insert a dummy paragraph heading. For instance, you may write a **GO TO** for a printing routine, which includes a line counter:

```
GO TO PRINTIT.
. . . . . . .
PRINTIT.
    WRITE PRINTLINE AFTER 1.
    ADD 1 TO LINE-COUNTER.
READITIN.
    GO TO READIT.
```

If you decide to use the **WRITE** in another part of the program, but without incrementing the line counter, you must insert a dummy paragraph heading:

```
PRINTIT.
    WRITE PRINTLINE AFTER 1.
CARRYON.
    ADD 1 TO LINE-COUNTER.
READITIN.
    GO TO READIT.
```

Now, after **GO TO PRINTIT**, the program will continue through **CARRYON**; but the **PERFORM** will 'return' after the single statement **WRITE**. **CARRYON** is an example of a procedure name which is (probably) never the operand of a **GO TO**; its only function is 'punctuation'.

A **PERFORM** can, however, cover more than one paragraph; we name the first and last paragraphs of the sequence we want to be **PERFORM**ed. We could write

PERFORM PRINTIT THRU CARRYON.

and both procedures will be executed, with a return after **ADD 1 TO LINE-COUNTER.** If we have three consecutive paragraphs **READIT, TESTIT.** and **COUNTIT**, then **PERFORM READIT THRU TESTIT** will execute all three, in sequence. (**THRU** is standard COBOL; some British compilers allow **THROUGH**!) There is no limit to the number of paragraphs that can be covered in a **PERFORM.**

We said just now that a routine can be 'in line', that is, accessed in the normal sequence, and used as the object of a **PERFORM** in another part of the program. This can lead to trouble if you put the procedure to be **PERFORM**ed immediately after the **PERFORM** instruction, as is quite natural:

PERFORM WRITIT.
WRITIT.
WRITE OUTRECORD AFTER 1.
NEXT-STEP.
  . . . . .

When the procedure **WRITIT** has been performed, the rule is that the next instruction to be obeyed is the one following the instruction containing the **PERFORM** verb, In this case it is the **WRITIT** paragraph, so the **WRITIT** will be done again before we arrive at the **NEXT-STEP** instruction. We must either write **GO TO NEXT-STEP** after **PERFORM WRITIT**, or, what is better and makes for a neater program, put all the paragraphs to be **PERFORMED** at the end of the program (after the **STOP RUN**—see 3.4.7). In other words, don't use a procedure in-line if it is also the object of a **PERFORM.**

3.4.6.1 PERFORM and transfer of control.

The last statement of the last paragraph named in a **PERFORM** must not be a **GO TO.**

There is no necessary relationship between the first and the second procedure names given in the **PERFORM**, except that a consecutive sequence of operations is to be executed beginning at the procedure with the first name and ending with the execution of the procedure with the last name. In particular, **GO TO** and **PERFORM** statements may occur between the first procedure-name and the end of the final procedure. If you have **PERFORMS** within a **PERFORM** (known as 'nesting') the 'inner' **PERFORM** must either be totally included in, or totally excluded from, the 'outer' **PERFORM**. Similarly you can **GO TO** statements either within the range of the **PERFORM** or outside it; but control must eventually return to the last statement of the last procedure specified in the **PERFORM**.

A special case arises when we want to terminate the **PERFORM**, that is, return to the statement following the **PERFORM**, before we have completed the range of statements specified in the **PERFORM**. This will obviously occur as the result of some test within the **PERFORM** procedures:

```
PERFORM PAGE-TEST THRU JUMPOUT.
WRITE PRINTLINE AFTER 1.
. . . . . . . .
PAGE-TEST.
    ADD 1 TO LINE-COUNTER.
    IF LINE-COUNTER LESS THAN 51 GO TO JUMPOUT.
    ADD 1 TO PAGE-NUMBER.
    MOVE 1 TO LINE-COUNTER.
    MOVE PAGE-NUMBER TO PRINT-NUMBER.
    WRITE PRINTLINE AFTER NEW-PAGE.
JUMPOUT.
    EXIT.
NEW-PARA.
```

Here we have a routine which tests whether 50 lines have been written on a page; if so a page-number is incremented and put in the printline, which is written after a move to a new page; a return is then made and another line is written and some more computation done; and we go back to the **PERFORM**. In the **PERFORM**, we have a test for the line-counter; if this has not yet reached 51 there are not yet 50 lines on the page so we don't want a new page; we want to return to the statement after the **PERFORM**, in other words jump out before the range is finished. The rule is that any transfer of control within the range must go to or return to the last statement of the last paragraph; so we have to put in a terminal paragraph **JUMPOUT** which consists of the one word **EXIT**. **EXIT** is a reserved word which must be in a separate paragraph and must be the only word in that paragraph; and we must not forget to give its paragraph name after **THRU** in the **PERFORM** statement. Whenever there is more than one possible path through a **PERFORM**, this clumsy device must be adopted to enable us to associate a procedure-name with the terminal point of the **PERFORM**.

The beginner is advised to avoid all but the simplest nested **PERFORM**, jumps to statements not within the procedures specified in the **PERFORM**, and so on. Unless the **PERFORM** will really save a lot of program or space, a simple old-fashioned loop will often do as well (as in Program EASY) especially if there are a lot of possible 'exits'. Don't forget that **READ INFILE AT END GO TO FINISH** is a conditional branch! But on the other hand when you have had some practice don't let the complications of the **PERFORM** deter you from using it; the use of **PERFORM**s is really the hallmark of the skilled programmer.

3.4.6.2 PERFORM with counter

A simple but useful option with **PERFORM** is:

> **PERFORM ALPHA THRU BETA N TIMES.**

where N is either a numeric literal or a data name with a numeric value. In either case, the number must not be zero or negative; if it is, the **PERFORM** is not carried out at all, and control passes to the next statement. This form saves all the counter-setting and testing that we have with the simpler type of loop; it is particularly useful in dealing with subscripted entries in tables, which we shall shortly deal with. Program EASY could be rewritten:

INITRUN.
    OPEN FILES, etc.
    MOVE SPACES TO PRINTLINE.
    PERFORM READEM THRU NOMORE 50 TIMES.

```
    GO TO FINISH.
READEM.
    READ CARDFILE AT END GO TO NOMORE.
    MOVE CARD-RECORD TO CARD-DATA.
    WRITE PRINTLINE AFTER 1.
NOMORE.
    EXIT.
FINISH.
    CLOSE FILES, etc.
    STOP RUN.
```

This will read in 50 cards and print them without our having to provide a counter for them.

If the counter of the **PERFORM** is a variable (like **N** above) it is illegal to attempt to modify it in the **PERFORM**ed procedures. You are not likely to do this, but the situation can arise.

.4.7 STOP

This is classified as a sequence-control verb. We have met it in the form **STOP RUN**; once the program reaches this point it cannot be restarted without reloading and beginning again from scratch. A milder form of **STOP**, however, has a literal as its operand, such as **STOP 12**, or

> IF COUNTER GREATER THAN PRESET-TOTAL STOP 'COUNTER ERROR'.

If this condition arises the computer prints out a message, including the literal, stops, and waits for the operator to type in a reply, supplied to him by the programmer (or abandon the run). The use of this form in 'diagnostics' is mentioned in 4.7.7.

STOP RUN, of course, *must* appear in the program. It doesn't have to be actually the last statement in the program; you can jump to routines that appear, physically, in the source program after **STOP RUN**, and it is, in fact, common practice to put standard routines and error routines etc., as well as paragraphs to be **PERFORM**ed after the main routine which ends with **STOP RUN**; but all such routines will contain a jump back to the main routine

99

(or be **PERFORM**ed), so that eventually you will reach the **STOP RUN.**

3.5 Table-Handling and the use of 'OCCURS'

3.5.1 Introduction

The facilities for Table-Handling in modern computer languages are among their most powerful features. They are not as prominent, perhaps, in COBOL as in mathematical languages such as Fortran and Algol, nor as consistent. This may be because there is less use for them in plain data-handling than there is in mathematical computation, but it is nevertheless true to say that a confident use of tables, like the use of **IF**s and **PERFORM**s, distinguishes the men from the boys in programming.

A *table* is merely an arrangement (or array, it is called in the mathematical languages) of data items which are to be treated in the same way, and have the same characteristics. As was pointed out early in this book, the distinguishing feature of computing is that we carry out the same process over and over again on constantly changing data, and this implies that since the process itself is the same on each 'pass', the data items must be of the same kind. Hitherto, we have dealt with records one or two at a time, but it is often convenient and indeed essential to have a whole set of data in store at the same time, as we shall shortly see; and if, as is generally the case, the data items are all of the same format—for example, numbers not exceeding six digits in length—this data can be read and stored in the form of a table, so that all the data is accessible to the program at all times. In technical terms, table handling allows 'direct access', whereas reading one item or record at a time allows only 'sequential access'. Naturally the size of the table, that is, the number of items of a given size in it, is limited by the size of the computer store, and this is one reason why large computers are more efficient than small ones: they can hold larger tables in store, and thus deal with more data at electronic speeds instead of waiting for the comparatively slow input devices and backing stores.

Table-Handling is so powerful and versatile a tool that is is impossible to illustrate adequately its capacities and applications in a

100

small book. The best we can do is to provide enough illustrations and rules to give the beginner a systematic understanding of tables that will enable him, as he gains experience, to use first principles to tackle the most complicated examples that may come his way.

5.2 An elementary example

We will whet the appetite of the reader with a simple example of the general idea of tables, and their value to the programmer.

Let us suppose that a certain firm has 125 branches, which supply voluminous information in the form of daily, weekly, and monthly returns. For our purposes, we will consider just one detail of these, the number of sales of some commodity. These are punched daily on cards, in the following format (as far as our example is concerned—we can ignore data such as commodity identifier, data, and so on which would undoubtedly also appear on the card):

cols. 4–7 Branch-number   cols. 9–12 Daily sales

and the first few cards in a given batch might have, under these heads:

78	469
5	25
7	123
107	89
79	209
78	46

and so on; there may be more than one card for each branch, in a particular run, and they are not in any order with respect to Branch-number.

Having accumulated a set of such cards, over a suitable period, we want to sum the totals by Branch—that is, to find out what each Branch has sold during the period; and to print out these totals, each with its Branch-number, in Branch-number order, one per line.

Our input format can be inferred from the above:

01 CARD-RECORD.
03 FILLER PIC X(3).

03 BRANCH-NUM PIC 999.
03 FILLER PIC X.
03 SALES PIC 9(4).

We allow three digits for Branch-number, as there are only 125 of them; and we expect not more than 9999 items to be sold by any Branch in any one day.

Since the records are not in order, we have got to accumulate totals in store until the end of the run—the last card of the file, for example, might refer to Branch 1. This means that we must set up a store location for each Branch's total. The size of the locations depends on the period over which the sales are accumulated: if a week, then we shall not expect more than 6×9999 items sold by any Branch, and five digits should be enough for each store location. So the Working-Storage entry will be:

WORKING-STORAGE SECTION.

. . . .

01 TOTALS-BY-BRANCH, VALUE IS ZEROS.
    03 BRANCH-001 PIC 9(5).
    03 BRANCH-002 PIC 9(5).
    03 BRANCH-003 PIC 9(5).
    03 BRANCH-004 PIC 9(5).

. . . and at this point, if not before, we begin to wonder: have we really got to write 125 practically identical entries? The answer is yes, with the techniques we have acquired so far.

This is not all. Even if we write out, or get someone to write out, the 125 entries for the Working-Storage, there will still be a problem in the Procedure Division, in which we read in each card and add the sales to the total for the branch designated by the Branch-number:

READIT.
    READ INFILE AT END GO TO NEXT-STEP.
    IF BRANCH-NUM EQUAL TO 1 ADD SALES TO BRANCH-
        001, GO TO READIT.
    IF BRANCH-NUM EQUAL TO 2 ADD SALES TO BRANCH-
        002, GO TO READIT.
    IF BRANCH-NUM EQUAL TO 3 ADD SALES TO BRANCH-
        003, GO TO READIT.

and so on up to IF BRANCH-NUM EQUAL TO 125 . . .

And you can expect the same trouble in the Write orders for printing out Branch-numbers and totals at the end of the run.

2.1 The solution

COBOL provides an easy way out. We are allowed to 'set up' the whole table, of 125 locations, by a single entry in the Data Division, using the **OCCURS** clause:

WORKING-STORAGE SECTION.

. . . .

01 SALES-TABLE VALUE IS ZERO.
   03 SALES-TOTAL PIC 9(5) OCCURS 125 TIMES.

The compiler will now set aside 125 locations, of five digits each, with an initial value of zero, to hold the accumulated sales-totals. (See Fig. 3.3 for a diagram of how this will appear in store.) We can refer to any individual location in this table by using the data-name **SALES-TOTAL** followed by a number in brackets, with a space between the name and the first bracket: thus **SALES-TOTAL (1)** is the first location in the table—what we previously called **BRANCH-001**; and **SALES-TOTAL (125)** is the last. The number in brackets is called a *subscript*.

This takes care of the setting up of the table, but you may wonder how this is going to help with the reading in of values from the cards: if we had to write 125 **IF**s of the form **IF BRANCH-NUM EQUAL TO 1 ADD SALES TO BRANCH-001**, shall we not have to write 125 similar **IF**s for **SALES-TOTAL (1)** up to **SALES-TOTAL (125)**? The secret is that we can write in the brackets, in the place of the numerical subscript, a data-name which can have a *variable* value; if I write, for example, **SALES-TOTAL (NUM)** in my program, then the location referred to is the one which would be referred to if we substituted for **NUM** the current numerical value of **NUM**. If the current value of **NUM** is 24, then **SALES-TOTAL (NUM)** means **SALES-TOTAL (24)**, the 24th location in **SALES-TABLE**.

Let us see how this helps. When we read in a **CARD-RECORD**, we want to add the **SALES** on it to the **SALES-TOTAL** for the appropriate branch. But the number of the Branch is given by the field

BRANCH-NUM, in the same record, on every card! So all we need write is:

READIT.
READ INFILE AT END GO TO NEXT-STEP.
ADD SALES TO SALES-TOTAL (BRANCH-NUM).
GO TO READIT.

This single instruction, **ADD SALES . . .**, takes the place of the 125 **IF BRANCH-NUM EQUAL TO . . .**

Now as each card is read in, the **SALES** on it will be added to the correct location, that is, the one that has the subscript with the same value as the **BRANCH-NUM** on the card. Taking the values given at the beginning of this section, the first **BRANCH-NUM** is 78, and **SALES** 469; so 469 is added to **SALES-TOTAL (78)**; the **BRANCH-NUM** becomes 5 when the second card is read in, so 25 is added to **SALES-TOTAL (5)**; then 123 is added to **SALES-TOTAL (7)**, and so on. This is what we mean by saying that the subscript takes on the current value of the variable **BRANCH-NUM**.

To conclude this example, let us apply the method to the writing out of the answers, in Branch-number order. The Branch-number and its total are to appear on the same line, with the format:
FD PRINTOUT.
01 PRINTLINE.
 03 FILLER PIC X(20).
 03 BRANCH-NUMBER PIC ZZ9.
 03 FILLER PIC X(10).
 03 BRANCH-SALES-TOTAL PIC Z(4)9.
 03 FILLER PIC X(82).

To produce these 125 lines *without* using a variable subscript, we would have to **MOVE 1 TO BRANCH-NUMBER, MOVE SALES-TOTAL (1) TO BRANCH-SALES-TOTAL,** and print; then **MOVE 2 TO BRANCH-NUMBER, MOVE SALES-TOTAL (2) TO BRANCH-SALES-TOTAL,** and print, and so on up to 125. But if we define a **COUNTER** in Working-Storage, with **PIC 999 VALUE IS ZERO**, and use it as a subscript, taking the values 1,2,3, . . . 125 in turn, then:

PRINT-PROCESS.
 ADD 1 TO COUNTER.

```
MOVE COUNTER TO BRANCH-NUMBER.
MOVE SALES-TOTAL (COUNTER) TO BRANCH-SALES-
   TOTAL.
WRITE PRINTLINE AFTER 1.
IF COUNTER EQUAL TO 125 GO TO NEXT-PROCESS.
GO TO PRINT-PROCESS.
```

Here we are reading each **SALES-TOTAL** in turn out of the table; each value in turn is moved to the single output location **BRANCH-SALES-TOTAL**, in the output record. We use the actual value of **COUNTER** itself for the Branch-number (**MOVE COUNTER TO BRANCH-NUMBER**); and **COUNTER** is used to 'number off' the items in the table. We use **COUNTER**, rather than **BRANCH-NUM**, because **BRANCH-NUM** was *not stored* when the cards were read in. The reason for this will be clear when we have given a fuller account of how the table is actually stored.

3.5.3 Subscripts

Subscripts are literals, or data-names; and they must be defined, if data-names, in the Data Division, and given a value, initially in the Data Division or by reading in data or by assigning a literal in the Procedure Division, just like other data-names. When not used as subscripts, that is, when not in brackets following a data-name, they can take on any value that is allowed by their **PICTURE**. However, as subscripts, there are certain restrictions on the value they can have. They must, of course, have a numerical **PICTURE** (made up of 9s and nothing else). They must be positive whole numbers, with values ranging from 1 to the number named in the **OCCURS**. If in the course of the program the data-name is assigned a value which is negative or zero, or which is larger than that named in the **OCCURS**, then if you use it as a subscript with that value the results will be unpredictable, that is, almost certainly wrong. We may also note (though a beginner is not likely to commit this error) that a subscript must not itself be subscripted.

The following example shows how easy it may be to fall into the trap of using an invalid subscript (here, zero); and what you can do to avoid it.

105

Example 1. Zero Subscript
In this example the records have a field **TIME-OF-REPORT**, which gives a time in hours and minutes (from 0000 to 2359) for each record. In the Data Division this appears as:

03 TIME-OF-REPORT.
  05 HOUR PIC 99.
  05 MIN PIC 99.

We want to count the number of records in each hour over a given period. We have a table in Working-Storage with one 'cell' for each of the 24 hours:

01 REPORT-TOTALS.
  03 HOURLY-TOTAL PIC 9999 OCCURS 24 TIMES.

We can have up to 9999 reports in each of the 24 cells of the table.
  Now, after reading in a record:

  ADD 1 TO HOURLY-TOTAL (HOUR).

The subscript value **HOUR** is taken from the input record, and directs the incrementing of the correct cell in **REPORT-TOTALS**, counting 1 for each record read in. But one snag is that every record which has a **TIME-OF-REPORT** between midnight and 0059 will have the hour 00, and we are not allowed to have a zero subscript. So we turn each hour 00 into 1, each 01 into 2, and so on:

READ INFILE AT END...
  ADD 1 TO HOUR.
  ADD 1 TO HOURLY-TOTAL (HOUR).

Now all the times from 0000 to 0059 will go into **HOURLY-TOTAL (1)**, all those from 0100 to 0159 into **HOURLY-TOTAL (2)**, up to 2300 to 2359 which will go into **HOURLY-TOTAL (24)**. You will have to make special arrangements for anyone who writes 2400: you could easily do this by having 25 cells (**OCCURS 25 TIMES**) and having **ADD HOURLY-TOTAL (25) TO HOURLY-TOTAL (24)** at the end of the run.

106

3.5.4 The table in store

A diagram of the store layout for the table we used in the introductory example is given in Fig. 3.3; it will help to explain the principles of table-handling. It shows the table in Working-Storage before any data is moved into it. It takes up 125 *contiguous* locations, of five digits each. The 'contiguous' is important, because the subscripts (1), (2), etc., are not actually stored in the computer. All that is actually stored is the labels **SALES-TABLE** and **SALES-TOTAL**, and the 125 'cells', with the machine address of the beginning of the table. Then if the whole table, **SALES-TABLE**, is, for example, subjected to a **MOVE** order, the whole block of 625 digits following that address is **MOVE**d; if we refer to a specific location, for example, **SALES-TOTAL (41)**, the program uses the subscript to *cal-*

	SALES-TABLE						
SALES-TOTAL	1	2	3	4		124	125
	00000	00000	00000	00000	....	00000	00000

	SALES-TOTAL	1	00000
		2	00000
		3	00000
		4	00000
SALES-TABLE		.	.....
		.	.....
		.	.....
		124	00000
		125	00000

Fig. 3.3. One-dimension tables
(a) Layout in store
(b) Alternative form for (a)

107

culate the position of the data in **SALES-TOTAL (41)** with respect to the location in store of the beginning of the table (that is, 40×5 characters from this beginning address). That is why the storage is contiguous.

It will generally be expedient to give these diagrams in vertical format, as shown in Fig. 3.3(*b*). The meaning is exactly the same; each location is contiguous to the one above it. You will find it helpful to visualise such tables as an array of pigeon-holes, each labelled with its subscript, into which data can be put.

Since the program calculates the position of the data in the table by means of the subscripts, it is obvious that the subscript series must be consecutive, without breaks. To illustrate this: let our company have 125 branches, as before, but let us assume that owing to closures, amalgamations, changes in numbering, and so on, the branch-numbers actually used (and punched on the cards) are no longer consecutive but cover the range 3–254. Though it would be 'natural' to use the branch number on the card at the subscript, it would be illegal if we had a table of 125 entries, i.e. one entry for each of the 125 actual branches. **SALES-TOTAL (126)** to **(254)**, for branches with numbers between 126 and 254, cannot be used because they violate the rule that the subscript must not exceed the value given in the **OCCURS**—there is no place for them in the table; and (though this is less serious) there will be locations in the table, with numbers less than 125, which no longer correspond to branches.

If we *do* want to use the branch-number as the subscript, then one of the solutions is to set up a table of 254 locations:

SALES-TOTAL PIC 9(5) OCCURS 254 TIMES.

This is wasteful of space, because there will be $254 - 125 = 129$ fields in the table which will never receive a value; you may tolerate this, if you are not short of space, for the convenience of having a ready-made subscript. There are methods, mentioned later (3.5.8 Ex.4) which will enable you to convert the branch-number to a true subscript, and avoid the inconvenience of having 129 blank lines in your print-out; but the point of this example is to warn you to be on the look-out for this trap when you have what appears to be a ready-made subscript in the record.

Under the heading of the Table in Store, it may be as well to remind you that each cell of your table must have a **PICTURE** large enough to occupy whatever data you want to put in it. This may be difficult to estimate if you are accumulating totals, or calculating them; in any case, since all the cells must be of the same size, they must all be of the largest size necessary for any one of them—if one of the cells is expected to reach four figures, and none of the others more than two, they must all be of four figures. This may be critical, with a small core. At all costs you must avoid 'overflow': you can use a **SIZE ERROR** clause, or test the sums as they are put in. Invariably, when you reach the limits of your computer, programming is tricky and messy.

5.5 OCCURS at group level

Another rule about **OCCURS** is that it must not be used with an item at **01** or **77** level. However, **OCCURS** are not necessarily used only with elementary items; they can be used at Group level.

In our first example, the **OCCURS** was attached to the elementary field **SALES-TOTAL**. There might, however, be more than one field on the card whose value we wished to store, for example, sales for three different varieties of the commodity, each occupying one field of the card:

```
01 CARD-RECORD.
   03 BRANCH-NUM PIC 999.
   03 FILLER PIC X.
   03 SALES.
      05 VARA PIC 9999.
      05 VARB PIC 9999.
      05 VARC PIC 9999.
```

We can set up the Working-Storage table in two ways. The first is exactly like the original, repeated three times:

```
01 SALES-TABLE VALUE IS ZERO.
   03 TABA PIC 9(5) OCCURS 125 TIMES.
   03 TABB PIC 9(5) OCCURS 125 TIMES.
   03 TABC PIC 9(5) OCCURS 125 TIMES.
```

109

The second method is to group the elementary items and attach the **OCCURS** to the group label:

```
01 SALES-TABLE VALUE IS ZERO.
   03 SALES-TOTAL OCCURS 125 TIMES.
      05 TABA PIC 9(5).
      05 TABB PIC 9(5).
      05 TABC PIC 9(5).
```

These are virtually equivalent (the second one has to have a 'dummy' group name, **SALES-TOTAL**, since we cannot append an **OCCURS** to an **01** level entry). Whichever we use, we shall have three **ADD**s, when we read in a record:

```
READIT.
   READ INFILE AT END GO TO NEXT-STEP.
   ADD VARA TO TABA (BRANCH-NUM).
   ADD VARB TO TABB (BRANCH-NUM).
   ADD VARC TO TABC (BRANCH-NUM).
```

The Procedure is the same, whichever way we write the Data Division entries. Note that when an **OCCURS** is used at Group level, all the subordinate items must be subscripted, exactly as if they had been given individual **OCCURS** as in the first example. Fig. 3.4 shows why this is so—there are in both cases three **TABA**s, three **TABB**s, three **TABC**s, and they must be distinguished. Fig. 3.4 also shows that the arrangement of the tables is different, for the two ways of giving the **OCCURS**. In most cases this will not matter to the programmer, but it is as well to know that there is a difference—we shall see in a moment how we have to allow for this in input and output, and it is also of importance in understanding two-dimensional tables.

If we do refer to **SALES-TOTAL**, the 'dummy' Group heading, it must be subscripted, as shown in the figure (3.4(*b*)). Such a data-item is probably meaningless in this case, but the next example shows a situation in which it makes sense to refer to such intermediate levels.

It was stated earlier that all items with an **OCCURS** must have the same form: for example, all the numbers in a table must have the same number of digits (or, rather, all the locations in the table must be of the size required to accommodate the *largest* item, which may be wasteful). It is obvious that this must be so, since we give the **PICTURE** only once, no matter how often the item **OCCURS**.

110

SALES-TABLE	TABA (1) (2) (3) (4) . . . . (125)	00000 00000 00000 00000 00000
	TABB (1) (2) . . . . (125)	00000 00000 00000
	TABC (1) (2) . . . . (125)	00000 00000 00000

SALES-TABLE	SALES-TOTAL (1)	TABA (1) TABB (1) TABC (1)	00000 00000 00000
	SALES-TOTAL (2)	TABA (2) TABB (2) TABC (2)	00000 00000 00000
	SALES-TOTAL (3)	TABA (3) TABB (3) TABC (3)	00000 00000 00000
		. . . .	. . . .
	SALES-TOTAL (125)	TABA (125) TABB (125) TABC (125)	00000 00000 00000

Fig. 3.4. Table layout
    (*a*) **OCCURS** *with elementary items*
    (*b*) **OCCURS** *with group item*

However, it is permissible, if we have a Group **OCCURS**, to have *subdivisions* of different size and character. We will take a personnel-record as an example:

We can legally write:

01 PERSONNEL-RECORD.
    03 PERSONNEL-NUMBER PIC 9999 OCCURS 500 TIMES.
    03 SURNAME PIC X(20) OCCURS 500 TIMES.
    03 FIRSTNAME PIC X(10) OCCURS 500 TIMES.
    03 SEX PIC 9 OCCURS 500 TIMES.

	PERSONNEL-NUMBER (1) PERSONNEL-NUMBER (2) . . . . PERSONNEL-NUMBER (500)	0012 0025 1207
PERSONNEL- RECORD	SURNAME (1) SURNAME (2) . . . . SURNAME (500)	WILLOUGHBY-JOHNSTONE COX . . . . MACFARLANE
	FIRSTNAME (1) FIRSTNAME (2) . . . . FIRSTNAME (500)	MARMADUKE ENGELBERT . . . . JOANNA
	SEX (1) SEX (2) . . . . . . SEX (500)	1 1 . 2

PERSONNEL- RECORD	DETAILS (1) DETAILS (2) DETAILS (3) . . . . DETAILS (500)	0012 0025 1207	WILLOUGHBY-JOHNSTONE COX . . . . MACFARLANE	MARMADUKE ENGELBERT . . . . JOANNA	1 1 . . 2

0012 is PERSONNEL-NUMBER (1); COX is SURNAME (2); JOANNA is FIRSTNAME (500).

Fig. 3.5. Store layout of multiple and group **OCCURS**
(a) Method 1
(b) Method 2

We could also write, with less labour:

01 PERSONNEL-RECORD.
   03 DETAILS, OCCURS 500 TIMES.
      05 PERSONNEL-NUMBER PIC 9999.
      05 SURNAME PIC X(20).
      05 FIRSTNAME PIC X(10).
      05 SEX PIC 9.

This satisfies the rule, because although the elementary fields are of different sizes and types, the **OCCURS** is attached to the Group field, and this is of constant size (namely the sum of the **PICTURE**s of the elementary fields, 4 digits followed by 30 letters followed by 1 digit). A diagram of the internal storage arrangements of the two methods is given in Fig. 3.5.

This is a case where the intermediate heading, **DETAILS**, which we have put in to carry the **OCCURS** (because we cannot put it at **01** level) might be used meaningfully as a data-name, unlike **SALES-TOTAL** in the last example. **MOVE DETAILS (1)**, for example, could be used instead of four individual **MOVE**s to copy **PERSONNEL-NUMBER (1), SURNAME (1), FIRSTNAME (1),** and **SEX (1)** to another part of the store.

5.6 Assigning values in Working-Storage

Hitherto, when we have defined tables with **OCCURS** in Working-Storage, the values, apart from the initial value of zero, have been assigned by reading in data to each location from an external medium, for example, a card-reader. We can, in fact, as with any other data, assign values in the Procedure Division, as literals:
   MOVE 5000 TO ITEM (23).
or as the result of computation:
   ADD BONUS (CUSTOMER), DISCOUNT (CUSTOMER), OLD-CREDIT (CUSTOMER), GIVING NEW-CREDIT (CUSTOMER).

We can set a whole table to some specific value: for example, if each item in a 10-long table called **ITEM** is to be set to an initial value of 1:

113

```
    MOVE ZERO TO N.
    PERFORM SET-TABLE 10 TIMES.
    . . . . . .
SET-TABLE.
    ADD 1 TO N.
    MOVE 1 TO ITEM (N).
NEXT-STEP.
```

The result of the **PERFORM** is that the value 1 is given to **ITEM (1)**, **ITEM (2)**, . . . in turn, up to **ITEM (10)**.

If the initial values we want to read in are *not* the same in every cell of the table, it is going to be rather a tedious business:

```
    MOVE 'JAN' TO MONTH-NAME (1).
    MOVE 'FEB' TO MONTH-NAME (2).
    MOVE 'MAR' TO MONTH-NAME (3). and so on.
```

Obviously in such a case you could read the names in as data, perhaps from 12 cards preceding the main run of transaction cards. We would have:

```
FILE SECTION.
01 MONTH-CARDS.
    03 M-NAME PIC XXX.
. . . . . .
WORKING-STORAGE SECTION.
01 MONTH-TABLE.
    03 MONTH-NAMES PIC XXX OCCURS 12 TIMES.
```

The 12 cards are read in, and the three-letter entry on each directed to the appropriate cell of **MONTH-TABLE**:

```
    MOVE ZERO TO MON.
    PERFORM FILL-TABLE 12 TIMES.
. . . . . .
FILL-TABLE.
    READ INFILE AT END GO TO ERROR-1.
    ADD 1 TO MON.
    MOVE M-NAME TO MONTH-NAMES (MON).
NEXT.
```

This is quite feasible, but it is a tiresome dodge—the operator may forget to put your **MONTH-CARDS** in each time the job is run, with consequent chaos, or the cards may get out of order.

114

6.1 REDEFINES

The best solution is the use of **REDEFINES**. The following example illustrates the principle, and is itself a useful device:

WORKING-STORAGE SECTION.
01 ALPHABETICAL.
   03 ALPHABET PICTURE IS X(26)
     VALUE IS 'ABCDEFGHIJKLMNOPQRSTUVWXYZ'.
   03 ATOZ REDEFINES ALPHABET PIC X OCCURS 26 TIMES.

The 26-letter sequence given in **ALPHABET** is *redefined* as a table of 26 cells, each containing one letter; now **ATOZ (1)** is **A, ATOZ (26)** is **Z.** This sort of thing is very useful, for example, if we want to check individual letters in references.

Again, we can write the month-table, shown in the last paragraph, permanently into the program.

WORKING-STORAGE SECTION.
01 MONTH-TABLE.
   03 STRING PIC X(36) VALUE IS
     'JANFEBMARAPLMAYJUNJULAUGSEPOCTNOVDEC'.
   03 MONTH-NAMES REDEFINES STRING PIC XXX OCCURS 12 TIMES.

Now, if we have a month in data written as two digits (as usual—051216 is 5 December 1916), we can use that two-digit reference as a subscript to pick out the required three-letter equivalent: if the month is given as **07, MONTH-NAMES (07)** is **'JUL'.** It is nowhere expressly stated that the subscript 7 indicates the letters **'JUL'**, or that (in the last example) the subscript for **'D'** is 4; this is implied by their *position* in the sequence.

We can use **REDEFINES** in the File Section, for reading in values of the table from external files:

01 OUTGOINGS.
   03 COST-ELEMENTS.
     05 LABOUR PIC 999.
     05 MATERIALS PIC 999.
     05 TRANSPORT PIC 999.
   03 COST-TABLE REDEFINES COST-ELEMENTS PIC 999 OCCURS 3 TIMES.

115

COST-TABLE (2), for example, is an alternative way of quoting the current value of materials, when this has been read in as part of the **OUTGOINGS** record.

Since the 'redefining' area occupies the same space as the 'redefined' area, we can use it to give different formats to parts of the same record. There can be, as a result, some saving of space and an increased flexibility of format, but the beginner is advised not to bother with this use of **REDEFINES**; there are, in particular, intricacies in the conversion of material from one form to another, rather like those involved in **MOVEs**, which may be a trap for those who do not fully understand what is going on. You will, however, find the uses of **REDEFINES** which enable you to treat a block of data as a string of individually addressable characters of use in all sorts of situations, and it is an invaluable device.

3.5.6.2   Rules about **REDEFINES**

The formal rules should not cause you any difficulty if you model your usage on the examples given.

1. **REDEFINES** must not be used at **01** level in the **FILE SECTION**. This is because there is 'implicit redefinition' at the **01** level: within the same **FD** there may be several Record Descriptions, and these all 'redefine' the same input area.

2. If we have a data-name **BULL**, and a redefining clause **GENTLE-MAN-COW REDEFINES BULL**, then **BULL** and **GENTLEMAN-COW** must have the same level number, and no higher levels (**01** being highest) can intervene between them.

3. **BULL** must not contain an **OCCURS**, but can contain a **VALUE**. Nor can any subordinate fields of **BULL** contain **OCCURS**; it cannot be the subordinate field of an entry containing an **OCCURS**.

4. **GENTLEMAN-COW** can contain an **OCCURS**, but not a **VALUE**; no VALUE can be specified for an entry containing an **OCCURS**, nor for an entry subordinate to an entry containing an **OCCURS**.

116

5. The entries defined for the two data-names must comprise the same total area, that is, the size of the redefining field, multiplied by its number of occurrences, must equal the redefined field area. (This is obvious: they are the *same* area, divided in different ways.)

3.5.7 Input and output in table form

Hitherto our use of **OCCURS** has been confined (with one minor exception) to the Working-Storage Section. It is perfectly feasible to set up tables in Input or Output areas, and entries in them can be manipulated exactly as they are in Working-Storage. There are, however, two points to note.

The contents of such tables are 'volatile': they will be erased and replaced each time we have a **READ** or a **WRITE**. They are therefore not useable, as Working-Storage tables are, for constant reference throughout the program.

The programmer is to some extent constrained by the form of the input and output record. Whereas in Working-Storage he can set up as large a table as he has room for in core, the size of the tables in input and output areas is limited by the size of the input and output records—not a serious limitation, perhaps, with paper or magnetic tape, but with card and print a limit of 80 or 120 characters is set. Moreover, the entries in input and output areas, as we well know, are a 'map' of the layout of the data on the card or print line, and the programmer may have little control over this, or may be governed by the customer's wishes. Let us illustrate this.

We already know that if we have a table of commodity numbers, each consisting of an **ALPHPART** and a **NUMPART**, we can set up a table in two different ways in Working-Storage, and these are to all intents and purposes equivalent:

   03 COMMODITY-NO OCCURS 8 TIMES.
     05 ALPHPART PIC XXX.
     05 NUMPART PIC 9999.

and

   03 COMMODITY-NO.
     05 ALPHPART PIC XXX OCCURS 8 TIMES.
     05 NUMPART PIC 9999 OCCURS 8 TIMES.

117

The first implies a storage layout in which **ALPHPART** and **NUM-PART** alternate:

ABC 1234 DEF 5678 . . . .

and the second in which all the **ALPHPARTS** are grouped, followed by all the **NUMPARTS**:

ABC DEF GHI JKL MNO PQR STU VWX 1234 5678 9012 . . . .

If these descriptions are used in an Input or Output Record Description, they imply also a card or print-line layout; both of them describe 56 columns of a card, or print, but only one of them will correspond to the actual layout of the data on the card, or to the layout we want in the print. The former is more likely, of course; but if we do use the wrong one we shall have serious errors in processing. Of course if the programmer wants to alter the layout in store, or to keep the data for reference, he can **MOVE** it to a Working-Storage area of whatever format he likes.

Program CHARLIE had an input format which invites the use of a table for input: it had 10 identical fields on each record. Instead of writing:

01 TABLEREC.

03 COMMOD-NO	**PIC X(6).**
03 FILLER	**PIC X(5).**
03 PRICE60	**PIC 9999.**
03 PRICE61	**PIC 9999.**
03 PRICE62	**PIC 9999.**
03 PRICE63	**PIC 9999.**
03 PRICE64	**PIC 9999.**
03 PRICE65	**PIC 9999.**
03 PRICE66	**PIC 9999.**
03 PRICE67	**PIC 9999.**
03 PRICE68	**PIC 9999.**
03 PRICE69	**PIC 9999.**

we write:

03 COMMOD-NO	**PIC X(6).**
03 FILLER	**PIC X(5).**
03 PRICE	**PIC 9999 OCCURS 10 TIMES.**

This version is equivalent to the original, setting up an input area of 51 characters (6 + 5 + 40); but it is significantly more concise. But remember that the former **PRICE60** is now **PRICE (1)**, not **PRICE (60)**!

An output record for the records of Program CHARLIE, printing 10 **PRICE**s on each line, might be:

```
01 PRINTLINE.
   03 FILLER PIC Z(20).
   03 COMMODITY PIC X(6).
   03 OUTPRICE PIC Z(6)9; OCCURS 10 TIMES.
   03 FILLER PIC X(24).
```

The table here consists of 10 fields of seven characters each, ample to hold the four digits of **PRICE** and separate them legibly.

To move the input record to output, you could write:

```
NEXTBIT.
   MOVE ZERO TO NUM.
   PERFORM MOVEOUT 10 TIMES.
   MOVE COMMOD-NO TO COMMODITY.
   WRITE PRINTLINE AFTER 1.
   GO TO NEXTBIT.
. . . . . .
MOVEOUT.
   ADD 1 TO NUM.
   MOVE PRICE (NUM) TO OUTPRICE (NUM).
ONWARD.
```

This procedure writes out one line; it is left to the reader to add the coding necessary to read in and write out the whole set of records.

5.8 Handling tables in the Procedure Division

The preceding sections have been concerned mainly with the *structure* of tables, and consequently with the Data Division. The Procedure Division has been involved because it is in that that we assign values to table locations from external files or literals.

We will now consider the *manipulation* of table entries. This can be considered independently of their structure, and the programmer will find it advantageous to do so, particularly when healing with Two-Dimensional tables. A rather trivial example of the distinction

119

between structure and manipulation can be found in the use of Fig. 3.4, which shows the different distribution of data for Group and Individual **OCCURS,** If we write

ADD TABA (NUM), TABB (NUM), TABC (NUM), GIVING COMTOTAL (NUM).

then in Group mode we are adding three contiguous items, and in Individual mode the three items are separated from each other by 124 other items; obviously a human clerk would much prefer the former, but it is unlikely to make any difference to the computer.

For the purposes of this section, we make a distinction, which must not be pressed too far, between two types of table usage: (1) Table Look-up, in which some item such as a reference number or commodity number, read in from an external file, is compared in turn with each entry in a table, so as to recover some associated entry in the table, such as a name or price; and (2) internal manipulation, in which the entries in the table are compared and combined with each other.

3.5.8.1 Table look-up

Example 2. The currency problem

A firm with an extensive foreign trade receives orders from many different foreign countries. Essential details of each order are punched in 'transaction' cards; each of these carries a three-letter abbreviation for the country of origin, for example, **JAP, GER, ITL,** and, with other details, the price in the currency of that country. Part of the processing is to convert that currency, by multiplication by the appropriate factor, into British currency. In a table held in core we have entries comprising the three-letter abbreviation and the necessary conversion factor; this table is read in at the beginning of each run. On each card we have an abbreviation and the conversion factor for that country:

AUS	.0161
BEL	.0085
DEN	.0588
FRA	.0769
. . .	. . . . .

There is a table in Working-Storage called **TABLAND**; it allows for 250 countries:

```
01 CONVERSION-TABLE.
   03 TABLAND OCCURS 250 TIMES.
      05 COUNTRY PIC XXX.
      05 FACTOR PIC 999V999999.
```

The input cards are called **T-ENTRIES** and are read in and **MOVE**d to Working-Storage. The reader will be familiar with this routine by now. The result is that we have **AUS** in **COUNTRY (1)**, **.0161** in **FACTOR (1)**, and so on.

Next we read in the transaction cards, and compare the country of origin on the card (**TRANSLAND**) with each **COUNTRY** entry in the table:

```
START-TABLE.
   MOVE 1 TO NUM.
   READ TRANSACTIONS AT END GO TO NEXTSTEP.
LOOK-UP.
   IF TRANSLAND EQUAL TO COUNTRY (NUM), MULTIPLY
      COST BY FACTOR (NUM) GIVING ENGLISH-MONEY,
      GO TO NEXT-PROCESS.
   ADD 1 TO NUM.
   GO TO LOOK-UP.
```

When a match is found, the conversion is done, and we go on to carry out further processing on this transaction card (**NEXT-PROCESS**). It is assumed that after this is done we return to **START-TABLE** to read in the next card and scan the table, starting with **NUM** equal to 1. When **TRANSLAND** does not match with **COUNTRY**, we add 1 to **NUM** and look at the next **COUNTRY**. Note then when the match *is* found, we 'jump out' of the table; there is no point in continuing the search. There may be applications where we don't do this; we might expect more than one match, so when we find an answer we record it and continue searching the table.

There is, at present, no test in this program to apply if we reach the end of the table without finding a match, as might happen if we had a country not represented in the table, or if the **TRANSLAND** name were misspelt. In that case the program would 'get into a loop', with **NUM** increasing indefinitely and generally raising hell in the core.

So we should put in a test: we can either have a special last entry (like **ZZZZZ** in our first exercise), or by recognising the last actual entry (**IF COUNTRY (NUM) EQUAL TO 'ZAM' . . .**) or by counting the number of comparisons till we reach 250.

Another point to note is that though the table was shown, in this example, in alphabetical order (**AUS, BEL, DEN, . . .**), we can have it in any order we like. If we expect the transactions to come mainly from **GER**, with **ZAM** next, and then **SPA**, and so on, then we shall save processing time by arranging the table in this frequency order, since the commonest **TRANSLAND**s will require the fewest comparisons before a hit is found.

If, on the other hand, the table is in alphabetical order as shown, we can jump out as soon as we have passed the correct place in the table, thus providing a safeguard against mispunched or non-existent entries. We would have:

IF TRANSLAND EQUAL TO COUNTRY (NUM) . . ., etc.
IF TRANSLAND LESS THAN COUNTRY (NUM) GO TO NOT-FOUND-ROUTINE.

and it is implied that if **TRANSLAND** is greater than the current country we add 1 to **NUM** and continue the search. Thus, if our table began **AUS BEL DEN FRA**, then if we had a transaction for **DER** (either a mispunch for **DEN** or a new country), we would compare up to **COUNTRY (4)**, which is **FRA**; and at that point the program would say, I have passed the point in the table at which this entry could have matched, and therefore it is not in the table.

Finally note the purely 'formal' nature of the subscript. It does not appear in any of the data, and it has no relation to the logical order of the table. The use of the subscript in reading in and scanning the table is precisely the same whether the table entries are in alphabetical order or frequency order or no order at all.

Example 3. Change-making

As we calculate each man's take-home pay in the pay program, we may want to produce a schedule showing how that pay is made up in actual currency—notes of £1 or £5 denomination, coins of 50p, 10p, 5p, and 1p (and ½p if we use them). Obviously we can calculate this by an arithmetical process, but a table has some advantages—for example we can bias our selection of currency towards a preponderance of popular coins and away from unpopular ones.

Our table for coins will consist of 100 entries:

```
01 CHANGE-TABLE.
   03 COINS OCCURS 100 TIMES.
      05 PENCE    PIC 99.
      05 FIFTIES  PIC 9.
      05 TENS     PIC 99.
      05 FIVES    PIC 99.
      05 ONES     PIC 99.
```

For each number of pence from 0 to 99, we have a table-card carrying the number of **PENCE**, and four entries (**FIFTIES, TENS, FIVES, ONES**) showing how we want that sum to be made up for example for 96 pence:

PENCE		FIFTIES	TENS	FIVES	ONES
96	(=)	1	3	2	6

This set of cards is read into **CHANGE-TABLE** at the beginning of each run of the program.

As each employee's card is read, the number of pence is compared with the table, by adding 1 to it (to avoid zero subscripts for zero pence). Alternatively we can have a 99-long table, from 1 to 99; each number of pence is used directly as a subscript to access the table; we have a routine to bypass zero pence if it occurs. In either case, we have to arrange to access the number of pence in the employee's pay record, and use this as a subscript; having found the right line, we move the elements to an out-record which shows, for each man, how his pay-packet is made up, and at the same time adds these elements to a schedule showing the distribution of coins for the entire payroll. The number of pence in the employee's record is **P**:

```
CHANGE-MAKING.
   READ EMPL-CARD AT END GO TO NEXT-CALC.
   IF P EQUAL TO ZERO MOVE ZERO TO Q50 (etc.), GO TO
      CHANGE-MAKING. MOVE FIFTIES (P) TO Q50.
   ADD FIFTIES (P) TO SUM50.
   MOVE TENS (P) TO Q10.
   ADD TENS (P) TO SUM10.
   etc.
```

If **P** = 96, **FIFTIES (P)** is 1 (see the previous example), **TENS (P)** is 3, and so on. **Q50, Q10, Q5, Q1** are fields in the employee's output record to indicate the number of coins in each denomination; **SUM50**, etc., are corresponding fields in the distribution schedule.

The table might be extended to cover amounts greater than 100p. A table to determine distribution of £1, £5, £10 notes is also feasible, but an arithmetic routine is probably simpler.

From the point of view of efficiency in running the program it would be much better to write

MOVE FIFTIES (P) TO Q50.
ADD Q50 TO SUM50.
MOVE TENS (P) TO Q10.
ADD Q10 TO SUM10.

and so on; referencing a subscripted data-name is much more expensive, in program time, than referencing a simple data-name, because the program calculates the position of the subscripted data-name each time it occurs.

Since the **MOVE** has put the value of **FIFTIES (P)** in the simple address **Q50**, we save time by using the simple data-name instead of the subscripted one for the **ADD**. Similarly, if you find that in a program you refer several times to a data-name from a table, with the same subscript, it is worth while **MOVE**ing the table-value to a location outside the table. This is a particular case of a general rule that if you have to do any work (computation) to find the value of a variable, you should move the answer to a location of its own if you want to use it at different points in the program, rather than re-calculate it each time you want to use it.

Example 4. Generating a subscript

In the original example in this section, with those Branch-numbers, we mentioned that if the numbers did not form a consecutive sequence from 1 to 125, we could not use them directly as subscripts. One way of handling this situation would be to set up a 125-long table in store, as before, and read in the actual branch-numbers (in the range 3 to 254) from table cards, at the beginning of the program (for convenience, in numerical order):

124

01 SALES-TABLE VALUE IS ZERO.
   03 SALES-TOTALS PIC 9(5) OCCURS 125 TIMES.
   03 BRANCH-NUM PIC 999 OCCURS 125 TIMES.

The table cards are placed at the head of the transaction file, and are read in with **INDX** starting at zero. Each has one entry, **BRANCH-NUMBER**:

READ-TABLE.
   READ INFILE AT END GO TO FINISH.
   ADD 1 TO INDX.
   IF INDX EQUAL TO 126 GO TO READ-CARDS.
   MOVE BRANCH-NUMBER TO BRANCH-NUM (INDX).

When the 125 cards have been read in, the table consists of 125 blank cells of five positions each, and 125 cells each containing one of the actual branch numbers.

INDX	1	2	3	4		124	125
SALES-TOTALS	00000	00000	00000	00000	....	00000	00000
BRANCH-NUM	3	8	10	11		353	354

The transaction cards, each carrying one of the actual branch-numbers and a sales figure for that branch (**BR-NUM** and **SALES**) are read in, and the **BR-NUM** is compared with each of the **BRANCH-NUM**s in the table: the **INDX** of that **BRANCH-NUM** is then used to add the **SALES** to the corresponding **SALES-TOTALS**:

READ-CARDS.
   MOVE ZERO TO INDX.
   READ INFILE AT END GO TO NEXT-STEP.
SEARCHIT.
   ADD 1 TO INDX.
   IF BRANCH-NUM (INDX) EQUAL TO BR-NUM, ADD SALES
     TO SALES-TOTALS (INDX), GO TO READ-CARDS.
   IF BRANCH-NUM (INDX) GREATER THAN BR-NUM, GO
     TO NOT-FOUND.
   IF INDX EQUAL TO 125 GO TO NOT-FOUND.
   GO TO SEARCHIT.

125

In some situations, the subscript could be *calculated* from data on the input. If for example we have a date in the usual form—two digits for day, month, and year—on each card and wish to assign data from each card to its appropriate date in a table for the whole year (that is, with subscript values from 1 to 365) we can use

> **GO TO R1, R2, R3, R4, R5, R6, R7, R8, R9, R10, R11, R12, DEPENDING ON MONTH-NUMBER.**
>
> **R2.**
> > **ADD 31 TO DAY-VALUE, GO TO R1.**
>
> **R3.**
> > **ADD 59 TO DAY-VALUE, GO TO R1.**
>
> **R4.**
> > **ADD 90 TO DAY-VALUE, GO TO R1.**

up to

> **R12.**
> > **ADD 334 TO DAY-VALUE.**
>
> **R1.**
> > **ADD DAY-NUMBER TO DAY-VALUE.**

where **DAY-NUMBER** is the two-digit entry for the day.

As well as finding a position in a table, this type of calculation may be used to find the position of a record in a disc file, in Direct Access working (3.7.1).

3.5.8.2 Internal manipulation

It is obvious that once we have got the table into core we carry out all sorts of computations without reference to input or output data. We can add up the contents of the table, to produce a grand-total—we might want to do this with our **SALES-TOTALS**:

> **MOVE ZERO TO NUM.**
>
> **ADDEMUP.**
> > **ADD 1 TO NUM.**
> > **ADD SALES-TOTAL (NUM) TO GRAND-TOTAL.**
> > **IF NUM LESS THAN 125 GO TO ADDEMUP.**

(Alternatively we could do this as each record was read in; it depends on the 'strategy' of the program.)

We might make special subtotals: for example, if Branches 5, 45, 99, and 7 all have something in common, such as being in the same city, we could, if management wanted it, write

ADD SALES-TOTAL (5), SALES-TOTAL (45), SALES TOTAL (99), SALES TOTAL (7) GIVING LEICESTER-TOTAL.

The 'increment' of the subscript need not be 1: **ADD 2 TO NUM** would pick out from the table every other entry–for example, all branches with odd numbers, supposing such an arrangement to be significant; **ADD 7 TO DAY-NO** will pick out the corresponding days of each week. We can read from the 'bottom' of a table and subtract 1 (or whatever), so that the table is read 'backwards'. The following examples illustrate these uses of the subscript.

Example 5. Space count

In this example we assume that we have a number of cards with a variable number of letters on each—COBOL source cards provide an excellent example: we can assume that each of the instructions we have written on a separate line will be punched on a separate card. We want to find out what is the average number of characters per card. We could start counting from the left of the card, as a human would, but there will be 'embedded' blanks in the text, between words, so we would have to count up to column 80 on every card to make sure there was no more text. So we count from the *right* until we find an actual non-blank character.

FD CARDFILE.
01 CARDREC.
   03 CHAR PIC X OCCURS 80 TIMES.

This defines the input record as a 'table' (in the input area) of 80 characters.

WORKING-STORAGE SECTION.
77 COLUMN PIC 99 VALUE IS ZEROS.
77 SUM-OF-CHARS PIC 9999 VALUE IS ZERO.
77 BLNK PIC X VALUE IS ' '.
77 NUMBER-OF-CARDS PIC 9999 VALUE IS 0.

SUM-OF-CHARS is the number of characters, over all cards; **BLANK** is a reserved word, so we use **BLNK** instead.

127

Now the process is to read in a card, and start at col 80 and test each column for blank, *decrementing* the subscript **COLUMN** each time. When we find a non-blank character, then **COLUMN** is the number of that column and is the required length of text on that card. So we add that to **SUM-OF-CHARS** and add 1 to **NUMBER-OF-CARDS**; at the end of the run we divide **SUM-OF-CHARS** by **NUMBER-OF-CARDS** and that will give us the average.

The Procedure is:

READIT.
   READ CARDFILE AT END GO TO CALC-AVERAGE.
   MOVE 81 TO COLUMN.
   ADD 1 TO NUMBER-OF-CARDS.

TESTIT.
   SUBTRACT 1 FROM COLUMN.
   IF CHAR (COLUMN) EQUAL TO BLNK GO TO TESTIT.
   ADD COLUMN TO SUM-OF-CHARS.
   GO TO READIT.

What we have assumed here is that none of the cards is entirely blank. If there is such a card, then the value of **COLUMN** will go from 80 (=81 – 1) to 1, and then to zero and to negative numbers, and there is no way of stopping it; the run will be wasted. This is the sort of error that will *not* be picked up in compilation; it will only become apparent at run-time. The solution is, of course, to put **IF COLUMN EQUAL TO ZERO** ... immediately after **SUBTRACT 1** ... The following action depends on what you want; if you want to include blank cards in **NUMBER-OF-CARDS** you merely go back to **READIT**; if not you will have to subtract 1 from **NUMBER-OF-CARDS**—and, if necessary, 'report' the finding of a blank card; and then go to **READIT**.

This sort of problem, of course, will not arise with paper tape records. In a wider sense, it does not arise with *human* processing: the human can see at once where the last column is. If we have a book which may have 70 lines per page, any or all of which lines may be blank, then a human will pick out blank pages much more efficiently than the computer will—the computer has to scan every line of every page.

128

Example 6. Sequence check

There is a sequence-number in each of the entries read into core into a table of 100 items. The sequence numbers are not necessarily consecutive, but they are unique in each entry and must be in order, for example, 3, 6, 7, 11, 15, 18 . . . . We wish to check that the sequence numbers (**SEQNO**) are actually in ascending order. Using the sequence quoted above, **SEQNO (1)** will be 3, **SEQNO (2)** will be 6, **SEQNO (3)** will be 7, and so on.

We define the subscripts **THISLINE** and **NEXTLINE** in Working-Storage, with **PIC 999** and **VALUE ZERO.** Now:

CHECKLIST.
    IF NEXTLINE EQUAL TO 100 GO TO NEXTSTAGE.
    ADD 1 TO THISLINE.
    ADD 1, THISLINE GIVING NEXTLINE.
    IF SEQNO (NEXTLINE) GREATER THAN SEQNO (THIS-LINE) GO TO CHECKLIST.
    GO TO SEQUENCE-ERROR.

Note that we jump out with **NEXTLINE** equal to 100; if we had said **THISLINE EQUAL TO 100**, then on the last pass we would have been comparing **SEQNO (100)** with **SEQNO (101)**, which doesn't exist, and we would have found ourselves (probably) in **SEQUENCE-ERROR.**

Example 7. Top price

We pointed out, earlier in this section, that such a format as that used in Program CHARLIE, with ten items per card, could be read in much more succinctly by the use of subscripts, that is, by treating each input record as a table. The use of subscripts also greatly simplifies the handling of such questions as: In what year did commodity XYZ123 reach its peak price? In how many years was the price of any commodity greater than in 1969? How many commodities reached a peak in 1969? and so on. Let us see how the subscript system can be used to answer this last question, how many commodities reached a peak in 1969. We will assume that we are doing this for each record in turn, and that we can safely do the table-handling in the input area. If, for any commodity, the price did reach a peak in 1969, we add 1 to a result-counter.

129

We have to compare **PRICE (1), PRICE (2), . . . PRICE (9)** with **PRICE (10)**, which is the price for 1969, in turn; if any of these is equal to or greater than **PRICE (10)**, then the Price for 1969 is not a peak.

```
READIT.
     READ CARDFILE AT END GO TO FINISH.
     MOVE 1 TO YEAR.
TESTEM.
     IF PRICE (10) NOT GREATER THAN PRICE (YEAR)
        GO TO READIT.
     ADD 1 TO YEAR.
     IF YEAR EQUAL TO 10 ADD 1 TO RESULT-COUNTER, GO
        TO READIT.
     GO TO TESTEM.
```

It would be very tedious to do this type of work without using subscripts. An obvious extension of operations illustrated here is the sorting of all the records in a file to some order; an example on sorting, and many other processes involving use of tables, will be found in Chapter 4. For the moment we will assume that the reader has a reasonable grasp of the elementary use of tables and subscripts, and we will go on to consider the Two-Dimensional Table.

3.5.9 Two-dimensional tables

These are allowed only in Level 2 Nucleus of COBOL and the beginner should not attempt to deal with them until he is completely at home with the setting up of one-dimensional tables and the manipulation of subscripts. This section is therefore confined to a brief exposition of the principles of 2D storage and manipulation, in a rather abstract form, which we hope will help the programmer when he feels confident enough to tackle them. If you find it hard going, skip to Chapter 4. Another reason for not giving more space to 2D tables is that the full demonstration of such tables, and their processing, in any sort of realistic form, is a long-winded and tedious business; an ounce of experience is worth a ton of exposition. The only practical example, therefore (which is, however, realistic and which you can expect to meet) is given in the form of a complete program with commentary.

9.1   Structure and storage

We will return, for an illustration, to the familiar Branch-totals problem. Let us assume that these records are organised in four-weekly periods, and that in each record we have a period number and a single digit (1,2,3,4) indicating the week-number within that period.

It is obvious that we can accumulate weekly totals, in a table of four 'cells' (either within one period, or overall; it doesn't matter). The table would be specified:

01 TOTALS-BY-WEEK.
   03 WSALES PIC 9(6) OCCURS 4 TIMES.

Now we could read in records and accumulate not only the **SALES-TOTALS** by Branch-number, as we did before, but also **WSALES** by week-number:

READIT.
   READ INFILE AT END TO GO NEXT-STEP.
   ADD SALES TO SALES-TOTAL (BRANCH-NUMBER).
   ADD SALES TO WSALES (WEEK-NUMBER).
   GO TO READIT.

The weakness of this procedure is that we cannot get totals such as branch totals broken down by week, or the highest scoring branch in any particular week. By accumulating totals by week in the **WSALES** table, we lose all the information that is on the cards about branches; and in accumulating branch totals we lose the information about distribution by week. But by *combining the two tables into one* we acquire immense power in squeezing the last bit of information out of the data.

This can be done by setting up a table with two **OCCURS**, one *subordinate* to the other:

01 SALES-TABLE.
   03 BRANCH OCCURS 125 TIMES.
     05 STOTALS PIC 9999 OCCURS 4 TIMES.

This is the normal COBOL form, but you will probably find it makes it easier to understand the storage and manipulation of tables if we adopt a slightly extended form, which is also quite legal:

131

SALES-TABLE	BRANCH (1)	WEEK (1,1)	STOTALS (1,1)	
		WEEK (1,2)	STOTALS (1,2)	
		WEEK (1,3)	STOTALS (1,3)	
		WEEK (1,4)	STOTALS (1,4)	
	BRANCH (2)	WEEK (2,1)	STOTALS (2,1)	
		WEEK (2,2)	STOTALS (2,2)	
		WEEK (2,3)	STOTALS (2,3)	
		WEEK (2,4)	STOTALS (2,4)	
	BRANCH (3)	WEEK (3,1)	STOTALS (3,1)	
		WEEK (3,2)	STOTALS (3,2)	
		WEEK (3,3)	STOTALS (3,3)	
		WEEK (3,4)	STOTALS (3,4)	
	BRANCH (4) to (124)			
	BRANCH (125)	WEEK(125,1)	STOTALS (125,1)	
		WEEK(125,2)	STOTALS (125,2)	
		WEEK(125,3)	STOTALS (125,3)	
		WEEK(125,4)	STOTALS (125,4)	

Fig. 3.6. Two-dimensional tables
(a) Branch major, week minor

01 SALES-TABLE.
  03 BRANCH OCCURS 125 TIMES.
    05 WEEK OCCURS 4 TIMES.
      07 STOTALS PIC 9999.

Both of these define a table of 125 locations, each location having four
subdivisions. The Storage picture for the second version is shown in
Fig. 3.6(*a*). Note the difference between this and the multiple
OCCURS previously described, in which all the **OCCURS** were at
the same level (Figs. 3.4, 3.5).

Each reference to the lower level must now have *two* subscripts
separated by a comma, one indicating the branch number, which can
range from 1 to 125, and the second the week number, which can

132

SALES-TABLE	WEEK (1)	BRANCH (1,1)	STOTALS (1,1)	
		BRANCH (1,2)	STOTALS (1,2)	
		BRANCH (1,3)	STOTALS (1,3)	
		BRANCH (1,4)	STOTALS (1,4)	
		BRANCH (1,5)	STOTALS (1,5)	
		. . . . . . BRANCH (1,125)	. . . . . . STOTALS(1,125)	
	WEEK (2)	BRANCH (2,1) BRANCH (2,2)	STOTALS (2,1) STOTALS (2,2)	
		BRANCH (2,125)	. . . . . . STOTALS (2,125)	
	WEEK (3)	BRANCH (3,1)	STOTALS (3,1)	
		. . . . . . BRANCH (3,125)	. . . . . . STOTALS (3,125)	
	WEEK (4)	BRANCH (4,1) BRANCH (4,2)	STOTALS (4,1) STOTALS (4,2)	
		. . . . . . BRANCH (4,125)	. . . . . . STOTALS (4,125)	

Fig. 3.6. Two-dimensional tables
(b) Week major, branch minor

range from one to four. Using either of the forms shown above, we have

STOTALS (BRANCH-NUM, WEEK-NUM).

For that matter, every reference to **BRANCH** must have a single subscript, in the range 1–125, but in this context such a reference does not mean very much since it refers to a *group* of totals. Our input routine will now be:

READIT.
   READ INFILE AT END GO TO NEXT-STEP.
   ADD SALES TO STOTALS (BRANCH-NUM, WEEK-NUM).
   GO TO READIT.

Before we consider what operations we can carry out on this 'two-dimensional' table, we will deal with some general points.

133

Totals for Weeks

Totals for Branch Numbers	1	2	3	4
1	STOTAL (1,1)	STOTAL (1,2)	STOTAL (1,3)	STOTAL (1,4)
2	(2,1)	(2,2)	(2,3)	(2,4)
3	(3,1)	(3,2)	(3,3)	(3,4)
4	(4,1)	(4,2)	(4,3)	(4,4)
125	(125,1)	(125,2)	(125,3)	(125,4)

Fig. 3.7. 2D table in row-column form

It will be seen from Fig. 3.6 that the table consists of $125 \times 4 = 500$ locations, each with a sufficient number of digits to hold the largest sales total likely to be required for any one branch in any one week. Since the number of locations in a table with more than one level (that is, with more than one **OCCURS**) is the *product* of the number of occurrences allowed at each level, one must take care not to set up tables so large that there is no room left in store for the rest of the program, or too large even to go into the store itself!

Some people prefer to think of such tables actually in two dimensions, that is, as a table with rows and columns, as shown in Fig. 3.7. While this is often very helpful, especially in discussing the customer's requirements with him and planning the form of the input and output, it must be remembered that it bears no relation to the way the table is stored in core, as a succession of doubly subscripted locations, each one being selected by calculations on the current values of the subscripts. The nomenclature 'row' and 'column' can sometimes be maddeningly confusing, if for example you have to 'turn the table on its side' for a more easily handled output, or take in on one card several data fields which you wish to handle as a 'column'. By convention, the first subscript, that is the one referred to by the first **OCCURS**, is said to be the row-subscript, and the second is the column-subscript; the elements of the table are said to be stored in row-order, or row-by-row. I myself prefer to call the first subscript the *major* subscript, and the second the *minor*. This corresponds to the order of storage, in which the first subscript is the major order ('by week within branch').

Beginners are often inclined to ask, what happens if I refer to

STOTALS (WEEK-NUM, BRANCH-NUM)

—reversing the order of the subscripts? The answer is that it makes no difference at all to the way the elements are stored. The expression means nothing in itself; it only has meaning when we assign actual numerical values to the subscripts. It is then the location indicated by the actual current values of **BRANCH-NUM** and **WEEK-NUM**. If **BRANCH-NUM** and **WEEK-NUM** are the same, it means the same as **STOTALS (BRANCH-NUM, WEEK-NUM)**. If **BRANCH-NUM** is 4 and **WEEK-NUM** is 2, it means **STOTALS (2,4)**. If **BRANCH** is 63 and **WEEK-NUM** is 3, it means **STOTALS (3, 63)** which is illegal since the minor suffix can only occur 4 times.

The order of storage is defined by the programmer when he writes the record description. Fig. 3.6(*b*) shows the storage layout produced when he writes

```
01 SALES-TABLE.
   03 WEEK OCCURS 4 TIMES.
      05 BRANCH OCCURS 125 TIMES.
         07 STOTALS PIC 9999.
```

Layout (*b*) is merely a rearrangement of layout (*a*), with the subscripts in reverse order. **STOTALS (125,1)** in the first table, in the 497th position, has the same contents as **STOTALS (1,125)** in the second, where it is in the 125th position. In both cases, the contents are the **SALES** for the 125th branch for the 1st week. We could, with equal validity, refer to the contents of this location as **WEEK (125,1)** in the first table, or **BRANCH (1,125)** in the second. The use of the elementary item **STOTALS**, however, helps to remove the confusion which is liable to arise if one uses a term associated with one of the subscripts to describe the item itself. The storage diagrams, which show the data stored in a linear, one-dimensional form, will also held you to avoid ambiguities arising from the description of 2D tables in terms of 'rows' and 'columns'.

135

Program A
TOTAL-SUMMING.
  MOVE ZERO TO WEEK-NUM.
NEW-WEEK.
  MOVE ZERO TO BRANCH-NUM.
  ADD 1 TO WEEK-NUM.
NEW-BRANCH.
  ADD 1 TO BRANCH-NUM.
  ADD STOTALS (BRANCH-NUM, WEEK-NUM) TO WTOTALS
    (WEEK-NUM).
  ADD STOTALS (BRANCH-NUM, WEEK-NUM) TO BTOTALS
    (BRANCH-NUM).
  IF BRANCH-NUM NOT EQUAL TO 125 GO TO NEW-BRANCH.
  IF WEEK-NUM NOT EQUAL TO 4 GO TO NEW-WEEK.
NEXT-STEP.

Program B
TOTAL-SUMMING.
  MOVE ZERO TO BRANCH-NUM.
NEW-BRANCH.
  MOVE ZERO TO WEEK-NUM.
  ADD 1 TO BRANCH-NUM.
NEW-WEEK.
  ADD 1 TO WEEK-NUM.
  ADD STOTALS as before to WTOTALS and BTOTALS.
  IF WEEK-NUM NOT EQUAL TO 4 GO TO NEW-WEEK.
  IF BRANCH-NUM NOT EQUAL TO 125 GO TO NEW-BRANCH.
NEXTSTEP.

Fig. 3.8. Programs for summing 2D table
(a) Branch inner loop, week outer
(b) Week inner loop, branch outer

3.5.9.2 The manipulation of 2D tables

Figs. 3.8 and 3.9 show programs and flow-charts for accumulating totals by Week in a table of four locations called **WTOTAL**, and totals by Branch in a table of 125 locations called **BTOTAL**, in the same program. The storage used is that of Fig. 3.6(a), with **BRANCH-NUM** major. You will see that the 'inner loop' is performed 125 times; when this is done, the **WEEK-NUM** is incremented by 1 and the inner loop is performed another 125 times. The order of extraction is

		added to	
STOTAL (1,1)	**BTOTAL** (1)	and **WTOTAL** (1)	
	(2,1)	(2)	(1)
	(3.1)	(3)	(1)
up to	(125,1)	(125)	(1)
then	(1,2)	(1)	(2)
	(2,2)	(2)	(2)
up to	(125,2)	(125)	(2)
then	(1,3)	(1)	(3)

and so on. 'Nested' loops like this are characteristic of 2D table handling.

An alternative way of doing this would be to have **BRANCH-NUM** as the outer loop, and **WEEK-NUM** as the inner (Program B, in Fig. 3.8(b)). We would then increment the outer loop index, **BRANCH-NUM**, each time the inner loop index reached 4; and the outer loop would be performed 125 times. The order of extraction is now:

	added to	
STOTAL (1,1)	**BTOTAL** (1) and **WTOTAL** (1)	
(1,2)	(1)	(2)
(1,3)	(1)	(3)
(1,4)	(1)	(4)
(2,1)	(2)	(1)

and so on. Write down the next few terms to assure yourself that you understand what is going on.

Which method we use makes no difference to the speed or efficiency of the program. Obviously, with the storage order in Branch-number major, the human would prefer the second, since the first involves reading the first entry, then the fifth, then the ninth, . . . and so on, returning to the second, sixth, . . . ; but to the computer, as long as the whole table is in core, it is all the same whether we read the records in sequence as stored or hop about from one to another.

We can use the programs with the **WEEK** Major storage, as shown in Fig. 3.8(b), as long as we reverse the order of the subscripts to correspond with that given in the Data Division. With Program A, all the totals for Week 1 (Branches 1–125) are accessed and added before any entry at all is made for Week 2; during this time each

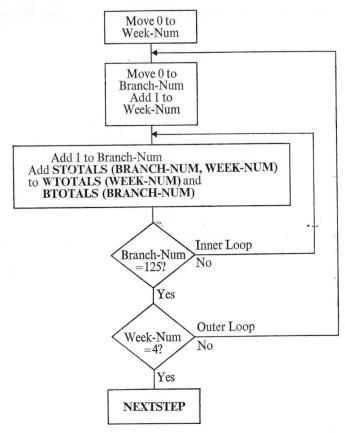

Fig. 3.9. Flow-charts for summing programs
(a) Branch inner loop, week outer

Branch total gets an entry, but four passes are needed to complete the sum. The order of extraction, in fact, is as shown in the Week Major diagram, Fig. 3.6(*b*). It is the same as the order of extraction of Program A, with the subscripts reversed. With Program B, the inner loop is the **WEEK-NUM**, and the order is the same as the previous Program B, with the subscripts in reverse order.

These bare bones are the skeleton of 2D table handling; if you can see how, given one form of storage, you can arrange a program to

138

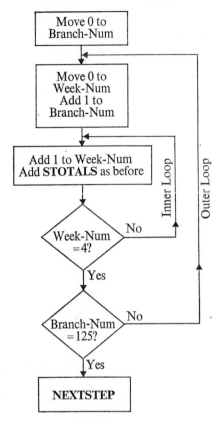

Fig. 3.9. Flow-charts for summing programs
(b) Week inner loop, branch outer

extract or process the data in the required order, you have conquered most of the difficulties of 2D tables.

Example 8. Program SKEW

The discussion of 2D tables has so far been rather theoretical, but a sound understanding of the way items are stored (dictated by the Data Division) and how they can be manipulated independently of the manner of storage, will help you to avoid some of the commonest errors and confusions of beginners. We will conclude, however, with

139

a program with running commentary illustrating a simple but typical and realistic exercise in table handling.

A certain factory has seven main divisions, numbered, for computer purposes, 1–7. Each division telephones a daily return of absentees to a central staff office; each day the numbers are entered on a card divided into seven fields, so that at the end of a five-day week we have five cards:

A		Div 1	Div 2	Div 3	Div 4	Div 5	Div 6	Div 7
	Day 1	5	12	3	2	9	4	0
	2	5	11	4	2	8	6	0
	3	4	11	3	1	9	6	1
	4	4	8	2	2	8	6	1
	5	5	12	3	5	9	5	0

In a weekly run these are read in, with a lot of other data, as part of a Management Information program, and at one stage in the program they are printed out. Printing out in five lines, one line per card, is of course very simple, but in order to conform to other tables in the report it is required to print them out in seven lines and five columns, that is, with columns for Day and lines for Div:

B		Day 1	Day 2	Day 3	Day 4	Day 5
	Div 1	5	5	4	4	5
	2	12	11	11	8	12

and so on. In other words the table is to be 'turned on its side'. First we define the input record format:

```
DATA DIVISION.
FILE SECTION.
FD CARDFILE.
01 ABSREC.
   03 DAY PIC 9.
   03 ABSNUM PIC 999 OCCURS 7 TIMES.
```

There are seven Division fields on the card, each of three columns—no Division is expected to have more than 999 absentees per day. This corresponds to a line of table A above.

We set up a table to receive this in Working-Storage: this is two-dimensional:

```
01 ABSTABLE.
   03 DIEM OCCURS 5 TIMES.
     05 DIV OCCURS 7 TIMES.
       07 ABS PIC 999.
```

The layout of **ABSTABLE** is (values have been entered to help relate it with the input data):

ABSTABLE	**DIEM (1)**	DIV (1,1)	ABS (1,1)	005
		DIV (1,2)	ABS (1,2)	012
		DIV (1,3)	ABS (1,3)	003
		DIV (1,4)	ABS (1,4)	002
		DIV (1,5)	ABS (1,5)	009
		DIV (1,6)	ABS (1,6)	004
		DIV (1,7)	ABS (1,7)	000
	DIEM (2)	DIV (2,1)	ABS (2,1)	005
		. . . . .	. . . . .	
		DIV (2,7)	ABS (2,7)	000
	DIEM (3), (4)	. . . . .	. . . . .	. . . . .
	DIEM (5)	DIV (5,1)	ABS (5,1)	008
		. . . . .	. . . . .	
		DIV (5,7)	ABS (5,7)	000

Now we can read in the data, card by card.

READIT.
   READ CARDFILE AT END GO TO . . .
   MOVE ZERO TO K.

K has been declared with **PIC 9** in Working-Storage; it is to be used as a subscript for the seven **ABSNUM** fields.

FILLITUP.
   ADD 1 TO K.
   MOVE ABSNUM (K) TO ABS (DAY, K).
   IF K LESS THAN 7 GO TO FILLITUP.

DAY is read from the card. The effect of **FILLITUP**, the first time it is done, is to pass **ABSNUM (1)** from the input area to the first line

141

(defined as **ABS (DAY, . . .)**) and the first position in this line (**ABS (DAY, 1)**) of the 2D table. The second time **FILLITUP** is done **ABSNUM (2)** is passed to **ABS (DAY, 2)**, and so on. The table will have been filled in when five cards, for **DAY**s **1–5**, have been read in; you should be familiar by now with the ways in which this can be done (with a **PERFORM**, or a counter, or a test for the last card (**IF DAY NOT EQUAL TO 5 GO TO READIT. GO TO WRITIT-1** (which is defined hereafter))).

When we have got the table filled up, with the 35 values from the cards, we must construct the lines of output. We will use the output format:

FD PRINTOUT.
01 PLINE.
  03 FILLER PIC X(9).
  03 DIVN PIC XXXXXX.
  03 ABSENTEES OCCURS 5 TIMES.
    05 FILLER PIC X(5).
    05 MENAWAY PIC ZZZZZ9.
  03 FILLER PIC X(10).
  03 DIV-TOTAL PIC ZZZZZ9.
  03 FILLER PIC X(39).

DIVN is a label for the Division Number in the printout; we allow six spaces because we shall want to write **TOTAL** there for the last line of the print, which gives the column-totals, that is, the total for each day and the grand total. We also have a **DIV-TOTAL** which will give the sum of the entries in each line, and will also hold the grand total on the last line.

We have made this generous allowance of digit spaces—far more than could be used up—partly to provide a decent spacing between columns, but also because the spacing of the individual columns, in such a table, depends not on the maximum possible size of the individual entries but on the maximum size allowed for the *totals*— which will almost certainly be greater than for the individual entries. If we allowed ZZZ9 for each of the individual line entries, and ZZZZ9 for the totals, the spacing would be such that the columns totals would be shifted progressively to the right of the columns to which they referred, which would look very ugly. So you always design the spacing of such a table as this starting with the column totals. A 'Printer Layout Chart' can be very useful here.

Before we go on to the Procedure, we will define some Working Storage whose use will become apparent shortly:

77 GRAND-TOTAL PIC 99999.
01 DTOTAL PIC 9999 OCCURS 7 TIMES.   (line-totals)
01 DAY-TOTAL PIC 9999 OCCURS 5 TIMES.   (column-totals)

.9.3   The procedure

Our strategy is to move items from the **ABSTABLE** in such a way that the Division is the same for each line, and each entry in the line has a Day entry with subscripts from 1 to 5. We shall also accumulate Division totals for each line in **DTOTAL (K)**, where **K** is the subscript indicating the Division; these will be **MOVE**d before the print to the edited field **DIV-TOTAL**, and at the same time added to **GRAND-TOTAL**. We have a table of five entries, **DAY-TOTAL**, to which we add each entry from the **ABS** table as it is moved into the output line; thus we are accumulating both line and column totals in the same pass. At the end of the run, when the seven Division lines have been written, we **MOVE** the **DAY-TOTAL** entries to their proper position in the output line, and **GRAND-TOTAL** to the **DIV-TOTAL** field, and print.

First, the **MOVE** from the **ABS** table to the output line. The trick is to think of the output we want, not in terms of rows and columns of the input—that way lies madness—but in terms of the *subscripts in the table*. The first subscript is for the Day, and the second is for Division, so in the first line we want the second subscript to be 1 for all entries, and the first subscript to run from 1 to 5. For the second line, the second subscript is 2, and the first subscripts again run from 1 to 5. So the first line is made up:

ABS (1,1), (2,1), (3,1), (4,1), (5,1) (summed to **DTOTAL (1)**)

which are to be moved to

MENAWAY   (1) (2) (3) (4) (5)   DIVN-TOTAL

The routine for the output is given below. There is a flow-chart in Fig. 3.10. In the Totals line, we write '**TOTAL**' under **DIVN**,

143

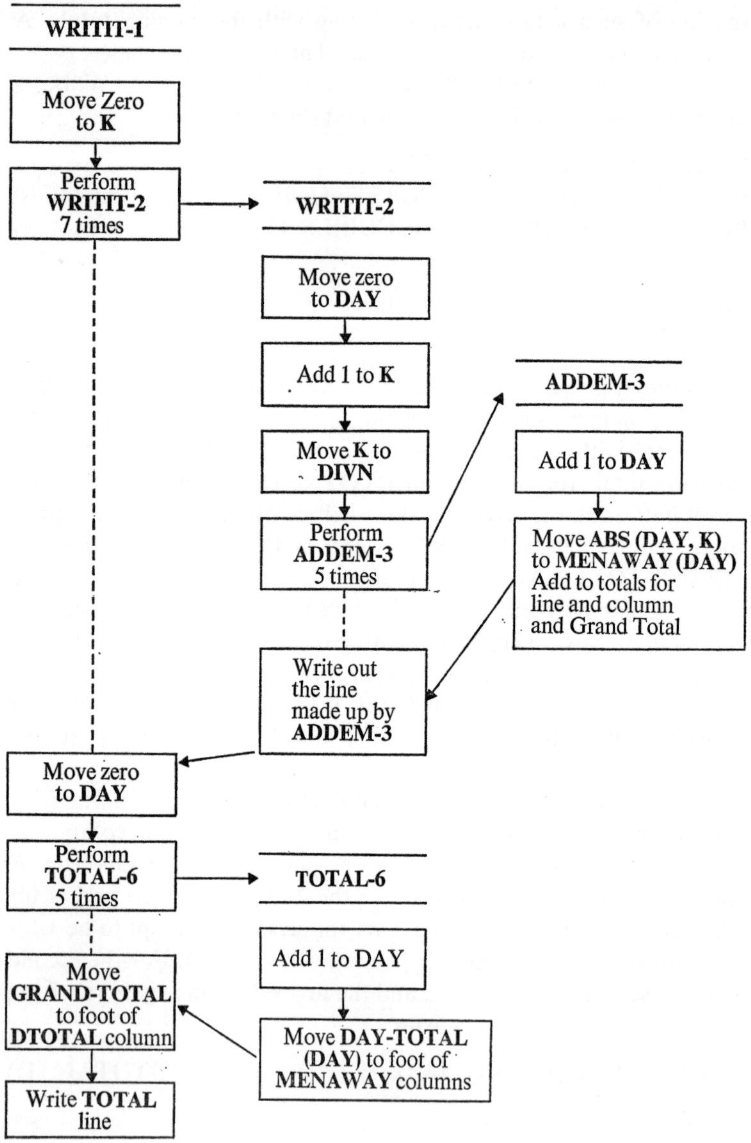

Fig. 3.10. Flow-chart for program SKEW

put **DAY-TOTAL (1)** to **(5)** in place of **MENAWAY (1)** to **(5)**, and put the **GRAND-TOTAL** in place of the **DIV-TOTAL**.

```
WRITIT-1.
    MOVE ZERO TO K.
    PERFORM WRITIT-2 7 TIMES.
    MOVE 'TOTAL' TO DIVN.
    MOVE ZERO TO DAY.
    PERFORM TOTAL-6 5 TIMES.
    MOVE GRAND-TOTAL TO DIV-TOTAL.
    WRITE PLINE AFTER 2.
 . . . . . . . . . . .
 . . . . . . . . . . .
ENDIT.
    CLOSE CARDFILE, PRINTOUT.
    STOP RUN.
WRITIT-2.
    MOVE ZERO TO DAY, ADD 1 TO K, MOVE K TO DIVN.
    PERFORM ADDEM-3 5 TIMES.
    MOVE DTOTAL (K) TO DIV-TOTAL.
    WRITE PLINE AFTER 1.
ADDEM-3.
    ADD 1 TO DAY.
    MOVE ABS (DAY, K) TO MENAWAY (DAY).
    ADD ABS (DAY, K) TO DTOTAL (K).
    ADD ABS (DAY, K) TO GRAND-TOTAL.
    ADD ABS (DAY, K) TO DAY-TOTAL (DAY).
TOTAL-6.
    ADD 1 TO DAY, MOVE DAY-TOTAL (DAY) TO MENAWAY
    (DAY).
```

We have used both **K** and **DAY** again as subscripts, this time generating **DAY** instead of reading it from the card. There is no need to invent a multiplicity of names for subscripts if you can use a data-name you already have, as long as you reset it.

The layout shows how **ADDEM-3** is 'nested': each time the outer **PERFORM (WRITIT-2)** is done, the inner **PERFORM** is done 5 times, each time building up one line of the output record (and accumulating totals for line (**DTOTAL**), column (**DAY-TOTAL**) and Grand Total). Don't put the **WRITE** in this inner **PERFORM**,

145

otherwise you will get 35 lines of print, filled with curious information.

As recommended in the section on **PERFORM** (3.4.6) we have put the paragraphs to be **PERFORM**ed at the end of the program, after **STOP RUN**. This is neater, and obviates the danger of accidentally 'dropping through' to them, as we might do if we had them 'in line'.

If you feel confident that you now understand how to manipulate the subscripts, you can try all sorts of embellishments like putting in a header line **DAY 1 DAY 2 DAY 3** and so on.

3.6   Magnetic tape

3.6.1   Introduction

In COBOL, the handling of input and output is defined in the two 'modules' Sequential Access and Random Access. The latter provides for the use of discs, drums, and other forms of 'mass storage' where access can be random or *direct* (3.7.1). The simplest definition of Sequential Access is that you read the records one after the other in the order in which they were written to the file. It is applied mainly to tapes, card, and printer, but can also be used with Mass Storage devices if they are used in sequential mode.

The methods we have used so far for reading card files and writing printer files are really subsets of the full Sequential Access facilities because certain features of card readers and printers are inflexible and do not need to be specified each time we use the file. The number of characters on a card or print line is fixed, for example; only one line can be printed, and only one card can pass through a reader at any one time.

We need to supply rather more information if we are dealing with files on magnetic tape (henceforward referred to simply as 'tape') or disc. Because we are dealing with peripheral devices, the methods of handling these files in the programming is to some extent machine oriented; the file descriptions given in the program itself are as simple as possible, and these are supplemented by 'control' cards, adapted to the machine's operating system and written in a language suitable to that machine. In this book we shall confine ourselves to the COBOL elements, but some general explanatory notes are given in 'Other magnetic tape considerations' for those to whom tape handling may be unfamiliar.

The information required is under the following heads:

> **FD** (followed by file-name);
> **LABEL RECORDS ARE** ...... ;
> **VALUE OF** .... ;
> **RECORD CONTAINS** ...... ;
> **BLOCK CONTAINS** ...... ;
> **DATA RECORDS ARE** ......

The clauses may be in any order, after the **FD**; the semicolons are optional but the final full stop must be there; the clauses can be written in line if you prefer: **FD TAPEFILE; LABEL RECORDS ARE STANDARD; VALUE OF** ... and so on.

The first three, **FD, LABEL RECORDS,** and **VALUE OF**, are concerned with the identification of the tape, and the information which is written on records of specified form at the beginning (the 'header record'), and the end (the 'trailer') of every tape. The next two concern the way the information is spaced out on the tape, much as we might say that a book consists of so many pages with so many lines on each page. The last is a list of the **01** level names that appear under that **FD**. We will describe these clauses in more detail.

6.2 The identification clauses

FD (File Description)

There is nothing to add to what we have already said about this for card and printer files. In the case of those files, it is the only information that is wanted.

LABEL RECORDS ARE ...

This can be followed by the word **STANDARD** or the word **OMIT-TED**. The beginner will rarely use anything except **STANDARD**. This means that each tape used in his program will have one or more records at the beginning (and end) containing information in a standard format laid down by the implementor, which is used by the Operating System of the computer in its 'housekeeping' or 'data

147

management'. The labels will carry such information as the 'accession number' of the tape, that is, the number by which it is recorded in the tape library irrespective of its contents; the retention date, which indicates how long the tape is to be kept before it can be used for other data; the date it is written; the title of the data-set written on it (see **VALUE OF**); and certain information for the use of engineers concerned with the maintenance of the tape decks. When the data on a tape is no longer required, the tape can be 'scratched', and used as a work-tape or for output of other data. When a tape is to be written on, the Operating System checks that it has been 'scratched', that is, that the label states that it can be written on, or that the retention period has expired.

VALUE OF

A typical entry would be **VALUE OF IDENTIFIER IS 'TRIAL TAPE '**, where **IDENTIFIER** is a data-name supplied by the implementor and **TRIAL TAPE** is the name entered in the label record by the program that wrote the tape; this name is a literal of a specified number of characters, here 12. When the tape is 'opened' for reading, the Operating System will check that the name given in the tape label record is the same as the literal in **VALUE OF**. This is, of course, a safeguard against the operator putting on the wrong tape (but it can be a nuisance, if you want to run your program with a tape which has a different label from the one originally used with the program; check with your installation how they get over this—they certainly will). When the tape is opened for writing, the name given in **VALUE OF** is entered in the label record. You may also need to enter other values for the label record, such as retention date, generation number, or sequence number if the reel is part of a file occupying more than one reel of tape. It is not possible to give general guidance on these points.

3.6.3 The format clauses

RECORD CONTAINS ...

This is followed by an integer and the word **CHARACTERS** (optionally); or two integers with the word **TO** between them. The integers show the number of characters in each record, or the range of the number of characters, between the shortest and longest record. ANSI COBOL states that this entry is never required, since the number of characters in a record (in a standard character form, irrespective of how they may be represented on the tape) is fully defined by the **PICTURE**s in the Record Description. You will probably find that your COBOL requires a clause **RECORDING MODE IS . . .** followed by **F, U, V,** or some other symbol. This is not a part of Standard Cobol, and is defined by your implementor. It allows for records of variable length (**V**), or Fixed (**F**), or unspecified (**U**). Usually the 'default value', if the **RECORDING MODE** is not stated, is taken to be **V**, in which case the length of the record is calculated by the computer when the record is written and is entered in a field at the beginning of the record. The programmer *may* have to allow for this field in moving and manipulating his record, and it is a frequent cause of diagnostic messages complaining of 'wrong record length' in compilation.

BLOCK CONTAINS...

This is followed by an integer and the word **RECORDS**. The compiler sets aside storage for the number of records thus specified. In card and printer files, we can have only one record per block, and as we know the input area is overwritten each time a new record is read in. In tape working, however, records are frequently grouped into 'blocks', and the object of this clause is to tell the compiler how much storage to allot. The upper limit of the number of records in a block depends on the number of characters in a record and the size of the core store, but a block size of 10 records is fairly typical.

The reason for blocking is that once we have read in enough data to fill the storage allotted to it we cannot read in any more until we have finished processing what we have. It is easy enough to hold up a card reader until we are ready to take the next card, but stopping a tape is not such a simple matter: the tape will be travelling (typically) at between 50 and 100 inches per second, and it cannot be stopped *instantaneously*; it must have time for deceleration, and during that time tape is passing under the reading heads and cannot be read because tape can only be read when passing at a specified constant speed. During this deceleration period, then, the tape that passes must not carry any data. Similarly, when the signal to start is given (when the program wants more data) there must be time, and blank tape, allowed for acceleration up to full speed. After each block, therefore, there must be a gap, known as an Inter-Block Gap. This gap is usually between two-thirds to three-quarters of an inch in length.

With a 'packing density' of 800 characters per inch, which is normal for modern tapes, an 80-column record will occupy one-tenth of an inch; if we have blocks of single records (**'BLOCK CONTAINS 1 RECORDS'**) there will be 0·66 inch blank tape for every 0·1 inch of data; and, also, since the tape *must* stop and start between each record, which may require about one-fiftieth of a second, during which time no reading or writing can take place, the arrangement of records in single blocks is not only wasteful of tape but the computer program may take much longer because it has to wait for the tape.

A high *blocking factor* is therefore economical of tape space and time, but since we must provide storage space for all the records in the block it uses up a lot of core. The decision on the optimum blocking factor is not altogether straightforward; but it is one the beginner is unlikely to have to make—for one thing it is only significant with large volumes of data, and for another he is likely to find the decision made for him if he handles tape made by other programs or is working as one of a team. If it is left to you, stick to smallish blocking factors, for example, not more than ten records to a block.

The fact that more than one record may be copied into store, in block reading, does not contradict the rule that the **READ** instruction makes available for processing, and the **WRITE** instruction makes available for output, one record at a time. The first time the **READ** statement is executed a whole block is brought in to fill up the input area; but the records are 'released' or 'made available' to the program singly, one each time a **READ** is executed, and when all the records in the input area have been released, the next **READ** brings in another whole block. Similarly a **WRITE** instruction releases one record to an output block which is built up in the store; when this area of store is full the block of records is written, preceded and followed by a gap, on to the tape. The programmer will be quite unaware of all this spoonfeeding; it is done by the computer, through its Operating system, or 'housekeeping', or the object program produced by the compiler.

DATA RECORDS ARE ...

This is followed by the list of the **01** names under that **FD**. In most
cases this is a mere formality, but the list could be useful, for example,
if the record descriptions have been taken from a library by a separate
ate process, to check that they have been correctly assembled.

5.4 Other magnetic tape considerations

Though tape handling requires more elaborate File Descriptions than
printer or card files, and presents many traps for the beginner, use of
tape files gives the programmer more flexibility than card. Input and
output records can be of whatever size you like, to suit the data. A
record like the Library Catalogue described in 3.2.2 can be written as
a single record on tape, with none of the apparatus of accession
numbers linking records, or code numbers to be tested:

```
FD MAIN-CATALOGUE; LABEL RECORDS ARE STANDARD;
    VALUE OF ID 'MAIN CATALOG'; BLOCK CONTAINS 10
    RECORDS; DATA RECORDS ARE CATALOGUE-ENTRIES.
01 CATALOGUE-ENTRIES.
    03 ACCESSION-NO, PIC X(10).
    03 AUTHOR.
    03 FULL-NAME (etc.)
    03 TITLE        PIC X(138).
    03 CLASS-NO     PIC X(20).
    03 PUBLISHER    PIC X(30).
    03 YEAR-PUB     PIC X(4).
    03 OTHER-INF    . . . . .
```

and so on. How to build up such single records from multiple input
records (and break them down again for printing) is described in
Chapter 4 (4.2.2, Reformatting).

Nor do you have to make output records up to 120 characters. You
can have different blocking factors for input and output tapes, and
indeed for every tape in the program if you like. Operating systems
generally impose a minimum and maximum length of record, something
thing like two characters minimum and several thousands maximum
mum. A record on tape is often referred to as a *logical record*, since

its length can be made to fit a logically independent, self contained section of data. (A block, or a card or line of print, is called a *physical record*.)

The ultimate restriction on the amount of data that can be written on a tape is the length of the tape itself. The standard length is 2400 feet (sometimes 3600); written at 800 bpi (bits per inch, which here means characters per inch), it can hold a maximum of about 23 million characters. However this total will be much reduced by the necessity to block the data so as to get it in manageable quantities into the core store: if we have 80 character records blocked in 10s (800 ch. per record) we shall get about 17000 such records (13600000 ch.) on a reel; if blocked in single 80 ch. records we would get about 41000 records (but only 3280000 ch.) on the reel.

It often happens, of course, that a file is so large that it fills more than one reel; the header label must then contain a sequence number which will be written and checked by the Operating System. The exact procedures for dealing with such multireel files depend on the implementation; they are not part of COBOL.

It is clear that the **OPEN** and **CLOSE** verbs do much more in tape handling than they do for cards or printer. The **OPEN** verb checks, or writes, the header label (according to whether **OPEN INPUT** or **OPEN OUTPUT** was specified), positions the tape so as to be ready for the first **READ** or **WRITE**, and performs other housekeeping; the **CLOSE** verb writes the trailer label, and carries out other procedures dependent upon tape-handling methods in your implementation.

The beginner will find that he will not go far wrong if he treats magnetic tape as if it were a card or paper tape file with certain additional facilities. He will get used to the idea that the amendment of a tape file always involves the creation of an entirely new tape. In a card file we can simply remove, manually or with a collator, the cards that have to be amended and insert new ones; to delete a record, all we do is remove the card. But to amend or delete entries in a tape file we must recopy the whole file, with no alteration except to those records which have to be amended or deleted (omitted).

Any amendment to a card file, and in fact any operation except reading and reproducing, destroys the order of the original file. If you make a mess of your amendment, you can't go back to the original file and start again. But you can in tape processing, precisely because all tape operations except reading involve making an entirely new

152

tape. This is the basis of the 'generation' system of tape handling, in which a tape used to create an amended tape is retained until the amended tape itself has begotten a descendant, so that if in this second amendment there is a disaster which destroys either of the tapes, they can be reconstituted from the 'grandfather'.

3.7 Direct access devices

7.1 Characteristics and applications

If you want to look up a reference in a book in which the contents are arranged alphabetically, as in a dictionary or encyclopaedia, or which has an index, you don't have to start at the beginning and read on until you come to the item you want: you can have 'direct access' either by virtue of the alphabetical arrangement or by the use of the index. You can't do this if you want to access a record on magnetic tape. Even if you *know* the position occupied by the wanted record on the tape—for example, the 147th—you still have to pass all the preceding records under the reading head and pass them into core, until you reach the one you want. If you want to do a series of amendments to records on the tape (as described in Chapter 4) you must sort the amendments to the same order as the records them-selves, because if you do an amendment, say, to the 140th record you can't turn the tape back and do an amendment on the 132nd. In the usual terminology, access is sequential on magnetic tape (as it is on punched cards and punched paper tape files, and in a slightly different sense on the printer—though in the case of cards and paper tape, the operator may be able to select the required point manually).

Direct Access Devices such as discs allow automatic access under program control, if not to single records, at least to segments of the file which contain the wanted records and an acceptable small num-ber of unwanted ones. The other main Direct Access Devices are drums and magnetic cards, but the use of these is far less widespread and more specialised than discs, and we will not deal with them here.

On discs, the records are written on tracks, much as on magnetic tape (but the binary digits of each character are written in sequence, not on six or eight parallel tracks as on tape). A track can be com-pared to a segment of magnetic tape, carrying a number of records,

153

which can be of fixed or variable length, blocked or unblocked, as on tape. Each track has an address, like an address in core store, which identifies it to the computer control system, so that if you know which track the wanted record is on, you can give an instruction in the program which will move a reading arm to that track, and the record you want can be selected from the records on the track. In a typical example of a modern disc store each track will hold about 7000 characters, equivalent to about 75 80-column cards. Each disc will have 200 tracks on each surface, upper and lower; there will be a number of discs in a pack, comprising say 20 surfaces. Whole disc packs can be removed, and others put in their place, just like magnetic tapes, so that the potential capacity of such a file is virtually unlimited. You might have say eight disc packs on line, that is, in direct communication with the computer—at any one time, each pack holding up to 30 million characters and thus allowing the computer to have access to over 200 million characters. Any record, in the whole device, can be accessed within say one-tenth of a second or less. The 'delay' in reading is due partly to the time it takes the reading arm to move to the proper track, and partly to the time it has to wait until the wanted record, or the start-read point on the track, revolves round to the reading head. The former is minimised by organising files in 'cylinders': when a track is full, we continue not on the adjacent track, which would involve moving the arm, but on the one above or below: since all the arms, one for each surface, move together, the arm is already in position and only electronic switching, which takes virtually no time, is required. The tracks on which a file is written may thus be compared to a cylinder. The rotation delay time can also be reduced by highly sophisticated design.

The enormous capacity of such files, with the possibility of access in a matter of milliseconds, has played a dominant role in the development of data processing since the middle 1960s (though discs and drums have been in use, in some form, since the earliest days of computers). In some installations, indeed, discs have entirely replaced tapes, though most computer managers at the present time would probably prefer to have both, because tapes provide cheaper storage if there is a mass of material to be 'archived' or referred to only infrequently, are more convenient than discs as a means of exchanging data and programs with other installations, and provide a good 'back-up' against failure of the discs.

Discs provide you with direct access to a file in much the same way as tables held in core, as we described in the last section, allow you to have access to data, on a much smaller scale, in no particular ('random') order. Some of the operations carried out with discs simply would not be feasible without them. Such are operations requiring immediate and 'unscheduled' access to files in order to answer queries, or to allow the immediate updating of a file or a number of files affected by one transaction, for example booking systems, where the clerk (often one of many clerks, all having access to the files through a 'remote terminal') needs to get the information about the availability of seats on a given route while the customer is still present, and must update the file as soon as the booking is complete so as the minimise the danger of overbooking. Direct Access devices are also used in place of Sequential Access devices in many applications where the latter provide a much less satisfactory and efficient means of doing the job. A transaction may involve the updating of many files—the notification of a file may lead to entries on an invoicing file, a commission file, a stock reorder file, and so on; these could be updated periodically, but in most situations the updating of all the files as soon as one transaction takes place will be preferable. Again, we may have a computer run which generates two or more printer files—in running a file of criminal records, for example, we want to print a list of all prisoners convicted of housebreaking followed by a list of prisoners convicted of burglary. We can extract and print the housebreakers and at the same time copy the burglars to another part of the disc, to be printed later; we shall not have to run through the main file again to find the burglars. This sort of thing can, of course, be done with tapes, but only for as many categories as we have spare tape units; with discs there is no effective limit to the number of such temporary files. We may have a few hundred amendments to make each day to a very large file, containing perhaps tens of thousands of records; with tape processing we would either have to 'batch' the amendments, that is, save them up until we had enough to make a run of the main file worth while, with a consequent risk that the main file may become dangerously out of date and inaccurate; or we must spend a lot of computer time on useless scanning of the file. Disc access provides a much more economical procedure. Finally, we may mention that such routines as sorting can be more efficient on disc than on tape, and the programmer can

155

benefit because he can organise his program into segments or over-lays which can be stored on disc until called for, when they can be brought into the core in any order and with a minimum delay. Discs thus provide a sort of slow-speed core.

A file on a Direct Access device can be used as if it were a Sequential Access File, and sometimes it is convenient or necessary to do this. The reading of the criminal records mentioned in the last paragraph would probably, though not necessarily, be carried out by reading all the records in sequence. We may have a file of medical records arranged in registration number order of patients; if we want to extract the records of all patients with measles, we shall have to examine each record in turn since there is no relation between the arrangement of the records and the feature we want to examine.

The advantage of a Direct Access File, however, lies in the fact that there can be a relation between the *key* (reference number, serial number, or other unique identifying feature) of a record, and its position on the tracks of the disc file. If we have simply filled in the tracks of the disc file with the records in key number order, we may be able to calculate, from the record key number, assuming so many records per track, what track the record is on, and thus give the program the track number which will enable it to retrieve the record. If the records are of variable length, however, or if there are gaps in the sequence of keys, this method won't work. We might be able to take advantage of the Direct Access feature by a 'binary search'—that is, we look at the middle of the file to see if the record number there is higher or lower than the one we are looking for; if it is higher we look at the middle record in the first half of the file; and so on. This is apt to be wasteful for more than a small number of such accesses. The main disadvantage of packing records in this way, however, is that if we want to insert any new records they either have to go at the end of the file, and are consequently out of order, or we have to remake the whole file. One method of getting round this, which we will mention briefly, is known as 'indexed sequential'. The records are written on the disc in key number sequence, with no gaps left even if the key numbers are discontinuous. There is a gap, how-ever, called an overflow area, at the end of each cylinder. One track is set aside as an index track; this has entries showing the highest record numbers on each of the other tracks. By means of this index we can find the position of a wanted record; if we want to add a record, it is written into a track in its proper sequence; the higher records are moved up to make room for it, and the highest record on the track is pushed off into the overflow area. The indexes are changed to show these new locations. The system can become complex to a degree that we cannot describe here; at some point, if the file goes on growing, it will be taken 'out of service' at some convenient time and rewritten so that all the records in the overflow area are now incorporated in the proper sequence; the indexes are remade and new, blank overflow areas allotted.

3.7.2 The Random Access Module in COBOL

We have not yet mentioned COBOL at all in this section. In ANSI COBOL, Direct Access is dealt with in the module called Random Access ('direct' access is the preferred term nowadays) and tapes, cards, printers, etc., are dealt with under Sequential Access. The differences between the two modules are not very evident—this is not surprising since COBOL tries to treat all files in the same way: card and printer files do not require the amount of information that tape or disc files do, and the logical characteristics of a Direct Access file are not so very different from those of a Sequential Access file. All that ANSI COBOL requires is an entry in the Environment Division

ACCESS MODE IS RANDOM, PROCESSING MODE IS SEQUENTIAL, ACTUAL KEY IS (data-name).

If we are not using Random Access, that is, if we are using the Direct Access file as a Sequential File, we write **ACCESS MODE IS SEQUENTIAL** (as we can, optionally and unnecessarily, for Sequential Access files). **PROCESSING MODE** is always **SEQUENTIAL**, both in Sequential and Direct Access; that is, the records are processed in the order in which they are **READ** and made available to the program.

The **ACTUAL KEY** is the location of the record that is to be **READ**, or the address at which it is to be written. The only feature of the Procedure Division that is peculiar to Random Access is the **SEEK** instruction, which places the reading arms in position so that the next **READ** or **WRITE** can be executed with a minimum of delay due to repositioning of the arm. It can be given while the record from the previous **READ** is still occupying the input buffer.

157

Most of the mechanics of Direct Access device handling are left to the implementor, which is reasonable enough since so much is dependent on the physical characteristics of the devices and on the operating system which controls them for all programs (not only COBOL). No doubt in time, as the handling of disc files becomes standardised to the extent that tape files have, we shall find COBOL extended to allow the COBOL programmer a more direct and detailed control over these files (as indeed he has now, in some implementations). At present, however, you will find that if you are handling Direct Access files, you do it either through additions to COBOL which are peculiar to your computer system, or through the 'operating' or 'control' system instructions which are not part of COBOL.

4 Using COBOL

4.1 Building blocks and little programs

The applications of computers nowadays cover almost every aspect of social and economic life, and for that reason it seems futile to select one 'application', carrying out specific tasks for one user, and use it as an illustration of the working of COBOL for the many other disciplines which will (I hope) be represented among the readers of this book. A doctor is not very likely to be interested in the scheduling of transport, nor the transport manager in the processing of medical records; the insurance broker will not be enlightened by the design of school timetables, nor the teacher by the calculation of premiums. Worse still, it is likely that a specific program, used as an example, would do little to satisfy even those who are interested in its subject matter, because they will see at once that a realistic program would need to be much more complicated and take far more factors into account.

All of these multifarious applications of computers, however diverse their purpose, have some things in common: they can be carried out on the same sort of hardware; they use the same programming language. In fact it is not going too far to say that they use the same verbs and data-structure; only the names given to the data-sets and procedures differ from one application to another. The doctor counts cells and the accountant counts money; the process, and the way the object of the counting is represented in the computer, is essentially the same in both applications.

The common features can be found at a higher level than COBOL language statements. If we look at a number of different applications, and discount the effect of the different data-names, we shall find that the same sequences of verbs, applied to the same types of data, occur in all of them. In scientific work, to be sure, we shall find a preponderance of 'computation', in the mathematical sense; in commercial work, a preponderance of comparisons and data-moves. And certainly some, if not all, applications will have some unique features; but by and large we shall be able to dissect out *routines* which are common to many programs, and which will correspond, very roughly, to paragraphs or sections in the program.

A high-level language is itself, of course, a set of common routines which are expressed in simple verbs; these verbs may represent whole sequences of machine language instructions. Various functions at a higher level than the high-level languages have been recognised and isolated; every manufacturer now provides a Sort routine for his machine; you can get file-handling routines, in which you fill in only the 'parameters' for the run—the parameters, in the modern use of the term, are the elements which can be varied from one run to another, such as the size of the file, the length of the records, the manner in which they are to be compared, and so on. Payroll 'packages' which calculate all tax and deductions are also commonly used. COBOL itself provides a Sort, a Report Writer, and a Library facility which enables you to call in pre-written routines as you need them.

It is fair to say that the computer world is still not entirely happy with packages that carry out standard functions at a higher level. One of the reasons is that such packages tend to be too general, in order to provide all the facilities that may be required in connection with a given function, and are therefore uneconomical in core store and running time—they include so many 'options' that a particular user does not want; or at the same time they may not be general enough, so that a user has to supplement them with code he has written himself.

Whatever the reason, we have not yet reached the day when all computer operation is provided in packages, and for some time yet we shall find that COBOL programmers write routines which carry out what we might call the common operations of data-handling; and the following pages describe typical examples of these common operations. They are not glamorous; you will not find a fully fledged Management Information System described here; often you will find that they are included in Report Writer or other ready-made and easily available forms. Nevertheless I still think you will find them extremely valuable and worth the study, not only because they are precisely the sort of routines that you will be writing as soon as you get on to operational COBOL programs, but also because they provide excellent supplementary examples of COBOL programming to illustrate the facilities you have learnt about in the previous pages.

160

At the end of the section, I try to show how these 'building blocks' can be put together to produce a complete functional program.

One thing that you will notice in these routines is that they are all based on Sequential Access, that is, they do not assume the use of discs and other Direct Access devices. It will be obvious in many cases—for example, in File Handling—that the process will be much simpler with Direct Access, and that a good deal of sorting of one file or another could be avoided. I have thought it best to retain the Sequential Access approach, partly because there are still some installations that don't have Direct Access, and partly because they are more valuable as illustrations in the more difficult mode of Sequential Access—if you can design a Sequential solution, you can certainly design a Direct one.

4.1.1 Arrangement of the routines

Whatever the application, then, you will find it contains routines for pagination and layout of output, for sorting, merging, deleting, and amending entries in files, for producing selective lists and totals and for searching files for entries specified by possibly very complicated criteria, for calculating percentages and averages and counting and summing and checking; and when you have taken these out there may not be much else!

These operations have to be classified somehow, for the purposes of description, and the classification I have adopted is based on 'the origin of the operands'. What this means is that all computer data-manipulations involve *two* operands—we compare A with B, we add A to B, we move A to B. Some operations, of course, can appear with more than two operands—**ADD A TO B GIVING C**—and in some, such as **READ** and **WRITE**, it is a bit pedantic to attempt to distinguish two operands. However, it is a useful basis for classification, because making these operands available to the program, ensuring that the records containing them are presented to the program in the right sequence and at the right time, while avoiding the hidden traps is one of the arts that the programmer has to practise, once he has learnt, as in Chapters 1–3, what the individual instructions do.

We have pointed out before that there are three ways in which data can be got into a program—or, in other words, in which operands can be given a value. The values can be assigned, by statement as a literal or use of a **VALUE** clause; they can be computed, by combination of other data values already assigned; and they can be read in, and the values stored in locations named in either the File Section or the Working-Storage section.

Data stored in the File section areas is normally *transient*; it is replaced each time a new record is read in. Data in Working-Storage is normally (though not necessarily) *static*. A typical example of a static file is a price-list read into a table in Working-Storage at the beginning of the program; orders are read in, a price is calculated for each one, and as each one is processed it is read out again and the store area used for the next order. The order file is *transient*.

As a general rule, we shall find that in any operation of computation or comparison involving two operands, one at least is read in from a transient file. Reading both operands by any other method does not seem to make much sense, if the object is to produce useful results, though it is easy enough to find borderline cases. Where *both* operands are read in from transient files we have the following possibilities:

1. Both operands are in the same record—for example, two fields of the same card.

2. The operands are in different records in the same file. They cannot both be in store in the same time unless one of them is moved to a working area. They may be counted, or added, or moved to a table; these operations do not imply any particular sequence in the records —like 1, they are handled independently of each other and need not be in order. If they are compared, we generally find that some sort of sequence is implied: it is an 'ordered file'.

3. The operands come from different files, from which records have to be read 'in step'.

This classification represents one possible measure of the complexity of the programs that you may have to write, and it is logical to treat the routines in that order. We do not adhere to it pedantically: output, for example, does not usually present any file-handling problems, but the arrangement of the output in an acceptable and attractive form may be a time-consuming and tricky business, which is best handled as a separate subject.

162

1.2 Classification by test and process

Before we leave the question of complexity, we may note that another method of classification, which is at least as valid as the 'origin of operands', could be based on the *use* made of the two operands. They may be *compared* with each other, as the operands of an **IF** statement; or they may be *combined*, as in an arithmetic statement (the case where the two data-names are the operands of a **MOVE** may be left out of account, since a **MOVE** is a 'housekeeping' operation that does not generally produce any new result, except in the trivial case of an editing **MOVE**). This distinction reflects what we may regard as the essential structure of computer routines, namely the *test* followed by the *process*: the process to be carried out is determined by the test.

Both the comparisons and the processes can range over a whole spectrum of complexity. We may have the very simplest tests, such as the test for End-of-File in **READ . . . . AT END . . .** , which is little more than a test for the existence of a record; we may have the very simplest processes, for example, a transfer of control to the next record if the data-item satisfies some test, as in a validation program, or a **WRITE** of the record to one file or another according to the result of some test. And of course we may have simple tests followed by simple processes, or complex tests and complex processes. On the whole, the learner will manage the complex processes without much trouble, once he has learnt the rules for handling data of different modes. He may not find it so easy to handle the decision logic in a sequence of **IF**s; we discuss briefly, at a later stage, the various aids he can call on to guide him through the maze. The programmer will find that what appears to be a complex problem is often simplified by deciding whether the complexity lies in the test or the process.

4.2 Operations on one file (non-sequenced)

Operations on a single file which is not assumed to be in any order present few difficulties, and the reader will be familiar with them. Both operands for comparisons or arithmetic will be found in the same record, or are supplied by simple constants and variables in

Working-Storage; computed results are stored in the same record, or in a single location in core; records are handled independently of their predecessors and successors.

4.2.1 Some common routines

Such routines are:

Counting the number of records in a file, up to an End-of-File or other marker, or counting the number of occurrences of a given entry;

Adding two or more fields in the same record, and storing the result in the same record;

Adding the contents of the same field throughout the file, and storing the result; more than one field in each record may be summed at the same time;

Finding the highest value in a given field in the file, or the second highest, or the lowest, etc.

Computation, such as finding an average of the sum of certain fields in a record, or over the whole file; calculating a percentage of some field; converting currency.

Carrying out the same amendment to a given field, all through the file, with or without 'testing'.

A few examples are appended, as a refresher.

4.2.1.1 Percentage

```
PERCENTAGE-CALC.
    MULTIPLY PRICE BY PERCENT.
    DIVIDE PRICE BY 100 GIVING PERCENTAGE ROUNDED.
```

PERCENT is a variable that will be given an appropriate value, for example, 5 for 5 per cent. **PRICE** will have a **PICTURE** say 9999V99, and **PERCENTAGE** the same. The percentage is rounded off to the nearest np.

164

1.2 Amendment

Each occurrence of catalogue number **DIN44** is to be changed to **RXE-56**:

IF CAT-NO EQUAL TO 'DIN44' MOVE 'RXE-56' TO CAT-NO.

This is obviously a specialised ('one-off') program since it will do this amendment and no other. A more generalised form is discussed later.

1.3 Comparisons within the record

We may use two fields in the same record as operands for a comparison:

IF FIELD-A GREATER THAN FIELD-B . . .

Such a test might be used for example to split a file in two, one output file containing records where **FIELD-A** is greater than **FIELD-B**, the other where it is less than or equal to. Or **FIELD-A** and **FIELD-B** might be debits and credits, and the result of the test would lead to two totally different procedures.

1.4 Average

Find the average of the five fields on the card:

ADD FIELDA, FIELDB, FIELDC, FIELDD, FIELDE GIVING FIELD-TOTAL.
DIVIDE FIELD-TOTAL BY 5 GIVING AVERAGE ROUNDED.

2.2 Reformatting, expanding, combining records

Records read in from card or tape almost always require some sort of reformatting for printing, if nothing more than the insertion of **FILLER**s as so to produce a readable line. It may be desirable to alter the order of the fields, or to move one field to the end of the line (for example, a reference number, used for 'looking up') or to omit fields that are of no interest to the reader (for example, an item

165

number used for internal machine checking in the program). None of these should need further description at this stage.

Two procedures which may be mentioned are 'closing up' and 'expansion'. Fields may be closed up by eliminating unwanted spaces, to make the text more presentable: for example, a list of names and initials, where 20 spaces are allotted to each name and three to initials, in store, might be printed out crudely as

CLOTWORTHY   JR
COLE   PMR
COLLINS   T

but would look better as

CLOTWORTHY, J.R.
COLE, P.M.R.
COLLINS, T.

This is not at all simple: the basic idea is to **REDEFINE** the fields as tables of 20 and 3, and to find the end of the surname as in Example 5, 'Space count', in Chapter 3. A note on how to insert commas and full stops will be found in 'Printing and presentation' (4.5.6).

In Expansion we make several records out of one: a familiar use is the **KWIC** index (keyword in context), so that a book entitled **CIVILISATION OF THE RENAISSANCE IN ITALY** can be indexed under three headings:

ITALY	**CIVILISATION OF THE RENAISSANCE IN**
CIVILISATION OF THE	**RENAISSANCE IN ITALY**
THE RENAISSANCE IN	**ITALY** **CIVILISATION OF**

(Words such as **OF, THE, IN, AND, A**, are generally suppressed, by means of a table look-up; in more elaborate indexes, other words carrying little information, such as **INTRODUCTION, GUIDE TO**, may also be suppressed). The three records made above will be merged with all the other expanded records made in the run and sorted to order on the 'key-word' so that we can look up the book under any of the three topics. Again, the basic process is the definition of the record as a table, finding the blanks, and moving the following letters one by one to an output area. It is a difficult and tedious process and the beginner should only try it in very simple cases.

In Chapter 3 (3.2.2) we described a Library Catalogue record which covered four cards; a single tape record embodying all four card-records was shown in the section on Magnetic Tape (3.6). The single record could be constructed by using the card-format as input and the tape format as output; each card, as it came in, would be tested to see what type of card it was, and would be **MOVE**d to the appropriate part of the tape record. (It would simplify the transfer to split the **03 TITLE PIC X(138)** into two sub fields each of **X(69)**.) Similarly, to print the tape record, you would have to split it, in core, into three or four print-formats and output them a line at a time.

.3 Reblocking

The output of 'expansion' is generally to a tape or disc, since the expanded records have to be sorted to order on the keywords. The commonest use of reformatting is for printer output, but there are other cases where the output is on tape, for example, where we have inputs recorded in several different formats and want to bring them all to the same format so as to facilitate processing. We may in this context mention *reblocking*; a tape written with one block-length may be rewritten with another. This might be done for economy in storage of archive material or it may be done to prepare the material for input to a program which has been written to cope with a different block-length. In any case, the block-lengths are merely declared in the usual way for the input and output tapes, in Data Division:

FD CUSTOMER-LIST; . . . . . . ; BLOCK CONTAINS 1 RECORDS;
     . . . 01 CUSTOMER-RECORD.
FD MAILING-LIST; . . . . . . ; BLOCK CONTAINS 10 RECORDS;
     . . . . 01 RECIPIENT.

where **CUSTOMER-RECORD** and **RECIPIENT** have compatible **PICTURES.**
Now the Procedure

REBLOCKING.
     READ CUSTOMER-LIST AT END . . . .
     MOVE CUSTOMER-RECORD TO RECIPIENT.
     WRITE RECIPIENT.
     GO TO REBLOCKING.

will write the output records exactly as they were in the input, but the blocking in tens is automatically seen to.

4.2.4 Validation

A practice that is becoming increasingly common, and which is to be encouraged, is the use of the computer to carry out checks ('validate') the data before it is allowed to enter the main program. Validation supplements the human activities of verification and checking; it cannot entirely replace them, since a wrong entry, which might be queried by a human intelligence, will be accepted as long as it conforms to the rules for valid data (on the other hand the computer will pick up errors which a tired or inattentive human would miss).

Some checks are very simple: we may know, for example, that we cannot have an account number greater than 4999, so that the program will signal an error if it finds an account number of 5234; but if the number has been punched as 1223 instead of 1233, the program will not pick up the error. To take one or two rather more sophisticated examples: if the sex of a patient is entered as M then if we find on his record a diagnosis-coding which indicates pregnancy, at least there is something that ought to be looked into. Nor, from the point of view of credibility, should we expect to find, in a police record, a sentence of 12 years for an offence coded as 'parking'; and it might be worth investigating if anyone on a weekly payroll got a payment of £500 or was allowed 200 hours overtime in the week. In a more general sense, validation is often used as a quality check—the number of errors shown up by a validation run is taken as an indication of the overall accuracy of the data, including those items for which we cannot devise a validity check.

The extent to which validation is used depends largely on the ingenuity of the systems analyst and the nature of the data, especially on the real need for accuracy. The programmer, for his part, will try to avoid cluttering up his programs with a great mass of tests, particularly if the errors that the Systems Analyst has thought of are such as might occur once in a blue moon, and might not matter much even then. The tests will usually consist of a long string of **IF**s, which have to be applied in sequence to *every* record, and may substantially increase the running time. This is one reason why validation is often done during the transcription of data from punched cards to tape, say; the speed of the card-reader is so slow compared with that of the computer that there is time for the execution of a lot of tests between the reading of one card and the next, without increasing the total time taken. (Another reason, of course, is that it is a good thing to check the records as far as possible and correct them before they get caught up in the main program.)

One commonly used check on input data is the *hash total*, in which the customer makes a total of all the entries in some field of his record —this may be a quite meaningless figure, like the total of personnel-numbers. The same total is calculated by the computer when it handles the input, and the two totals are compared; this provides some check that all the data, and no more than the authorised data, has been read in. Another type of check, which provides rather more interesting COBOL than the hash total, is the check-digit, which is described next.

Example 9. Check-digit

A check-digit is a digit calculated from the digits of a numerical item which it is important to get right, for example, an account number or patient's registration number, and appended to the number when it is punched, or before. Generally the computer will calculate the check-digit in the first place, perhaps producing a list of 'valid' numbers which the clerk selects as necessary. Systems to give really secure checks against garbling or mutilation can be quite elaborate, and there is an extensive literature on the subject. Alphabetical items can also be given a check letter, by assigning numerical values to the letters, but we will not consider them here.

We will illustrate one of the simpler routines used to calculate a check digit, and show how it could be checked. The original number is of four digits, and a check digit is added to make it up to five. Each of the four digits is multiplied by a factor, which is fixed in the system, and the results are summed:

```
Number 4 6 8 3          Factors 5 4 3 2
       4      times          5      = 20
       6      times          4      = 24
       8      times          3      = 24
          3 times              2 =   6 : total 74
```

The program adds a digit to make this up to the next highest multiple of 11, which is 77, so the check digit is 3 (74 + 3 = 77) and the complete number with check digit is 46833.

169

On reading in the number, say from a punched card, we can reproduce the calculation on the first four digits to see if we get the same check digit. In the Data Division we **REDEFINE** the five digit number (**REG-NO**) as five separate digits, so that they can be accessed separately. We also set up another table, to hold the factor-digits 5,4,3,2.

```
DATA DIVISION.
FILE SECTION.
FD INFILE.
01 MED-RECORD.
   03 REG-NO.
   03 CHECK-NO REDEFINES REG-NO.
      05 DIGIT PIC 9 OCCURS 5 TIMES.
. . . . . . . . . . . .
WORKING-STORAGE SECTION.
77 CHECKSUM PIC 999 VALUE IS ZEROS.
77 POS PIC 9 VALUE IS ZERO.
77 CHECK-RESULTS PIC 99.
01 FACTOR-LIST.
   03 FACTOR-NUMBER PIC 9999 VALUE IS 5432.
   03 FACTOR REDEFINES FACTOR-NUMBER PIC 9 OCCURS
      4 TIMES.
```

Then in the Procedure Division:

```
CHECK-DIGIT-ROUTINE.
   MOVE 1 TO POS.
   MOVE ZERO TO CHECKSUM.
   PERFORM MULTIPLICATIONS 4 TIMES.
   ADD DIGIT (5) TO CHECKSUM.
   GO TO TESTIT.
MULTIPLICATIONS.
   MULTIPLY DIGIT (POS) BY FACTOR (POS) GIVING
      CHECK-RESULTS.
   ADD CHECK-RESULTS TO CHECKSUM.
   ADD 1 TO POS.
```

TESTIT.
   SUBTRACT 11 FROM CHECKSUM.
   IF CHECKSUM GREATER THAN ZERO GO TO TESTIT.
   IF CHECKSUM EQUAL TO ZERO GO TO CHECK-OK.
CHECK-FAILED.

CHECK-FAILED is the routine to be followed if a registration number has the wrong check-digit.

The repeated subtractions are, of course, merely a way of dividing by 11; if the **CHECKSUM** is an exact multiple of 11 we shall end with a remainder of zero, and go to **CHECK-OK**. COBOL Level 2 actually allows **DIVIDE . . GIVING . . . . REMAINDER . . . ,** so that you can divide by 11 and test for a zero remainder; but the repeated subtraction is necessary in Level 1, and it is not so very wasteful if the dividend is not large compared with the divisor—as here, where the registration number is of five digits, including check-digit, and so cannot be greater than 99999, which gives a **CHECKSUM** of 135 (that is, $9(5 + 4 + 3 + 2) + 9$). The highest *legal* registration number will be 99996, which gives a **CHECKSUM** of 132.

4.2.5 Sorting

It is natural to conclude the section on operations on files that are not in sequence with the operation that turns such files into files that are sequenced.

You will never have to write a full-scale sort program yourself. There is a COBOL Sort module, described later, and even if this is not included in your subset of COBOL, you would use the Sort routine every manufacturer provides. Nevertheless you may sometimes want to put four or five items—for example, the year-prices in Program CHARLIE—into order without going to the bother of using a separate Sort routine, and it is useful to know a method of doing it.

We will illustrate the process with a set of five items, which we will call **D E A C B** : these are to be sorted to the natural order **A B C D E**. These might be the 'keys', for example, reference numbers or dates or **KWIC** keywords, of records, so that sorting the keys implies sorting the records too.

Example 10. String Sort

We first scan the keys in pairs: when we find a pair in the wrong order, we interchange them:

1. **D E A C B**	D and E are compared: no change.
2. **D E A C B**	E and A are compared and interchanged.
3. **D A E C B**	E and C are compared and interchanged.
4. **D A C E B**	E and B are compared and interchanged.
5. **D A C B E**	This is the result of the first pass.

Note that the effect of this is that the highest letter (**E**) is 'picked up and carried' to its proper position. This being done, there is no need to do any more comparisons involving the fifth place—we know this is right. So we now repeat the process on the first four items only.

1. **D A C B**	Interchange **D** and **A**.
2. **A D C B**	Interchange **D** and **C**.
3. **A C D B**	Interchange **D** and **B**.
4. **A C B D**	Result.

and it is not difficult to see the final stages.

Third Pass		Fourth Pass	
1. **A C B**	No change.	1. **A B**	No change.
2. **A C B**	B and C are interchanged.	2. **A B**	Result.
3. **A B C**	Result of third pass.		

In the first pass there are four comparisons for five items; in the second, three comparisons for four items; in the third, two comparisons for three items and in the fourth one for two. So we need four passes for five items. Let us now design a COBOL program for sorting these five items—it would not be too difficult to generalise it to take in any reasonable number of items. A flow-chart will be found in Fig. 4.1. We define the items to be sorted as a table, **LETTER PIC X OCCURS 5 TIMES,** so that in the original sequence **D** is **LETTER (1)**.

We set **TOTAL** equal to 6; this is one more than the total number of items to be sorted. We reduce **TOTAL** by one for each pass, and obviously when it is reduced to 1 the sort is complete. We also set two subscripts, **M** equal to 0 and **N** equal to 1:

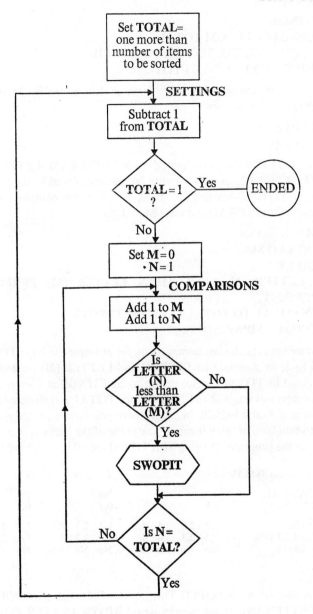

Fig. 4.1. Flow-chart for string sort

173

SETTINGS.
    SUBTRACT 1 FROM TOTAL.
    IF TOTAL EQUAL TO 1 GO TO ENDED.
    MOVE 0 TO M, MOVE 1 TO N.

Now we compare two successive keys, as determined by **M** and **N**, which take on the values

    M   01234
    N   12345

so that **LETTER (1)** is compared with **LETTER (2)**, **LETTER (2)** with **LETTER (3)**, and so on until **M** becomes equal to the current value of **TOTAL**—on the first pass, 5. After this comparison, we subtract 1 from **TOTAL** and reset **M** and **N**:

COMPARISONS.
    ADD 1 TO M.
    ADD 1 TO N.
    IF LETTER (N) LESS THAN LETTER (M) PERFORM SWOPIT.
    IF N EQUAL TO TOTAL GO TO SETTINGS.
    GO TO COMPARISONS.

When we come to the last comparison, for example, we have **TOTAL** equal to 2; we compare **LETTER (1)** and **LETTER (2)**; we find that **N** is equal to **TOTAL**, so we return to **SETTINGS** and subtract 1; but the next test sends us to **ENDED** since **TOTAL** is now equal to 1.

You may find it helpful, in cases where you have a procedure like this, to tabulate, or 'play through' the value of the items at successive stages in the program. Starting with **TOTAL** equal to 6 we have:

Subtract 1 from **TOTAL**	5				4			3	
Is **TOTAL** = 1?	No				No			No	
Set **M, N**	0,1				0,1			0,1	
Add 1 to **M, N**	1,2	2,3	3,4	4,5	1,2	2,3	3,4	1,2	2,3
Compare **LETTER**	1,2	2,3	3,4	4,5	1,2	2,3	3,4	1,2	2,3
Is **N** = Total?	No	No	No	Yes	No	No	Yes	No	Yes

and so on.

One more routine: **SWOPIT**. This merely exchanges **LETTER (M)** and **LETTER (N)**. If we merely wrote **MOVE LETTER (M) TO LETTER (N), MOVE LETTER (N) to LETTER (M)**, we don't get the result we want. (What do we get, remembering that **LETTER (M)** means the contents of the Mth location in the **LETTER** table?) What we have to do is move one letter to a siding, move the other letter to its original place, and move the original letter to its new place:

SWOPIT.
    MOVE LETTER (M) TO SIDING.
    MOVE LETTER (N) TO LETTER (M).
    MOVE SIDING TO LETTER (N).

Playing this through, where we are comparing **E** and **A** in **D E A C B**:

	LETTER (M)	LETTER (N)	SIDING
	E	A	—
Move (M) to Siding	E	A	E
Move (N) to (M)	A	A	E
Move Siding to (N)	A	E	E

You will see that if two 'keys', that is, here, two letters, are the same we do not go to **SWOPIT** and they are not interchanged. Since they are indistinguishable to the computer this is reasonable.

This sort routine is obviously a crude affair, and would be very uneconomic if applied to more than a few items. You can probably see improvements: how about jumping out of the routine if we do a whole pass without making any interchanges—for example, if we start with **E A B C D** we shall have **A B C D E** at the end of the first pass, so why do any more! Can you put in a check to achieve this? Can you generalise the routine to deal with any number of items?

2.5.1   Sort and merge

The commonest form of sort employs the method of sorting records in short strings (the length of string depends on many factors, including the amount of store available; the strings may be only 10 or 12 records). The records are read in from the input file in strings of the required size, and after each string is sorted in the store, perhaps by the method just described, it is output, each successive string to alternate tapes. Thus the first string of records, string A, is read out to tape 1; string **B** goes to tape 2; string **C** goes to tape 1, string **D** to tape 2, and so on, until all the input has been sorted in strings. The

175

output tapes, 1 and 2, are now read as input, taking one string from each: thus string **A** and **B** are read in and *merged*, and put out as one string on to tape 3. C and **D** are merged and put out on to tape 4. Thus we finish this part of the operation with strings of double the original length. This process continues until we end up with a single string containing all the records in order.

Sorting, therefore, is confined to the first operation, the first sort of the short strings. The other operations involve only merging, which is a much quicker operation than sorting. If two of the strings are (after the primary sort) are:

    BKRTUV. . . .
    ADEPSX. . . .

B and **A** are compared, and **A** read out since it is 'lower' than **B**; then **B** and **D** are compared and **B** read out; **D** and **K** are compared and **D** read out, and so on, so the resulting string is:

    ABDEKPRSTUVX. . .

A COBOL program for a merge is described in 4.4.2.

4.2.5.2   The COBOL Sort Module

Sorting on a large scale is such a time-consuming business that system programmers go to great lengths, using highly sophisticated mathematical techniques, to 'optimise' the Sort routine; and the use of discs instead of tapes has greatly improved sorting methods (while, to some extent, making it less necessary to sort files before processing them). The COBOL programmer will sooner or later have to handle one of these Sort routines, so we include a short description and explanation of the COBOL Sort Module.

No particular technique of sorting is prescribed; this is left to the implementor.

The programmer describes the input and output files in the usual way in the Data Division, with their **FD**s; he also writes a Sort-Description preceded by the letters **SD**. This is followed by a Record Description (level **01**, with lower levels as necessary) of the records to be sorted. It *must* contain details of the 'sort-keys', that is, the fields which determine the order in which the records are to be after the file is sorted. They are described as data-fields in the ordinary way, each with its **PICTURE**.

In the Procedure Division, the verb **SORT** is followed by the file-name which follows **SD**, and then the sorting keys are specified. For each key, the programmer says whether the order is to be **ASCENDING** (that is 0,1,2,3, . . for digits and A,B,C,D, . . for letters; as stated in 3.3.4, the order of digits and letters relative to each other, and the order of 'symbols', depends on the collating sequence of the system, and it is important to bear this in mind if you sort the same data on two different machines); or **DESCENDING**, which is the reverse order. The order in which the keys are named determines the order in which the sort is done: the first key named is the major sort, the last is the minor sort. The fields named as keys can be in any order within the record (but must be in the same position in every record: this will not worry the programmer who is not dealing with variable length records); generally up to 12 keys are allowed.

The specification of the order of the keys is followed by details of the files to be used for input and output, by the **SORT** procedure. In the simplest case, the input is specified by the word **USING** followed by the file name of the input file. Then each record or the input is taken by the **SORT** procedure, as it stands, and the fields for sorting are selected from it according to the data descriptions given in the **SD** (which, in a sense, **REDEFINES** the input record) The output file is specified by **GIVING** followed by the file name o the output file defined in the Data Division. Again, the records from the **SORT** are moved to the output areas, when sorted, and redefined by the output record description. This can be illustrated by the following little program, which takes as input a set of records which have a **COUNTY**, a **TOWN**, and a **POPULATION**, and sorts them into ascending order of **COUNTY** (Aberdeenshire, Antrim, Armagh, . . .) and, within **COUNTY**, into **TOWNS** in descending order of **POPULATION**.

Example 11. The COBOL Sort

DATA DIVISION.

FILE SECTION.
FD INFILE; LABEL RECORDS ARE STANDARD; BLOCK CONTAINS 10 RECORDS; DATA RECORDS ARE INREC.

01 INREC.

03 COUNTY-1	PIC X(20).
03 TOWN-1	PIC X(20).
03 POP-1	PIC 9(7).

FD OUTFILE; LABEL RECORDS ARE STANDARD; BLOCK CONTAINS 10 RECORDS; DATA RECORDS ARE OUTREC.
01 OUTREC.

03 COUNTY-2	PIC X(20).
03 TOWN-2	PIC X(20).
03 POP-2	PIC 9(7).

SD SORTFILE; DATA RECORDS ARE SORTREC.
01 SORTREC.

03 COUNTY-3	PIC X(20).
03 TOWN-3	PIC X(20).
03 POP-3	PIC 9(7).

The only entry after the **SORT** File-name is **DATA-RECORDS**; it cannot have labels.

The Procedure Division entries will be:

PROCEDURE DIVISION.
SORTEM.
   OPEN INPUT INFILE; OUTPUT OUTFILE.
   SORT SORTFILE ASCENDING COUNTY-3, DESCENDING
      POP-3, USING INFILE, GIVING OUTFILE.
   CLOSE INFILE, OUTFILE.
   STOP RUN.

This program, of course, does nothing but sort; the output tape could be processed to put it into a form ready for printing, or it might be used as it stood for the next stage in the program.

The **SORT** can be used as a step in any ordinary program, or as an independent program as above. It is possible, however, to specify instead of the **USING** or **GIVING** clauses an **INPUT PROCEDURE** (for **USING**) or an **OUTPUT PROCEDURE** (for **GIVING**). Following this there is the name of a *section* which processes the records before they are read into the **SORT**, or on output from it. It is thus possible, for example, to reformat the input records before they go into the **SORT**, and on coming from it. We can also *select* records on input and output—in fact we can do anything in these Procedures that any COBOL Procedure can do, except **SORT**. The beginner should not try them until he has had some experience of the simple **SORT** and has studied the COBOL implementation for his installation.

One point to note is that in the COBOL Sort module, ANSI specifically states that it soes not dictate what is to be done with records that are equal on the sorting keys; it assumes that it doesn't matter what order they are put in by the **SORT** (which is reasonable enough, if the programmer hasn't bothered to distinguish them). One consequence of this is that records which are identical on sorting fields, such as dates, but different on others (and are thus distinguishable, to the human) may appear in different orders if the sort is carried out more than once (for example, if a file is sorted periodically, after updating). You could write an input procedure to put a unique number on all records, to be used as the lowest order sorting key (that is, it is only used if all other sorting fields are equal). This would ensure that all 'equals' came out in the same order each time.

4.3 The ordered file

In the following routines we assume that the file is sorted to order on a given field or fields, and we take that into account in handling the file: for example, it is sorted on the field **PLACE**, and we compare the **PLACE** in each record with the **PLACE** in the previous record. If the file is sorted on **PLACE** and no other field, and we carry out some operation on say **RECORD-DATE**, then this is not a sorted file as far as that operation is concerned.

For convenience, we assume (where necessary) that the ascending collation order is space, 0–9, A–Z, with no assumption about special characters and symbols. The routines are written for ascending sequence; the amendments to cope with descending sequence are trivial. You should have no difficulty in adapting these routines to to your own collation sequence.

3.1 Sequencing

It is not usually necessary to check that a file has been sorted correctly by the computer. However this simple operation will serve as a model for other operations on successive records.

The file is supposed to be in order on **PLACE**; we wish to check this. We set up a temporary store in Working-Storage, **TEMPORARY-PLACE**, and initialise it to **SPACE**. This is on the assumption that **SPACE** is the lowest element in the collating sequence; if **SPACE** is not the lowest element, then the temporary store must be initially set with whatever character is the lowest, for example, if the lowest is A:

```
77 TEMPORARY-PLACE PIC X(10)
   VALUE IS 'AAAAAAAAAA'.
```

Now we read in the first record, and compare its **PLACE** with the temporary field:

```
READEM.
   READ INFILE AT END GO TO LASTBIT.
   IF PLACE LESS THAN TEMPORARY-PLACE GO TO
       SEQUENCE-ERROR.
   MOVE PLACE TO TEMPORARY-PLACE.
   GO TO READEM.
```

The first **PLACE** *cannot* be less than **TEMPORARY-PLACE**, so it is moved to the temporary store; the **PLACE** from the next record is compared with it, and takes its place if it is equal or greater, and so on.

There is no output in this routine, except of course for any necessary error-notification. When there is an output the temporary store is often unnecessary since we can compare the input record with the previous record after the latter has been moved to the output area.

4.3.1.1   Checking for gaps

In the previous example, we made no check to see if any place-names were missing; as long as a place-name was greater than or equal to the place-name on the previous record, we were satisfied. A more practical application is checking for gaps in the sequence, that is, ensuring that the items in the series are not only in order, but are also consecutive. We might, for example, want to check that all 125 branches, in the Table-Handling example, have sent in returns. With a small number like 125, and given the routines that we used there, the simplest thing would be to 'tick off' each branch number as it appeared, and then check the table to see that all branch-numbers are ticked off. But for large files it may not be practicable to set up a table of sufficient size in core, so we check each number with the preceding one.

This type of routine would be more appropriate if we were generating and *assigning* serial numbers, e.g. line-numbers for a print-out. The routine would then be:

A Working-Storage variable, **LAST-SERIAL**, is set up, with an initial value of zero (or, in general, one less than the first value of the sequence to be tested). We now test that each **SERIAL** read in is one more than the previous one:

```
READEMIN.
    READ INFILE AT END GO TO THATSTHELOT.
    ADD 1 TO LAST-SERIAL.
    IF LAST-SERIAL NOT EQUAL TO SERIAL PERFORM
        SEQUENCE-ERROR.
    MOVE SERIAL TO LAST-SERIAL.
    GO TO READEMIN.
```

Thus if we get the sequence 132, 133, 135, 136 we shall get an indication (according to what we have prescribed, in the **SEQUENCE-ERROR** routine, for example, a **DISPLAY WRONG SEQUENCE' SERIAL**) when 135 is read in; after **PERFORM**ing the **SEQUENCE-ERROR** control returns to the next statement in line, **MOVE SERIAL TO LAST-SERIAL**, so that when 136 is read in the program continues normally. Similarly, a repeated **SERIAL**, for example, 132 133 133 134, will cause the first 133 to be increased to 134; comparison with the second 133 causes an **ERROR** notification; the second 133 is **MOVE**d to **LAST-SERIAL**, and gives a correct comparison with 134. Check what happens with a transposition: 132 134 133 135; and with a complete intruder: 132 133 784 134 135. The analyst must always ask, of course, whether duplicates and gaps are allowed or expected. If duplicates (or any number of repetitions of the same number) are allowed, we merely insert, after **READ INFILE . . .** and before **ADD 1 TO LAST-SERIAL**, the check for equality: **IF SERIAL EQUAL TO LAST SERIAL GO TO READEMIN**. If there are any errors, it will probably be necessary to inspect the file and correct the errors by hand; after all, if an incorrect sequence appears in a file which is supposed to be sorted, there is something badly wrong, and if there are a lot of errors it would be best to do the sort again (with the correct parameters this time, someone will say unkindly).

Where there are known to be gaps in the series, especially if it is expected that they will be filled in at a later date, it is sometimes useful to print out the serials that do occur, with the data associated with each serial, and to print the missing entries in their correct place in the sequence, with the missing numbers blank; the print can then be used as a working document in which the user can enter the details of the missing items, as and when they become available. At some convenient time the print is returned to the data preparation section and used as a punching document, the manually entered details being punched and merged into a new machine run. The following routine uses a variable called **COUNTER** which is very similar to **LAST-SERIAL** in the previous example:

READAREC.
   READ INREC AT END GO TO FINISH.
CHECKIT.
    ADD 1 TO COUNTER.
    IF SERIAL EQUAL TO COUNTER MOVE INRECORD TO
       OUTRECORD, PERFORM WRITEIT, GO TO READAREC.
    MOVE SPACES TO OUTRECORD.
    MOVE COUNTER TO OUT-SERIAL.
    PERFORM WRITEIT.
    GO TO CHECKIT.

The **WRITEIT** routine should **WRITE OUTRECORD AFTER 2**, so as to provide space for handwriting. Again we will check the routine with an actual example. Let the serial numbers in the file be 10, 11, 12, 15, 17, 20. Then if we start with **COUNTER** equal to 9:

COUNTER:	9	10	11	12	13	14	15	16	17	18	19	20
Current **SERIAL** following **READ:**		10	11	12	15	15	15	17	17	20	20	20

Whenever the **COUNTER** differs from the current serial, which it does when it has values 13 14 16 18 19, the **COUNTER** is written out, followed by a blank line. When **COUNTER** and **SERIAL** are the same, the **SERIAL** is written out with the current record.

This routine could be wrecked by duplicates or mis-sorts and we must be careful that they do not occur (though it is possible to modify the routine to deal with duplicate **SERIALs**). Another snag is that there may be unexpectedly large (genuine) gaps, of several hundred or even thousands of **SERIALs**; we would wish to avoid printing whole volumes of blank entries. One remedy is to subtract each actual serial from the previous one: if the gap exceeds an acceptable figure, we don't print all the intervening values of **COUNTER** but put in a row of asterisks or some such symbol to show that the series is discontinuous. If we are to have a constant number of entries per page of print, for example, 25, a sophisticated solution is to omit all complete pages that have no data entry. We will leave it to the reader to work out this rather tedious routine.

Assigning serial numbers to records, as they appear in the file, is a routine which it is sometimes useful to carry out. As each record is read in we **MOVE COUNTER TO SERIAL** (a field in the record) and **ADD 1 TO COUNTER** before reading the next record.

.1.2 Alphabetical sequencing

Where the items to be checked are numbers, it is easy to generate the sequence, by simple addition. In some cases, however, alphabetical sequences may have to be checked. Such cases are not very common, but they do occur especially where the system was devised without computer processing in mind, or where it is important to save space —two characters, for example, can be used to reference up to 676 records, which would require three digits.

We can't generate the sequence by simple addition, as in the case of numerical sequences; adding letters doesn't make sense without some rather sophisticated programming. What we can do is assign a numerical value to each letter:

```
01 TABULA.
   03 ALPHA PIC X(26)
      VALUE IS 'ABCDEFGHIJKLMNOPQRSTUVWXYZ'.
   03 TAB REDFINES ALPHA PIC X OCCURS 26 TIMES.
```

(You have seen this before.) Now to find the numerical value of a specified **LETTER** we can scan the sequence until we find the letter

183

and the current value of the subscript is the numerical value of that letter:

```
MOVE ZERO TO IND.
SCANNIT.
    ADD 1 TO IND.
    IF LETTER EQUAL TO TAB (IND) MOVE IND TO WANTED-
        VALUE, GO TO NEXT.
    ADD 1 TO IND.
    IF IND EQUAL TO 27 GO TO LETTER-NOT-FOUND.
    GO TO SCANNIT.
NEXT.
```

Obviously you can extend this to two-letter references by giving the first letter a factor of 26.

4.3.2 Removing duplicates

It is sometimes feasible to compare successive records by comparing the contents of the input area with the contents of the output area, without making use of Working-Storage.

The following routine removes duplicates, that is, it copies a file, omitting the second, third, etc., versions of any identical successive records. There is a flow-chart in Fig. 4.2.

```
OPENER.
    OPEN INPUT INFILE, OUTPUT OUTFILE.
    MOVE SPACE TO OUTREC.
PROCESSIT.
    READ INFILE AT END GO TO FINISH.
    IF INFILE EQUAL TO OUTREC GO TO PROCESSIT.
    WRITE OUTREC AFTER 1.
    MOVE INREC TO OUTREC.
    GO TO PROCESSIT.
```

We start by filling the output area with spaces. A record is read in, and compared; it will (presumably) be different, so the blank record is printed and the read-in record takes its place; and the process is repeated. If the input record does match the output record, it is over-written by the next **READ**.

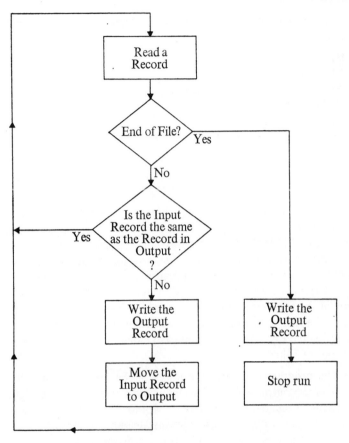

Fig. 4.2. Flow-chart: removing duplicates

The routine needs some cleaning-up:

(*a*) The output record cannot be edited, with **FILLERS**, etc. If it were it would be difficult to do a simple **MOVE INREC TO OUTREC**, and we could not compare them. This does not matter, however, if we are outputting to tape rather than printer.

(*b*) The 'dummy' first record, of spaces, is put in to provide a comparison for the first 'real' record, and is copied out at the head of the

185

output file. This may be a nuisance and it is possible to add coding to avoid this:

PROCESS-FIRST.
  PERFORM READIT.
  MOVE INREC TO OUTREC.
PROCESSIT.
  PERFORM READIT.
  IF INREC EQUAL TO OUTREC GO TO PROCESSIT.
  etc.

It is not necessary to 'initialise' the output area with spaces; the first record is moved to it, in **PROCESS-FIRST**, as soon as it is read in.

(*c*) This is *very important*: the program, as is normal, tests each input record to see if it is an End-of-File record; if it is, the program jumps straight to **FINISH**. But when this happens there will be a record waiting in the output area, and as the program stands this record will not be printed, and it should be because it is certainly not a duplicate (—OK?). So we must put in an additional **WRITE OUTREC** at the start of the **FINISH** routine; otherwise the last record in the file will simply be lost. You must *always* be on the look-out for this sort of thing: 'Have I cleared my output (and working) areas when I act on the End-of-File?'

(*d*) The program compares the *whole* of the input record with the *whole* of the output record. This may be a waste of time; it might be sufficient to compare say **SERIAL**. Moreover it may be too strict a test, because the slightest difference may lead the program to say they are not duplicates—for example, two words separated by a space in one record and two spaces in the other, the sort of difference that can easily arise through recording at different times. The exact logical definition of a duplicate may indeed be a very tricky matter, and it is probably best to select the alleged duplicates on **SERIAL**, say, and print them out for human inspection. The processes are quite intricate and are described at various points in this chapter.

4.3.3 Extracting singles

This is a complementary routine to the previous one. We wish to know which entries occur only once in the file—for example, if we want a list of agents who have sent in only one order in the period covered by the file, or the number of prisoners who have had only one sentence, or people who have seen the doctor only once. In the jargon, we want to 'extract singles'.

It is not enough to test whether a record is different from the next, on the analogy of the previous routine: for example we might have a sequence 112 112 113 113 113 114 114 115 116 116.

115 is the only single, but we get non-equal comparisons each time there is a change of number. What we need to act on is the appearance of a number which is different from both the preceding and following one.

To do this we adopt a very common programming device, the 'switch' or 'flag'. The switch is a variable that can take on one of two values—conventionally 0 or 1 (it can be a single bit). After a test, we set the switch to 0 if the condition is not satisfied, 1 if it is (or vice versa, as you please). We can say that the switch *remembers* the result

```
PROCEDURE DIVISION
INITRUN.
    OPEN INPUT INFILE (etc.)
    MOVE SPACES TO OUTREC.
    MOVE SPACES TO INREC.


PICKEMOUT.
    MOVE INREC TO OUTREC.
    READ INFILE AT END GO TO FINISH.
    IF SERIAL EQUAL TO OUTSERIAL, MOVE ZERO TO FLAG,
        GO TO PICKEMOUT.
    IF FLAG EQUAL TO 1 WRITE OUTREC AFTER 1,
        GO TO PICKEMOUT.
    MOVE 1 TO FLAG.
    GO TO PICKEMOUT.


FINISH.
    IF FLAG EQUAL TO 1 WRITE OUTREC AFTER 1.
    CLOSE INFILE OUTFILE.
        STOP RUN.
```

Fig. 4.3. (a) Program: extracting singles

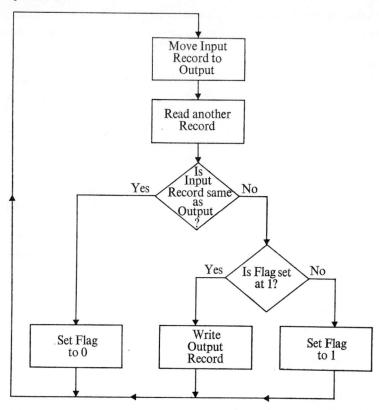

Fig. 4.3. (b) Flow-chart: extracting singles

of the test. We must declare the switch, here called **FLAG**, in Working-Storage:

77 FLAG PIC 9 VALUE IS ZERO.

As in the previous program, we compare the record just read in, in the input area, with the preceding record which has been moved to the output area. If they are the same, we are not interested because they are not singles; so we **MOVE** the input record to the output area, overwriting the record already there. This **MOVE** is not for the

188

purpose of output, because we know we are not going to output this particular record; it is merely so that we can compare it with the next record read in. At the same time, we set the Flag to zero, which means 'the record in the output area is not a singleton'. Note that we set it to zero without bothering to test whether it is already at zero; it is less trouble to do it this way.

If the records are not the same, we test the Flag. If it is 1, this means that the record in the output area was different from the preceding one, and since it is also different from the following one it is a single; so we write it out and **MOVE** the input record to the output area, leaving the Flag at 1. If the Flag is not already set at 1, we set it to 1 and **MOVE** the input record to output without writing the record already there. Then we read in another record and repeat the comparison. The program and flow-chart are given in Fig. 4.3.

Let us see how it works with the sequence already given, in which we will distinguish each occurrence of the same serial by a small letter:

Current **SERIAL** (in Input area)	Last **SERIAL** (in output area)	Comparison	Set Flag to 0	
112b	112a	Equal	0	**MOVE** and
113a	112b	Unequal	1	**READ**
113b	113a	Equal	0	
113c	113b	Equal	0	
114a	113c	Unequal	1	
114b	114a	Equal	0	
115	114b	Unequal	1	
116a	115	Unequal		Flag was set to 1 and current pair are unequal; therefore print 115. Flag remains set at 1.
116b	116a	Equal	0	

It is clear from this that when the two records in the input and output area are different, *and* the flag is already set to 1, we have a singleton —the 1 'remembers' that the previous comparison was also Unequal. If 116 were a singleton, it would conform to these conditions and would be printed out as well as 115.

The switch is a very useful device for remembering the result of a test when it is inconvenient or impossible to act on it at once. But remember to check what happens at the end of the run when the End-of-File record is read in. No comparison is done; we have to decide what to do with the record sitting in the output area. If the flag is set at 0, the record in the output area was the same as the preceding one, was not a single, and can be forgotten about; if the flag is set to 1, it was different from the preceding one and as it is the last data record in the file it must be a singleton. So at the beginning of **FINISH** we write **IF FLAG EQUAL TO 1 WRITE OUTREC AFTER 1.**

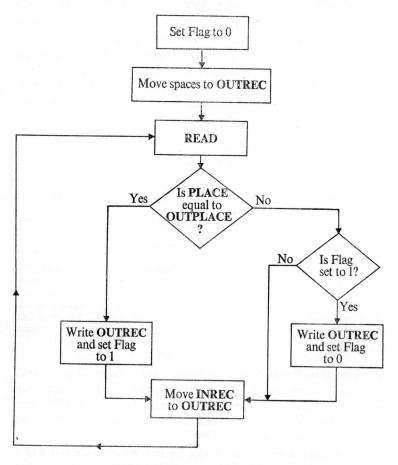

Fig. 4.4. Extracting multiples (flow-chart)

4.3.4 Extracting multiples

The object of the coding is to extract all sequences, that is, all records *except* singles; we print out the duplicates, instead of deleting them. Let us assume that the file is sorted to order on **PLACE** and we want to extract all sequences of records that have the same **PLACE**.

We proceed much as in the previous example, as might be expected, with the use of a flag to indicate that the record in the input area is the *same* as the output. An outline flow-chart (Fig. 4.4) should suffice; you can write the coding if you like. If the records in the input and output are not the same and the flag is not set, then the record in output is a singleton; and we overwrite it with the input record.

This is a routine you would use in the processes for removal of duplicates described at the beginning of this section: when all the duplicates (that is, multiples) had been extracted and printed, you would examine them individually to see if they were, in fact, duplicates.

4.3.5 Space on change of field

This is a routine you will always find useful, in printing out a file that is sorted on some field such as **PLACE**. All records with the same **PLACE** are to be grouped together, with a space each time the **PLACE** changes:

> **LEEDS**
> **LEEDS**
>
> **LEICESTER**
>
> **LIVERPOOL**
> **LIVERPOOL**
> **LIVERPOOL**
>
> **LONDON**
> etc.

Such a layout is much easier for the user, in looking up a place name, than a solid print (it would also be a good way of printing out the duplicate listing we have been discussing).

191

The process is simple: if the **PLACE** is the same in input and output, write the output and move the input record to output. If they are different, write a blank line, and then move the input record. For interest we give alternative ways of doing this:

READ IT.
   READ . . . .
   IF PLACE EQUAL TO OUTPLACE GO TO GAMMA.
   WRITE OUTREC AFTER 1.
   MOVE SPACE TO OUTREC.
GAMMA.
   WRITE OUTREC AFTER 1.
   MOVE INREC TO OUTREC.
   GO TO READIT.

It would be more economical to write:

READIT
   READ . . . . . .
   IF PLACE NOT EQUAL TO OUTPLACE, PERFORM WRITE-IT, MOVE SPACE TO OUTREC.
   PERFORM WRITEIT, MOVE INREC TO OUTREC, GO TO READIT.

You should draw up a table like that we used for the 112 113 114 sequence to check each stage of the process—and to decide what to do when the EOF record turns up.

The second method makes use of a flag. The flag is set to indicate that the input is different from the output. If it is set, the output is printed 'after 2', that is, after moving the printer two vertical lines, so that there is a blank line above the line printed. If the flag is not set only one line-feed is given:

INITRUN.
   OPEN INPUT, etc.
   MOVE ZERO TO FLAG.
   MOVE SPACE TO PRINTLINE.
TESTIT.
   IF FLAG EQUAL TO 1 GO TO SPACEIT.
   WRITE PRINTLINE AFTER 1.
   GO TO READIT.

```
SPACEIT.
    WRITE PRINTLINE AFTER 2.
    MOVE ZERO TO FLAG.
READIT.
    READ CARDFILE AT END GO TO FINISH.
    IF PLACE NOT EQUAL TO OUTPLACE MOVE 1 TO
      FLAG.
    MOVE CARDREC TO PRINTLINE.
    GO TO TESTIT.
```

One method uses **MOVE SPACE TO OUTREC** in order to get a blank line, the other advances the printer two lines instead of 1. A third alternative is to define a blank line as a constant in Working-Storage:

01 BLINE PIC X(120) VALUE IS SPACE.

You can put a second output record description in the File Section:

FD PRINTFILE.
01 OUTREC.
   03 OUTPLACE, etc.
01 BLANKLINE PIC X(120).

You can then **MOVE BLINE TO BLANKLINE** and print, whenever you want a blank line, without any complications about numeric and alphanumeric items in **OUTREC**.

4.3.6 Tabulation

Tabulation covers a very wide range of facilities that will almost certainly be provided in the COBOL Report Writer feature, or, if you haven't got that, in 'languages' known as Report Program Generator or some such name. In this book we will therefore cover only a small section of the field, because these features will be useful in themselves and will provide useful examples in COBOL.

The data consists of cards (**CARDREC**) each of which carries a date in six figure form (010270 = 1 February 1970) and a figure which represents some daily total, for example. value of sales. There may be no cards, or a number of cards, for any particular day. The cards are assumed to be sorted to date order. We require to *tabulate* them,

193

that is, to print out one line for each data that occurs, with one figure giving the total of sales for that day; where that entry is the last in the month, the total for the month is given as well on the same line; this is followed by a blank line. When the entry is the last in a year, the total for the day, month, and year are printed, and a new page is started for the next entry; at the head of each page, on the right, we print the year. The output will look something like this:

```
                                                      1969

          · ·   · ·   · ·     · ·
          02   11   69     45
          23   11   69     28
          29   11   69     10     83

          29   12   69     27
          30   12   69     34     61     144
(new page)                                            1970
           2    1   70     12    etc.
```

In the Procedure Division, after the usual preliminaries, we test to see if the Year in the record read is in the same as the Year in Working-Storage (see Fig. 4.5(a), the Data Division), that is, the Year of the previous record. If it is not, then we move the sales totals for the old year to the output record, and move the total from the new record into Working-Storage (this move saves zeroing and adding—it has the same effect). We then proceed to do the same for month totals and day totals, without any further date-testing, because if the year has changed, the day and month must be reprinted too. If we had started by testing for day-change, we might have had to cope with successive records like

```
          01   01   69
          01   01   70
```

—unlikely, but as you know, if it can happen it will. We are similarly guarded against a change of year without a change of month.

If the Year *is* the same, we add the day's total to the Year total, and test for change of Month. If this is different we enter the following routine at **NEW-MONTH**, skipping over **NEW-YEAR**, and then 'drop through' as before to **NEW-DAY**. If only the day has changed, we go straight to **NEW-DAY**. In any case, if there is no change, we add the day's totals to the relevant counters. If the dates of the input

194

Program TABULA

DATA DIVISION.
FILE SECTION.
FD INFILE.
01 CARDREC.
   03 INDATE.
      05 INDAY   PIC 99.
      05 INMTH   PIC 99.
      05 INYR   PIC 99.
   03 SALES,   PIC 9999.

FD OUTFILE.
01 PLINE.
   03 FILLER   PIC X(50).
   03 OUTDAY   PIC Z9.
   03 OUTMTH   PIC ZZ9.
   03 OUTYR   PIC ZZ9.
   03 FILLER   PIC X(5).
   03 ODAYTOTAL   PIC ZZZ9.
   03 FILLER   PIC XXX.
   03 OMTHTOTAL   PIC ZZZ9.
   03 FILLER   PIC XXX.
   03 OYRTOTAL   PIC Z(5)9.
   03 FILLER   PIC X(28).
   03 CENTURY   PIC X(7).
   03 PAGE-YEAR   PIC 99.

WORKING-STORAGE SECTION.
77 TABSWITCH   PIC 9 VALUE IS ZERO.
01 WREC VALUE IS ZERO.
   03 WDATE.
      05 WDAY   PIC 99.
      05 WMTH   PIC 99.
      05 WYR   PIC 99.
   03 WDAYTOTAL   PIC 9999.
   03 WMTHTOTAL   PIC 9999.
   03 WYRTOTAL   PIC 9(6).

Fig. 4.5. Tabulating: (a) Data Division

195

```
PROCEDURE DIVISION.
INITRUN.
  OPEN INPUT, etc.
  PERFORM CLEARIT.
READIT.
  MOVE ZEROS TO TABSWITCH.
  READ INFILE AT END GO TO FINISH.
  IF INYR NOT EQUAL TO WYR GO TO NEW-YEAR.
  ADD SALES TO WYRTOTAL.
  IF INMTH NOT EQUAL TO WMTH GO TO NEW-MONTH.
  ADD SALES TO WMTHTOTAL.
  IF INDAY NOT EQUAL TO WDAY GO TO NEW-DAY.
  ADD SALES TO WDAYTOTAL.
  GO TO READIT.
NEW-YEAR.
  MOVE WYRTOTAL TO OYRTOTAL.
  MOVE SALES TO WYRTOTAL.
  ADD 2 TO TABSWITCH.
NEW-MONTH.
  MOVE WMTHTOTAL TO OMTHTOTAL.
  MOVE SALES TO WMTHTOTAL.
  ADD 1 TO TABSWITCH.
NEW-DAY.
  MOVE WDAYTOTAL TO ODAYTOTAL.
  MOVE SALES TO WDAYTOTAL.
SHIFTDATE.
  MOVE WDAY TO OUTDAY (etc.).
  MOVE INDAY TO WDAY (etc.).
WRITA.
  WRITE PLINE AFTER 1.
CLEARIT.
  MOVE SPACES TO PLINE.
TESTSWITCH.
  IF TABSWITCH EQUAL TO 3 GO TO FASTFEED.
  IF TABSWITCH EQUAL TO 1 PERFORM WRITA.
  GO TO READIT.
```

Fig. 4.5. Tabulating: (b) Procedure Division (continued on page 197)

```
FASTFEED.
    MOVE 'YEAR 19' TO CENTURY.
    MOVE INYR TO PAGE-YEAR.
    WRITE PLINE AFTER NEW-PAGE.
    PERFORM CLEARIT.
    PERFORM WRITA.
    GO TO READIT.
FINISH.
    MOVE WYRTOTAL TO OYRTOTAL.
    MOVE WMTHTOTAL TO OMTHTOTAL.
    MOVE WDAYTOTAL TO ODAYTOTAL.
    PERFORM WRITA.
    CLOSE INFILE, OUTFILE.
    STOP RUN.
```

Fig. 4.5. Tabulating: (b) Procedure Division (continued from page 196)

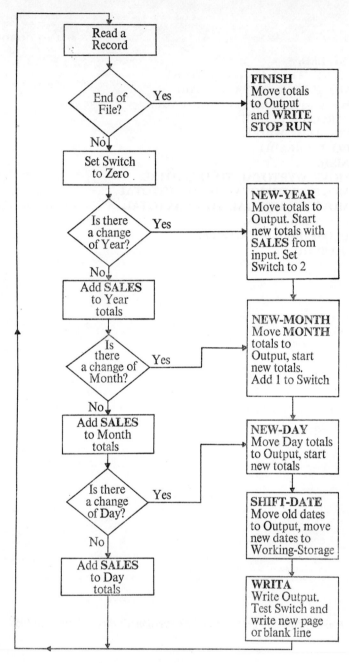

Fig. 4.5. Tabulating: (c) Flow-chart

and the Working-Storage records are the same, the totals are incremented without printing, and another record is read in—there is no need for any date-move since they are the same.

If there has been a change of date, we move the whole date in Working-Storage to the output—there is no point in trying to move each element individually since the effort is trivial—and write the output. We then test to see if we have had (*a*) a change of month, which requires a blank line, or (*b*) a change of year, which requires a new page. It should be fairly clear that if we entered at **NEW-YEAR**, the Switch will be at 3; if at **NEW-MONTH**, at 1; if at **NEW-DAY**, at zero. If we want a blank line, we merely **PERFORM WRITA**; since **PLINE** now contains blanks, this does the trick. If we want a new page, we form the year heading '**YEAR 1970**' or whatever it may be, write it at the top of a new page, write a blank line, and read another record.

.3.7 The Trailer Record

Let us consider the following problem, which can crop up in many forms. We have a file of records sorted to some reference, such as **PLACE**, so that they form sequences with the same reference, as in the Extract Multiples program. But somewhere in each sequence— beginning, middle, or end—there is a record called a **MASTER** record, which carries some sort of discriminant to show that it is a Master. We wish to print out the file, with the Master at the *end* of sequence to which it belongs, followed by a space. We can assume that every sequence has a Master, and no more than one, and there is no sequence consisting of a Master only.

We might achieve this result by sorting; but this may be inconvenient, especially if the Masters occurred only rarely and not in every sequence; or it may be that the discriminant is such that if we sort on it it will not place the Master record behind all the others. There are ways round this: we could have a special run to put a discriminant on the records so that the Masters *would* come last, or we could extract all the Masters and then merge them back at the end of each sequence (this is dealt with in the section on Two-file working); or we might find we could do it with an Input or Output Procedure in the sort.

199

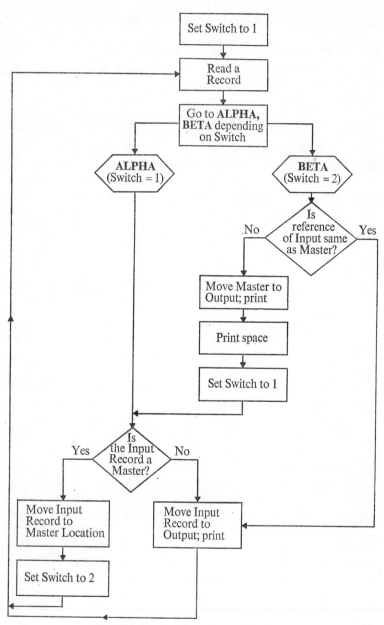

Fig. 4.6. The Trailer Record: flow-chart

However it is quite easy to devise a routine which will do it. A flow-chart is shown in Fig. 4.6. After reading a card, we go to one of two routines **DEPENDING ON** a switch or flag, which is initially set to 1 (we use 1 and 2 for the switch, rather than 0 or 1, because it is the operand of the **DEPENDING ON**). We test the input record to see if it is a **MASTER**; if it is, we move it to a 'siding' in Working-Storage, set the switch to 2 (which means 'I have found the Master for this sequence') and read another record. It it is not a Master, we just move it to output and print. In either case we then read another card. If the switch is still set at 1, we go to routine 1 again; if it is set to 2, we check to see whether its reference—for example, **PLACE**, if that is what the file is sorted on—is the same as that of the Master in the siding, that is, whether it belongs to the same sequence. If it is we again just move it to output and print. If it is not, this means that we have come to the end of the sequence, so we move the Master to output and print, print a space, and set the switch to 1 to mean 'I have not got a Master record (for the coming sequence)'. Then we check at once to see if the incoming record is a Master: if it is, we move it to the siding and set switch back to 2.

As a matter of fact it is not very serious if our assumptions were unjustified; nothing disastrous happens if we get more than one Master in a sequence, or no Master, or a Master without other records in the sequence. Can you work out what does happen? As you will see, there are untidinesses, but we shan't get into a loop, or print out wrong answers, or lose data, which are the things the programmer must really guard against.

You should, however, ask the customer if the occurrence of a sequence with no Masters, or more than one Master, is a situation which he would like brought to his notice. You will find it possible to test for these situations, but awkward—as it always is when you design a program on one set of assumptions and then try to make it cope with cases where these assumptions are not true.

4.3.8 The Header Record and others

The preceding problem of the Trailer Record appears more often, and in a more difficult form, as the Header Record; in terms of the previous problem, the Master Record is to be printed out *first*. Germane

201

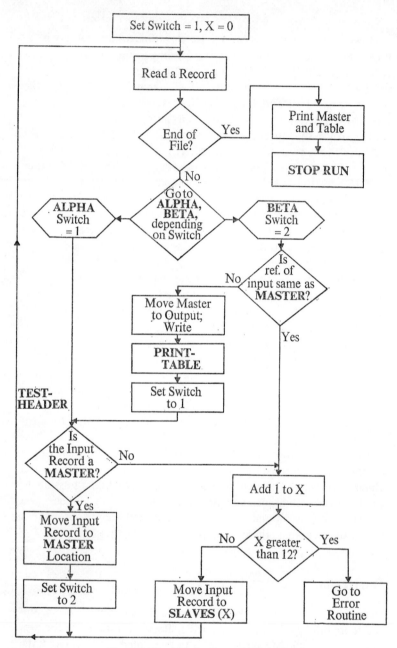

Fig. 4.7. The Header Record: flow-chart

forms of this are requests for printouts of sequences which have more than (say) 2000 entries; printing out a sequence if one record in it has the entry **MEASLES** and another (before or after it) has the entry **TEETOTALLER**. The characteristic of such cases is that we cannot print out anything until (possibly) the whole of the sequence has been read in and examined.

The solution we shall adopt is to set up a table in core of a size large enough to hold the maximum number of records that can occur in a sequence. For this to be feasible, we have to be certain about the maximum number, and it must not be so large that we have no room for the table in core (though the advanced programmer may be able to get round this). We will assume that we have a maximum size of 12 records (for example, as if there were one record for each month, and in each sequence one and one only bore the entry **SUBSCRIP-TION PAID**).

The strategy is the same as for the previous program, with a few alterations. In particular there is a temptation to start printing as soon as the **MASTER** record appears, but resist it; it only complicates the program. It is simpler to read in the whole sequence before printing. A flow chart is given in Fig. 4.7.

In Working-Storage we have a Master Location, as before, and a table of 12 positions called **SLAVES**; this holds the records which are not Masters and which must therefore be stored until the Master is printed. When we find a non-Master record, we do not, as in the previous program, print it at once. We increment the index (**X**) of the **SLAVES** table, and thus **MOVE** the record into the next highest position in that table; if we find that we have more than 12 **SLAVE**s for any one Master we must go to an Error Routine.

When we find the end of a sequence (because of a change of serial, or whatever it is that is common to all records in a sequence) we carry out the Print-Table routine. First we **MOVE** the Master to the output area and print it, and then print the **SLAVES** table, clearing it at the same time:

PRINT-TABLE.
    IF X EQUAL TO ZERO, MOVE 1 TO SWITCH, GO TO TEST-HEADER.
    MOVE SLAVES (X) TO OUTPUT-AREA.
    PERFORM PRINT-OUT.

> MOVE SPACES TO SLAVES (X).
> SUBTRACT 1 FROM X.
> GO TO PRINT-TABLE.

TEST-HEADER is the first test in **ALPHA** (see Fig. 4.7); we use it to see if the record which has been sitting in the input area, during the Print-table routine, and is the first of the new sequence, is the Master for that sequence. If we want to print a blank line at the end of a sequence, to separate it from the Master of the following sequence, it can conveniently be done at the beginning of the Print-Table routine.

Note how X gets reset to zero in Print-Table. The value of X with which we start the routine is the result of accumulating non-Master records in **SLAVES**. where we **ADD 1 TO X** each time we read in a Slave. Thus when we come to print out the table the value of X tells us, without any scanning of the table, how many entries there are (if any; there may be 0–12). In other words we build X up to a maximum in reading in Slave entries, then decrement it to zero in reading them out. The locations in the table, too, are cleared as the table is printed out. This is strictly unnecessary, but is a wise precaution.

This means, of course, that the records are printed in the reverse order of their occurrence in the input file, since the first **SLAVE** read into the table, with $X = 1$, is the last out. If this is unacceptable, it is not much more difficult to read out the table starting at 1. The same method is used for filling up the table, adding 1 to X for each entry made; then when we want to read it out we set a subscript Z equal to 1:

> PRINT-TABLE.
>   **IF Z GREATER THAN X MOVE 1 TO SWITCH, GO TO
>   TEST-HEADER.**
>   **MOVE SLAVES (Z) TO OUTPUT-AREA.**
>   **PERFORM PRINT-OUT.**
>   **ADD 1 TO Z.**
>   **GO TO PRINT-TABLE.**

Don't forget to reset Z and X before starting the next sequence; and don't forget to clear the Master Location and the Table when you find the End of File record.

This method is a good deal more sensitive to errors in the file than the 'trailer' programs. You should work out what will happen if we get a sequence with no Master—this incidentally will be the likeliest cause of the number of records exceeding the size of the table. The Error Routine will probably consist of a printout of a warning, either in the main listing or by a **DISPLAY** on the console typewriter, that more than 12 **SLAVES** have been found; after which the program continues normally with the next sequence. If you don't know how many records there will be in a sequence, or there are too many to hold in a table, you have to do the job indirectly, for example, extracting the Masters in one run and merging them at the head of the appropriate sequence in the next, as described in the section on Two-File working; or do a count of each sequence; or (where you are looking for **MEASLES** in one record and **TEETOTALLER** in another, in the same sequence) do a run to select all sequences that satisfy this test, note the sequence number of each, and extract by sequence number.

4.4 Operations on two files

The commonest use of two files is in File Maintenance, where a **CHANGES** file is used to update an **OLD** file, so as to produce a single **NEW** file. If the number of changes is small, we can put them into core, either in sorted or unsorted order, as described in Table Look-up; or of course if we have discs we can use much more sophisticated techniques that are outside the scope of this book. If, however, we have a number of changes that is more than a certain percentage of the main file, say about 3 per cent, it is not unreasonable to sort the two files to the same order and compare them sequentially, record by record, as described in this section. After all, most files are kept in some sort of order, and it is generally only necessary to sort the **CHANGES** file (which is the smaller) to the same order as the **OLD** file.

We are not concerned, in this section, with the nature of the comparison made between records; nor with the action that is the result of a match. The former is dealt with in Selection; the latter covers the whole range of this book. All we are concerned with here is the mechanics of the comparison sequence, the **READ**s, **MOVE**s, and **WRITE**s that ensure that the files are 'kept in step'. The 'match' may be the result of an extremely complicated set of comparisons; the

'WRITE' may be a simple extraction on to an output file or the signal for a long sequence of instructions.

Operations with two tape files are in one way easier than operations with successive records in the same file, since the two tapes, as distinct peripherals, are assigned, in the Environment Division, to different files and therefore have their own **FDs** in the Data Division and their own input areas; thus reading from one file does not overwrite what has just been read in from the other, and there is no need to move a record to the Working area, at least in the simpler operations.

4.4.1 Deletion

This is the simplest process of all. The **CHANGES** file consists of a list of Serials (or whatever the selection field may be: in this section, we will use 'Serial' to mean 'the field or fields which are being compared and on which the files are sorted'). We want to delete from the Old file all those records with serials that appear in the Changes file, that is, we want to *copy* the Old file on to a new tape, omitting all those records that have the Serials appearing on the Changes tape.

We will call the 'match' fields **CHASER** (for Change Serial) and **OLDSER** (for Old Serial) respectively.

We begin by reading in a Changes Record and an Old Record, and compare the two serials:

1. If they are the same, the next record from the Old File is read in overwriting the first; then we read in another serial from the Change file, and compare again.

2. If the Change serial is *smaller* than the Old Serial, this means that a deletion has been specified for a serial which is not in the Old file. This may or may not be alarming; if it is we go to an Error Routine and put up a danger signal; in any case, we read in the next **CHASER** ('feed the changes file') so as to bring the serials into step with the Old file.

3. If the **CHASER** is larger than the **OLDSER**, the Old record is not one that has to be deleted; so we **MOVE** it to output, and Write; and then read in another Old Record.

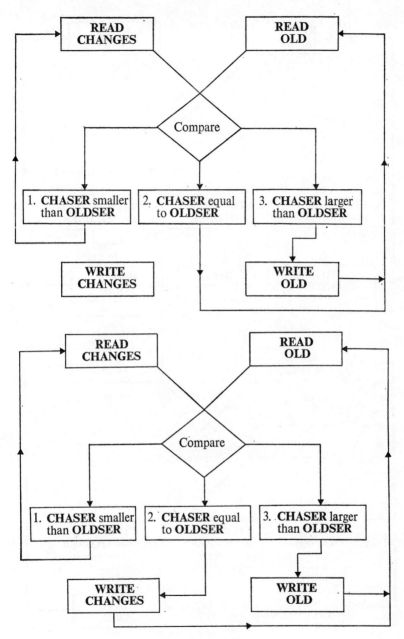

Fig. 4.8. (*a*) *Deletion flow-chart*
(*b*) *Replacement*

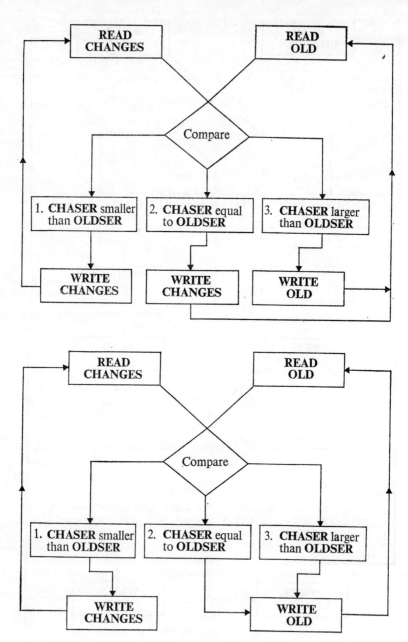

Fig. 4.8. (c) *Replace and Insert*
(d) *Merge*

We can represent the process diagrammatically, as in Fig. 4.8(*a*): 'Play it through' with a simple sequence. In COBOL the process is:

COMPARISON.
    IF CHASER LESS THAN OLDSER GO TO READ-CHANGES.
    IF CHASER EQUAL TO OLDSER GO TO READ-OLD.
    IF CHASER GREATER THAN OLDSER, MOVE OLDREC TO TAPEOUT, WRITE TAPEOUT, GO TO READ-OLD.

where **READ-CHANGES** is merely **READ CHANGE-FILE AT END GO TO FINISH**, and similarly for **READ-OLD**; which should make you think—if **OLD-FILE** comes to an end first, implying that there are still serials left in **CHANGE-FILE**, do we want to know, and if so what do we do about it; and what is more important, if **CHANGE-FILE** comes to an end first, we must ensure that the remaining records on **OLD-FILE** are copied out—otherwise we shall have deleted everything in **OLD-FILE** which has a higher serial than the last one in **CHANGE-FILE**! So our input routines can be improved:

READ-CHANGES.
    READ CHANGE-FILE AT END GO TO FINISH-1.
    GO TO COMPARISON.
READ-OLD.
    READ OLD-FILE AT END GO TO FINISH-2.
    GO TO COMPARISON.

and the **FINISH** routines are:

FINISH-1.
    READ OLD-FILE AT END GO TO FINISH-3.
    MOVE OLD-REC TO TAPEOUT.
    WRITE TAPEOUT.
    GO TO FINISH-1.

FINISH-2 is a routine which notifies the user that there were serials remaining, not matched; it may list them, and other unmatched serials found during the run. **FINISH-3** is merely **CLOSE OLD-FILE, CHANGE-FILE, OUTTAPE, STOP RUN.**

4.4.2 Replacement

As can be seen from Fig. 4.8(*b*), the diagram given for Deletion serves as a framework or paradigm for all two-file operations. If, for example, we want to *replace* the record in the Old file with the record from the Changes file when the serials match, we proceed as in Fig. 4.8(*b*). The COBOL coding is left as an exercise to the reader.

The **CHANGES** file here, of course, is a file of complete records, not just serials. A very similar operation is shown in Fig. 4.8(*c*), where we write the Changes to the New file in case 1 also. We then replace if we have a match, insert if there is no match; in other words we have a Merge of the two files, with the Changes overriding the Old where they coincide.

4.4.3 Merge

All records from both files are to appear in the output file, in their proper order. The diagram is given in Fig. 4.8(*d*). Note the differences between this and replacement. When a Changes record has the same serial as the Old, the Old record is written first, and the Changes second. If we alter Case 2 to lead to **WRITE CHANGES** followed by **READ CHANGES**, the records from the **CHANGES** will 'lead' the matching records from the Old file. It is for the customer to say which he wants.

4.4.4 Amendment

This is a very similar process to replacement. If we want to amend a record, we can, of course, repunch the whole of it, and use the replacement program, but this is a lot of unnecessary work if we only want to amend one field.

Where the amendment is to the same field in every record, the problem is trivial. A common form of this is *extension* of the record: the output record is a combination of the old and the Changes record, containing elements from both.

In some difficult cases of preparation of technical data, the originator of the data will require to have a proof print, which he will scan to see that the data has been correctly transcribed; a doctor, for example, whose case-notes are being entered into a computer by his receptionist, will want to check that she has read his handwriting correctly. It will generally be agreed that he should adopt some standard method of marking the proofs for correction; if the data is fielded (that is, not in free language form) a program can be devised which will allow the use of correction cards which indicate the record to be corrected, the field affected, and the correct version. In a simple version, we might number the fields 1, 2, 3, 4, 5, etc; then, having matched the Changes and Old records on their serials (or whatever means we have adopted to give a unique reference to the lines of the proof print), we can write

GO TO UNO, DOS, TRES, CUATRO, CINCO, . . . DEPEND-ING ON FIELDNUM.

Here **UNO** is a procedure for use in amending field 1:

UNO.
    MOVE CORRECTION-FIELD TO FIELD-1; GO TO . . .

and similarly for **DOS, TRES**, etc.

One difficult question is the amendment of serials, where serials are used to select records for matching. We may find that there are two records with the same serial, owing to a mispunch; how are we going to select the one with the wrong serial so as to amend it? You could, of course, do a **DELETE** for that serial, and put only the right one back; or you can select on the serial, then select the record for amendment by some entry which it does not have in common with the genuine record, and then alter the serial. Requirements for amendment are, however, enormously varied, and a general treatment is not really possible. Moreover, in all of this we are getting rather a long way from COBOL because the are questions which are common to all data processing, so we will not go into the subject in any more depth.

There are two general considerations:

There may be duplicates in the Old file or the Changes file or both. By duplicates we mean more than one record having the same entry in the field which is used for matching; this means, of course, that they are consecutive in the file since we have assumed that the files are sorted on that field. It is very likely that there will be duplicates in the Old File if it is sorted on a field such as **PLACE**, where we may

211

get long sequences of the same **PLACE**; in that case, a Delete run with a Change file quoting the **PLACE** would result in the deletion of the entire sequence; in a Replacement run, the Changes entry would replace every entry in the Old sequence; in a Merge, the Change entry would come at the head or tail of each sequence. There may similarly be sequences in the **CHANGES** file. Where there are duplicates in both files, you should play through the sequence to make sure the result will be what you want.

We may, or may not, expect to find unmatched records in either file. In an Amendment or Delete run we shall on the whole expect every record in the Changes file to be matched with a record in the Old File; if there are unmatched changes, we ought to be notified. On the other hand, in a Merge, unmatched records will be normal.

The illustrations given do not exhaust all the possibilities of two-file handling. It is an amusing exercise to define various paths through this framework, starting from the three possible results of the comparison, and see whether the resulting operation makes any sense or not.

4.4.5 Selection

This is another subject, like Two-File Handling, which is not confined to COBOL, but which the aspiring programmer has to know about. Selection is the heart of what is known as Information Retrieval. The term is nowadays applied to programs which review immense files of data and select records according to (possibly) very complicated logical criteria, designed to retrieve all the relevant items with a minimum of irrelevant ones. We shall not deal with these techniques in detail: the files are usually so large that some form of disc storage is necessary in order to make them accessible in any reasonable length of time (these programs are characteristic of 'real time' operations); the use of a low-level language is generally considered to be advisable. But, as in the case of all the routines in this section, the COBOL beginner, while he will never want to write a full-fledged program, may occasionally find it necessary to run through a tape file and pick out records on criteria that are not as simple as the one ('serial', 'place') we have used so far.

The Logical Operators **AND** and **OR**, which are allowed in COBOL

Level 2 Nucleus, were mentioned in the section on Change of Sequence, in Chapter 3. Whether you use them in this form, or simulate them by a sequence of **IF**s, you may be able to carry out the comparisons a good deal faster by thinking about the order in which the tests are carried out. If you have to look for a record which has a date earlier than 1967 (recorded as 67) and also contains the word **PENICILLIN** in a given field, it is obvious that you should test for 67 first, because this test will be much quicker than a thirteen-letter comparison. In fact you may sometimes be able to speed up tests by splitting up long names in the Data Division:

03 PLACE-NAME.
    05 FIRST-LETTER PIC X.
    05 REST-OF-NAME PIC X(19).

You can then write:

IF FIRST-LETTER NOT EQUAL TO 'L' GO TO NEXT-RECORD.
IF REST-OF-NAME EQUAL TO 'LANDUDNO' GO TO FOUNDIT.

Then the second test is only carried out if the first letter is **L**. Obviously in any but an *ad hoc* program you would have variable-names for the query record, instead of the literals.

You can save time if you know the relative probability of the criteria. Suppose you want to extract the records of all males aged 90 or over. You might write:

IF SEX EQUAL TO 'M' GO TO NEXT-TEST.
GO TO NEXT-RECORD.
NEXT-TEST.
    IF AGE GREATER THAN 89 GO TO FOUNDIT.

The first test will be carried out on all records, and about half (presumably) will pass the test, so that the second test is carried out on half of the records. But if you carry out the 90-up test first, you will get through to the second test only in a very small proportion of the records. In other words, where the criteria are in an **AND** relation ('Male *and* over 89') test for the *less* likely criterion first.

If you have an **OR** relation, the test most likely to give an affirmative answer is put first, because if that is satisfied there is no need to test the other alternatives. So if you are searching the records of an English firm for representatives who speak French or Balinese, you put French first; when 'French' is found you don't need to test for Balinese—this is only done when the subject doesn't speak French.

If you do use **AND** and **OR**, watch out for the traps that arise from the usage in common speech. If a customer asks for a list of orders from Paris and New York, he means Paris *or* New York: **IF PLACE EQUAL TO PARIS AND PLACE EQUAL TO NEW YORK** will get you nowhere. Similarly 'orders in March and April' don't exist as such.

A *range* of values is sometimes asked for: 'serials between 1000 and 2000', 'orders between 1967 and 1970'. Remember that the form will be

IF SERIAL LESS THAN 1000 GO TO NEXT.
IF SERIAL GREATER THAN 2000 GO TO NEXT.
MOVE INREC TO OUTREC . . .

Using the logical operator, this is

IF SERIAL LESS THAN 1000 OR GREATER THAN 2000 GO TO NEXT.

Always ask the customer whether he wants to include one or other or both of the terminal values.

4.4.6 Variants and garbles

It was mentioned in Chapter 3, in the section on Comparisons (3.3.4), that the computer will recognise that two words are **EQUAL** only if they are identical in every respect, to a much greater degree than humans expect. If you are not sure of the spelling of a name in a file you can adopt some such device as the 'joker' character, for example, you can say that '&' stands for any character whatsoever, so that **SM&TH** will select **SMITH** and **SMYTH**. But this is of limited use (and, in fact, is pretty difficult to program in COBOL); it will not help, for example, if we have to pick out **PHILIPS** which might be spelt **PHILLIPS** or **PHILIPPS**. In the latter case we would have to write three IFs, testing each version in turn. It is sometimes feasible to use a computer program to avoid the use of multiple tests of this sort: one makes a preliminary listing of the file and notes all the variants that occur, and then a program is written to add a common version to all variants of the same name, for example, the name **PHILIPS** will be added to all records with variants of that name, and that field will be used in searching. The same device can be used to cope with variants in data prepared at different times by different people. The list of variants and standard forms is sometimes called a *thesaurus*.

.4.7 File handling

The operations just described—replacement, amendment, merge, etc.—are often known as 'file handling' or 'updating' programs, and in most operational usage you will find them combined in one program—obviously you don't want to do separate runs to delete and to amend and to insert. Such programs can be very flexible and complicated, especially with 'real time' response, where you have to be certain, for example, that amendment is done as quickly as possible so that the file is up-to-date when 'interrogated', or that amendments, deletions, etc., are done in a logical order and do not conflict with each other.

One of the commonest uses of two-file working, which does not really fall under any of the above, is a form of table look-up. We may, for example, have orders represented by product codes and customer codes, written to a magnetic tape. We wish to associate each product code with its full description, and other relevant details such as price, discounts, stock level, etc. If there are more than a few such products, it will probably be impracticable to hold this table in store, so we sort the orders to the same sequence as the product file—for example, product code order—and 'collate' the two, running them in step with each other. The output is a combination of the matching records from the two tapes. Both of the input tapes may well remain in use as operational files in their original form; this is one way that the 'collation' or 'association' process differs from those previously described.

It is quite possible that a file-handling program will have several inputs and several outputs running simultaneously, but the beginner should master the simple cases first.

4.5 Printing and presentation

For 'working results', or the output of your own programs where you know what each entry means and no one besides yourself is going to see it, the minimum of explanatory material will be necessary (beyond printing out some title to tell the computer room, or despatch staff, who is to receive the print). For prints which are to be presented to the upper echelons of management it will be worth while spending a good deal of effort—sometimes more than on the 'meat' of the program!—in the embellishment of the print, for the two-fold reason that upper echelons are likely to be better impressed by, and take notice of, prints that are elegantly presented, and that they won't understand them unless they are lavishly annotated. Prints that are to be copied and given a wide circulation should also be carefully laid out.

As with several of the routines we have used as examples, many of the processes that are described here will be found in one of the versions of the Report Writer. Report Writer is described as a method in which the output is defined by the physical appearance of the output record, rather than by the procedures that lead to it from the input. It is concerned with the format of the printed output; it deals with headings, footings, line counts; page overflow and accumulation of totals are automatically taken care of.

4.5.1 The printer

While I have tried, in this book, to avoid dealing with specific hardware, a section on printing is so tied up with the device that does it— the line printer—that we cannot avoid making some assumptions about it. If your printer does not conform to this description, you will find it easy to make the necessary conversions, to suit your printer.

The printer prints 10 letters per inch, horizontally; this is a very useful figure because it enables you to use an ordinary ruler if you want to find out the position of a letter in a printed line, and this is useful for designing formats and setting up tables for output. It will print either six or eight lines to the inch, vertically, six being much commoner. The number of letters that can be printed on a line varies according to what the customer wants: 96, 120, 132, 160 are available from different manufacturers and there may be others. We have fixed on the 120-position printer for our illustrations: this will usually print on paper 15 inches wide by 11 inches deep. The print will occupy up to 12 inches of the width of the paper, and we can get 66 lines per page. The paper is usually in 'fanfold' form, the sheets being continuous, but separated by perforations: you can treat the whole thing as one large continuous sheet or you can have it divided into pages. Generally the printer will contain a paper loop which controls the line spacing and page feeding; most installations have a standard loop, allowing about 50 lines per page with a space at top and bottom, and this will be used unless the programmer wants something else. Oddly enough, COBOL has no official phrase meaning 'start a new page'; you will sometimes see an odd command like **WRITE AFTER CHANNEL-1**' which is a reference to the paper loop, which has a number of 'channels' controlling various paper movements. In this book we shall write **'AFTER NEW-PAGE'**.

4.5.2   Paper economy

An odd heading, you may think. Certainly paper is not all that cheap, but it is not generally one of the main preoccupations of the computer manager! But there is a cogent reason for trying to cut down the volume of paper: a print that makes the best use of the paper area takes up less room in the customers' cupboards and desks; it is often easier to read since it presents more information to the eye at once; and since it takes no longer to print 120 letters on a line, than one letter and 119 blanks, you can save printer time and computer time by making the fullest use of each line.

Example 12. Two-up

When we need more than one copy of an output where the lines are short, none exceeding, say, 50 characters, we can print 'two-up': that is, the output record is printed in positions 1–50, and repeated, without change, in 71–120 (say):

217

position 1   71

    12725 COLEMAN MRS M. 12725 COLEMAN MRS M.
    12728 CONOLLY MISS J. 12728 CONOLLY MISS J.
    12735 COWLEY MR A.B.   12735 COWLEY MR A.B.

and so on. After printing, the paper is sliced vertically so as to provide two prints half the width of the original paper; remember that a margin may be needed for binding, to the left of each column. By this means ordinary 'three-ply' paper can be made to yield six copies in one run. 'Three-up' or even more is, of course, feasible, provided that the entries are short enough. The Data Division for the example given would be:

```
01 PRINTLINE
   03 REG-NO        PIC 9(5).
   03 FILLER        PIC XX.
   03 SURNAME-ETC   PIC X(30).
   03 FILLER        PIC X(34).
   03 REG-2         PIC 9(5).
   03 FILLER        PIC XX.
   03 NAME-2        PIC X(30).
   03 FILLER        PIC X(12).
```

And in the Procedure Division, whenever we **MOVE** an entry to **REG-NO** and **SURNAME-ETC**, we put in two more moves of the same items to **REG-2** and **NAME-2**.

Example 13. Printing in columns

Though this looks, superficially, the same as two-up, it is not at all the same, and is in fact a much more complicated process. The object is paper economy and convenience for the user, as in two-up, but the columns on the page are not the same. The advantage to the user is that he has only one quarter (say, if we print four columns per page) of the volume of paper to handle, compared with printing only one column per page, and only one-quarter of the page-turning to do. You can even print columns more closely than in two-up, since you don't have to allow space for cutting and binding between each column.

If we have a file of names, each of 30 characters (that is, the maximum length of name is 30 characters) we can print four columns. The names are assumed to be sorted to alphabetical order. We could take four names at a time and print them in a single line:

218

COLEMAN MRS M.   COLEMAN MR T.J.   COLEMAN MR W.D.   COLLINS MISS J.
COLLINS MR S.S.   COLLINSON MR M.   COLT MISS J.D.   . . . . . .

and so on, but unfortunately users don't take at all kindly to this sort of layout. It is much more difficult to scan than where the names are laid out *vertically* in alphabetical order, as in a telephone directory:

COLEMAN MRS M.   CONNOLLY MR J.D.   COWLEY MRS T.   CRAIG MR E.G.
COLEMAN MR T.J.   CONNOLLY MISS M.T.   COX MR G.R.   CREIGHTON MR T.S.
COLEMAN MR W.D . . . .
COLLINS MISS J.
COLLINS MR S.S.
COLLINSON MR M.
COLT MISS J.D.
. . . .

with say 50 names in each column.

Obviously the first line cannot be printed until the 51st, 101st, and 151st names have all been read into store. There is hardly any alternative to a table which contains a number of cells equal to the number of columns times the number of entries in a column—in our example, $4 \times 50 = 200$ cells. The whole page, so to speak is made up in store

```
DATA DIVISION.
FILE SECTION.
FD INFILE.
01 INREC PIC X(30).

FD OUTFILE.
01 PLINE PIC X(120).

WORKING-STORAGE SECTION.
77 NROW PIC 99 VALUE IS 1.
77 NCOL PIC 9 VALUE IS 1.

01 PAGE-FORM.
    03 ROW OCCURS 50 TIMES.
        05 COL OCCURS 4 TIMES.
            07 NOMEN PIC X(30).

01 HEADER.
    03 FILLER PIC X(90).
    03 FIRST-NAME PIC X(30) JUSTIFIED RIGHT.
```

Fig. 4.9. Printing in columns
(a) Program—data division

219

and then printed out line by line. The Data Division is shown in Fig. 4.9(a).

NROW and NCOL are to be used as subscripts for row and column, with maximum values of 50 and 4, respectively. PAGE-FORM is a table of 50 rows and 4 columns, the cells of which are called NOMEN. Note that it is a large table, of 30 × 200 = 6000 characters.

```
PROCEDURE DIVISION.
OPENUP.
    OPEN INPUT INFILE, OUTPUT OUTFILE.
ALPHA.
    MOVE 1 TO NCOL.
BETA.
    MOVE 1 TO NROW.
FILLUPTABLE.
    READ INFILE AT END GO TO FINISH.
    MOVE INREC TO NOMEN (NROW, NCOL).
    IF NROW LESS THAN 50 ADD 1 TO NROW,
        GO TO FILLUP-TABLE.
    IF NCOL LESS THAN 4 ADD 1 TO NCOL, GO TO BETA.
WRITE-PAGE.
    MOVE SPACES TO PAGE-FORM.
    MOVE NOMEN (1, 1) TO FIRST-NAME.
    MOVE HEADER TO PLINE.
    WRITE PLINE AFTER NEW-PAGE.
    MOVE SPACES TO PLINE.
    WRITE PLINE AFTER 1.
    MOVE ZERO TO NROW.
    PERFORM PRINTOUT 50 TIMES.
    GO TO ALPHA.
FINISH.
    MOVE ZERO TO NROW.
    PERFORM PRINTOUT 50 TIMES.
    STOP RUN.
PRINTOUT.
    ADD 1 TO NROW.
    MOVE ROW (NROW) TO PLINE.
    WRITE PLINE AFTER 1.
```

Fig. 4.9. (b) Program—procedure

HEADER is a record which is put at the head of each page; the first name on each page, **NOMEN (1,1)**, is printed at the extreme right (**JUSTIFIED RIGHT**), as a guide to the user. It is also a handy device for controlling the move to a new page!

In the Procedure Division, Fig. 4.9(*b*), we read in names to fill up each column in turn. When the table is full, we move the first name to the header line, print it, clear the header line, and print a blank line after it. Then we start printing out the rows of the table, one complete **ROW** at a time. This is done 50 times.

When we have read in the last name from the file, we shall not have a complete page in the store, unless the number of names is an exact multiple of 200; we could have, say, two complete columns, one incomplete one, and one blank. We have to print these out when we reach **FINISH**, otherwise the listing will be incomplete. Since we have already cleared the whole page-area before printing from it (**MOVE SPACE TO PAGE-FORM**), we can safely assume that any cell to which we have not yet moved a name is blank, and so we can print out the lines exactly as before.

The elegant thing to do, of course, would be to rearrange the names on the last page so as to produce four columns of equal, or nearly equal, length. You might like to try your hand at this; and at other embellishments, such as printing out the last name on the page underneath **FIRST-NAME**, numbering the pages, and starting a new page (with, consequently, the previous page left incomplete) after each change in the initial of the surname. These processes are not all that easy, but you know enough COBOL now to do them, and they lie in the area where you have to find out for yourself how to do things.

Example 14. Layout in lines

We read in a number of records, each of which carries a date and a small number associated with that date, for example, the temperature at a given place. If we print these out one item to a line, the output will be bulky, difficult to handle, and wasteful of paper:

MARCH
1 12
2 14
3 12
4 13

and so on. A much better layout would be *across* the page;

DATE	1	2	3	4	5	6	.	.	.	.	.	.	30	31
MARCH	12	14	12	13	.	.	.	.					14	15
APRIL	14	15	17	14	.	.	.	.					.	. .
MAY	16	16	19	20	.	.	.	.					.	. .

and so on. We shall get perhaps two years' readings on one page, whereas with one-item-per-line layout we would not get more than two months on a page.

We must assure ourselves that there is enough room on the line; at all costs we must avoid 'overflow', in which the most significant digit of an entry is covered up by the least significant digit of the entry on its left. We have 31 days, in each of which there can be a temperature of two digits (centigrade); we may also have to allow for minus temperatures. There ought also to be a space between each item, for legibility. This means four spaces per item, which is too much for a 120-position printer; in any case we want a little space at the left for Month. On the whole it is a fair bet that we shan't get a temperature less than -9, so we can cut ourselves down to three positions (space, sign or digit, digit) for each item, making 93 positions per line. If we do get temperatures below -9, all that will happen will be that the minus will occupy the space between the items. (Most manufacturers supply a 'Printer Layout Chart', which helps in designing formats like this.)

The input data will be something like:

```
DATA DIVISION.
FILE SECTION.
FD INFILE.
01 TEMPREC.
   03 INDATE.
      05 DAY PIC 99.
      05 MTH PIC 99.
      05 YR PIC 99.
   03 INTEMP PIC S99.
```

We can use the same output format for both the 'header' line, carrying the dates, and the **TEMP** lines carrying the month-name and the temperature for each day.

```
FD OUTFILE.
01 OUTREC.
   03 FILLER PIC X(5).
   03 LABEL-AREA PIC X(12).
   03 TEMP PIC – 99, OCCURS 31 TIMES.
   03 FILLER PIC X(10).
```

You will remember (perhaps) that – **9** means that a value, say, ' – **5**' will be printed as '(space) – **5**', while ' **+5**' will be printed as '**5**' preceded by two spaces, which is what we want (3.2.4).

First of all we will generate a line of dates, 1–31, for the header line:

```
MOVE ZERO TO N.
PERFORM DATEGEN 31 TIMES.
MOVE 'DATE' TO LABEL-AREA.
PERFORM PRINTOUT.
MOVE SPACES TO OUTREC.
. . . . . . . . . .
```

The **DATEGEN** paragraph, **PERFORM**ed 31 times, is:

```
DATEGEN.
   ADD 1 TO N.
   MOVE N TO TEMP (N).
```

The result is the printout of a line:

DATE 1 2 3 4 5 6 31

Note the interesting and satisfying use of N both as a data item for printout and as the subscript indicating its place in the printout. To make this introductory routine complete you should ensure that it starts at the head of a new page (see 4.5.1).

Now we begin to read in the data. We can assume that the records are in date order. As we read in each card, we transfer its **INTEMP** to **TEMP (DAY)** in the output format, **DAY** being taken from the input record. We have to count in the appropriate number of days for the month (28, 30, 31); there are various ingenious ways of doing this (for example, reading the correct value from a table store; using a **GO TO . . . DEPENDING ON MTH**, as in 3.4.5, where if **MTH = 1** we go to a routine which says '**MOVE 31 TO NO-OF-DAYS**' and then **PERFORM . . . NO-OF-DAYS TIMES**) but the simplest,

223

perhaps, is to read in each record and print out the printline when we detect a change of **MTH**.

We can print the month-name at the left of each line, using a three-letter form as in 3.5.6 (under **REDEFINES**); or we might use a fuller, more elegant form:

01 **MONTH-TABLE.**
   03 **MOIS-1 PIC X(12) VALUE IS 'JANUARY**   '.
   03 **MOIS-2 PIC X(12) VALUE IS 'FEBRUARY**   '.
   03 **MOIS-3 PIC X(12) VALUE IS 'MARCH**   '.
  . . . .
   03 **MOIS-12 PIC X(12) VALUE IS 'DECEMBER** '.
01 **MONAT REDEFINES MONTH-TABLE PIC X(12) OCCURS 12 TIMES.**

Now we can **MOVE MONAT (MTH) TO LABEL-AREA** before each print.

4.5.3   Group indicate

This is a process which greatly improves the readability of prints where there may be long sequences of entries which have some element in common. The element is printed once, on its first occurrence, and the field is left blank as long as there is no change in that element. For example, we may have a file whose 'major sort' is on **PLACE**, with a 'minor sort' on date, so that we might get sequences like:

```
NEWBURY     21.05.71  ........data........
NEWBURY     21.05.71  ........data........
NEWBURY     03.07.71  ........data........
NEWCASTLE   23.01.71  ........data........
NEWCASTLE   24.02.71
NEWCASTLE   24.02.71
NEWCASTLE   24.02.71
NEWPORT     18.04.71
```

which we print as:

NEWBURY	21.05.71	....
		....
	03.07.71	....
NEWCASTLE	23.01.71	....
	24.02.71	....
		....
		....
NEWPORT	18.04.71	....

—with Group-indicate on Place and date, and a space on change of Place. You could, of course, Group-indicate month and year, even where there is a change of day, if you wished.

There is not much to be said about this feature; it is usual to repeat all the data, whether there has been a change or not, at the head of a new page; if there is a change in the major field, the minor field is repeated, whether there has been a change or not (for example, if the date of the last entry for Newbury were the same as the first for Newcastle, the Newcastle date entry would be printed notwithstanding). The reader should be familiar enough with this type of routine: the basis is the Working-Storage siding into which we move the Serial or Place (or whatever field it is we wish to Group-indicate) from the first record. We compare it with the same field in the next record; if they are the same we move the second record to output and move spaces to the group-indicated field:

```
READIT.
   READ INFILE AT END GO TO FINISH.
   IF INPLACE EQUAL TO WPLACE MOVE SPACE TO
      INPLACE, GO TO WRITEIT.
   MOVE INPLACE TO WPLACE.
WRITEIT.
   MOVE INREC TO OUTREC.
   WRITE OUTREC AFTER 1.
   GO TO READIT.
```

where **WPLACE** is, of course, the 'siding'.

If we have two fields we wish to group-indicate, with the Date field minor to the Place (so that Date is always printed on change of Place), we can vary our strategy a little to achieve a neater program:

225

```
READIT.
    READ INFILE AT END GO TO FINISH.
    IF INPLACE NOT EQUAL TO WPLACE, MOVE INPLACE
        TO WPLACE, MOVE INDATE TO WDATE GO TO WRITEIT.
    MOVE SPACE TO INPLACE.
    IF INDATE NOT EQUAL TO WDATE, MOVE INDATE TO
        WDATE, GO TO WRITEIT.
    MOVE SPACE TO INDATE.
WRITEIT.
    MOVE INREC TO OUTREC.
    WRITE OUTREC AFTER 1.
    GO TO READIT.
```

And so on, for as many fields as you wish. Don't forget that you should repeat the whole record at the top of a new page (to be really clever, you could write **CONTINUED** there).

4.5.4 Page control

The change to a new page is generally determined by one of two factors: a logical change in the sequence of items—for example, when the date changes to a new year; and, failing that, a specified number of lines. If we did not have the latter, the print would be continuous, without any break at the perforation; if this is what you want (for example, for 'graphical' output, see 4.5.5) it is up to the operating staff to see that the perforation falls exactly between two lines so that no line is illegible. Often it is the custom of the house to print with a standard printer-tape which will move the printer to a new page at some fixed number of lines, say 50, so that the programmer only has to bother about his 'logical' changes. Of course there is often conflict between the logical and automatic changes; it is annoying when the automatic change gives you a new page after 50 lines, prints one line on the new page, and then finds a logical change which causes it to move to a new page—when one could easily have got the odd line on to the bottom of the first page. The programmer can attempt to avoid this sort of thing by programming both logical and line-controlled changes, but it can be extraordinarily difficult to handle—again, a case where the human, who can look ahead to see how near the logical change is, does better than the computer—and the be-

226

ginner is advised to put up with any inelegancies of this kind. The same sort of trouble can arise after 'change of control' in Tabulation: you get a blank line at the end of a sequence, print the first line of the next, and then the automatic change takes you to the top of the next page; it would have been so much neater to finish the page at the blank line. This is not so difficult to handle, but needs some care.

Sometimes it is just impossible to achieve the right logical result by processing each record as it comes in; the only solution is to set up the whole page as a table in store, and 'format' it before outputting any lines (cf. Printing in Columns, 4.5.2).

You should always precede your first **WRITE** order for the printer with a **NEW-PAGE**; this makes things easier for the operating staff. Make sure you don't carry out a **NEW-PAGE** when you write a new line—a rather easy thing to do. In modern printers the results are spectacular.

4.5.5 Graphical output

You have no doubt heard of 'graphical plotters' which can be attached to computers so as to present the output in graphical form (for example, as a set of lines or curves) instead of digital. You can achieve something of the same sort on an ordinary printer. You may, for example, have returns relating to each month of the year:

JAN	1405
FEB	1689
MAR	1787
APL	2034
MAY	2106
JUN	2099
JUL	1985
AUG	1743
SEP	1439
OCT	1200
NOV	1458
DEC	1690

The pattern—a rise until early summer, then a drop, and a recovery towards Christmas—can be more clearly shown by plotting these quantities as points on a graph. On a printer it can be done with a

227

horizontal layout, but a vertical layout like this much simpler and is not so restricted by the width of the paper:

		110	12	13	14	15	16	17	18	19	20	21	22
		·	·	·	·	·	·	·	·	·	·	·	·
JAN	1405				*								
FEB	1689							*					
MAR	1787								*				
APL	2034										*		
MAY	2106											*	
JUN	2099											*	
JUL	1985										*		
AUG	1743							*					
SEP	1439				*								
OCT	1200		*										
NOV	1458					*							
DEC	1690							*					

If you now join up the points, by hand, you have an acceptable graph. Points to note are:

(a) Print the lines in double spacing; otherwise you will find that graph points for adjacent entries, if widely separated horizontally, are liable to confusion.

(b) You are, of course, constrained by the width of the paper in that you have to scale the entries so as to fit in (even so this is easier than printing horizontally because quite often the number of entries is fixed, as here at 12, and you can't alter it). In this graph we have decided that the range we have to allow for is between 1000 and 2200, and this is represented by about 110 printer positions; so we scale the values accordingly. We shall see shortly how this is done.

(c) Remember that the representation of the value, as a distance along a line, is only very approximate and is restricted by the fact that you can only print at intervals of 0·1 inch in any case. So don't try to be too meticulously accurate; simplicity in scaling down and converting the value to a subscript is more important. In some cases, in order to achieve a simple scaling conversion, you may find it pays not to use the whole width of the paper. On the other hand, rather than allow for extreme values which would mean reducing the scale and squashing up the common values, one can allow a 'high zone' and a 'low zone' to accommodate the extreme values.

(*d*) With continuous stationery the graph can of course extend over more than one page, and this will be useful when there are a lot of entries, for example, several years to plot as above.

The basis of the program is that the output area is defined as a table with one cell corresponding to each print-position; here the table is 110 long:

FD OUTFILE.
01 OUTREC.
    03 MONAT PIC XXX.
    03 AMOUNT PIC ZZZZ9.
    03 FILLER PIC XX.
    03 GRAPH PIC X OCCURS 110 TIMES.

Since we have a range of 1100 values to fit into this—very conveniently!—we can allow one print position for a range of 10 values, that is, if we round off the last digit and divide by 10 for each value we shall reduce the 1100 values to a range of 110 in all. The lowest value will be 110 and the highest 219; value 110 goes in cell 1 of the table, value 219 in cell 110; so if we subtract 109 from the scaled value we shall get the subscript.

We assume that the figures are held in a 12-long table, **SCORE**, in Working-Storage, and the month-names are held in a similar table. The outline of the main routine is (with **RES** defined as **PIC 999** and **ASTERISK** as **PIC X, VALUE '*'**):

    MOVE ZERO TO MONTH.
    PERFORM PRINTOUT 12 TIMES.

    . . . .
PRINTOUT.
    ADD 1 TO MONTH.
    MOVE SPACE TO OUTREC.
    DIVIDE SCORE (MONTH) BY 10 GIVING RES ROUNDED.
    SUBTRACT 109 FROM RES.
    MOVE ASTERISK TO GRAPH (RES).
    MOVE MONTH-NAME (MONTH) TO MONAT.
    MOVE SCORE (MONTH) TO AMOUNT.
    WRITE OUTREC AFTER 2.

Example 15. Histograms

A variation on the graph is the *histogram*. This is often clearer, and it saves the manual joining up of points which is sometimes necessary to make a graph intelligible. Instead of printing a single point for a value, we print asterisks (or whatever symbol we choose) right up to that value:

```
JAN   1406   **********************
FEB   1689   *****************************
MAR   1787   *********************************
APL   2034   *****************************************
```

and so on. After clearing the table in output, we proceed as follows:

```
MOVE ZERO TO VAL.
FILLEMIN.
    ADD 1 TO VAL.
    MOVE ASTERISK TO POSITION(VAL).
    IF VAL EQUAL TO RES GO TO WRITEIT.
    GO TO FILLEMIN.
```

where **RES** is calculated as in the Graph program.

The histogram sometimes looks better if it is more solid:

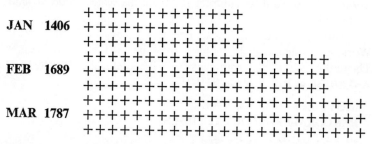

That is, each line is repeated three times. The modification is simple, as long as you remember that a **WRITE** may destroy the output area!

4.5.6 Other trimmings

It is literally true, as we have said before, that you can spend more time on the embellishment of the print than on the program itself.

You really have to watch yourself—you may write and test a perfectly acceptable and accurate program in a couple of days, then spend a week putting in headings, underlinings, thumb indexes, the lot—and find that the program produces blank output! It's happened to me.

However: we mentioned underlinings. These are best declared as literals, of the requisite length, in Working-Storage:

77 HEADERLINE PIC X(14) VALUE IS '_ _ _ _ _ _ _ _ _'.

will give us an underline for

MONTHLY RETURN

A hyphen does well enough for horizontal lines; some printers have a vertical stroke (used in some programming languages) which can be used for making up vertical lines. If you haven't got it you can use a 1, but vertical lining is a messy business and you are advised to indicate columns by full stops in the line.

We have already had an example of a heading with a fixed part and a variable part, in the Tabulator program, where ' **YEAR 19'** was followed immediately by the two digits of the year. It is possible to mix up literals and variables in the same line: if you want to print out a line like

COMPUTER-NAME KLUDGE, CORE SIZE 3 MILLION WORDS, CYCLE TIME 10 NANOSECONDS.

in a catalogue of computers, in which the entries **COMPUTER-NAME, CORE SIZE, WORDS, CYCLE TIME** and **NANO-SECONDS** are constant, you can write a Record Description:

01 CATALOGUE.
    03 COMP-NAME PIC X(14) VALUE IS 'COMPUTER-NAME'.
    03 C-NAME PIC X(10) VALUE IS SPACE JUSTIFIED RIGHT.
    03 CORE-SIZE PIC X(12) VALUE IS ', CORE SIZE'.
    03 C-SIZE PIC 999 VALUE IS ZERO.
    03 MILLORTHOU PIC X(9) VALUE IS SPACE JUSTIFIED RIGHT.
    03 WDSETC PIC X(19) VALUE IS ' WORDS, CYCLE TIME '.
    03 C-TIME PIC 999 VALUE IS ZERO.
    03 N-SECS PIC X(13) VALUE IS ' NANOSECONDS.'.
    03 FILLER PIC X(37).

231

Note how commas, spaces, etc., have been allotted in the literals. In Procedure, we move the variables to the appropriate slots, and then when we want to print we move the whole **CATALOGUE** record to output. To me, this sort of output always looks artificial and contrived; I prefer the constants used as headers, especially of course if there is a long list of items. It's simpler to program and easier to read. You can write the whole heading as a single literal (see 'The COBOL Coding Sheet', 4.7.2, for instructions on how to write 120-long literals).

The opportunities for wasting time on embellishment are endless, and you will soon find your own favourite gimmicks, so we won't spend any more time on the subject. If you want a bit of practice, try putting brackets round the **AMOUNT** in the Graph exercise: **JAN (1405)**, etc.

4.6 The blocks in the program

Before going on to deal with the practical aspects of getting a program ready for compilation, I will try to show that the routines or 'building blocks' described in this section, petty though they may seem, are in fact adequate for building up 'proper' programs, and such functions are, as I stated in the Introduction (4.1) the stuff from which such programs are made. To analyse a fully fledged applications program in detail would take far too long; I will briefly describe the sequence of processes in an invoicing and stock control program, and point to the routines which will be involved. I can only urge, as I have done before, that you should think all the time of the applications you are interested in and how you would use the routines to deal with them.

Orders received from the customer are 'coded', that is, a product number and customer number replace the literal form on the order. This will probably be done manually, but the *table look-up* could be used to facilitate this.

The coded versions are punched and verified. A *validation* program could be used to reinforce the checking.

The cards are *copied to magnetic tape*; a standard COBOL procedure, perhaps involving *blocking* of records; probably the Validation would be incorporated in this process.

232

The primary order file is now *sorted* to product-number order. It is *collated* with a Master Product File, which is in product-number order and for each product gives a description, price, discount rates, and present stock level. There are two outputs: an order-file which *combines the data* from the primary coded order file and the Master Product File, and a new Master Product File which has been *updated* by *subtracting* from the stock levels the amounts shown in the order file.

The new orders may cause stock levels to fall below re-order point; *a printout* (and possibly a tape record too) is made of such items, for re-ordering from the factory. Possibly some orders cannot be filled at once; until the re-ordering has been completed and the new stocks received this will be *noted* on the new order tape. When new stocks are received, the Master Product file must be *updated*.

The new order tape is now *sorted* to customer-coding sequence, and is run against a Master Customer File. This program takes full details of customer's name and address from the Master File, and uses these and the details from the order file to produce order/invoice documents. Where an order cannot be filled until stocks are replenished, a note to that effect is printed. We might have, at this stage, a *check* against the customer's credit rating or outstanding debit balance, to give an 'early warning' before goods are despatched.

At monthly intervals this order tape will be used to create and print statements to be sent to customers, and it may produce an up-to-date list of outstanding debts.

The order tape can also be used to help the sales manager and production controllers; the details required can be *abstracted* from it and the resultant file used in statistical analyses and breakdowns.

There is nothing in any of the processing which you should not now be able to do in COBOL, and most of it will involve, in some form, the routines dealt with in this Chapter 4. Where the complexity really arises is not in the programming but in the systems design: putting details of previously unfilled orders back in to the system is simple enough, but at what stage do you do it? If a large order, which necessitates re-ordering from the factory, is cancelled after the documents are produced, what steps are you going to take to put the files in order again? Once the systems analyst has decided what the programs are to do in such cases, the programmer will find, in all probability, that the 'standard routines' will do the job.

4.7 Practical Programming

4.7.1 The structure of the program

The invoice/stock control procedure briefly described in the pre-ceding section is really a 'suite' of programs; the output of one stage becomes the input of the next. Since there may have to be a time gap between certain stages, the processing cannot be continuous (although, with modern disc files, we may well find that the program is merely suspended during these time gaps; the data produced at intermediate stages will be stored on disc until the program resumes).

Each of the programs in the suite can be written as an independent COBOL program. Much of the data will be common to more than one program, and we may find the same data formats merely copied from one program to another (a good reason for standardisation). A COBOL module, **LIBRARY**, permits the automatic copying of segments of source program from a tape or disc, at compilation time, but the programmer can equally well use reproduced packs of cards. You will soon find by experience which routines and formats you use repeatedly, in the same form, and you will soon build up standard packs of cards or sections of tape which you incorporate wherever required. You will have to be careful with sequence numbers (see 4.7.2) but by a skilful use of the **PERFORM** you will find that you can insert such routines into your source program without violating the rules about sequencing.

In early stages you should not worry too much about the elegance of your program. If you find that you have written the same short routine twice, or the structure is so clumsy that the same test is carried out at two or more different points in the program, don't worry about it; you can spend hours reconstructing the program to save the odd branch or instruction, and it makes not a ha'porth of difference to the efficiency of the final version. At a later stage, how-ever, you will begin to find that a well-constructed program, with economical and symmetrical procedures, is less liable to contain errors, and that the errors are easier to trace if they do occur. The **PERFORM** verb is an invaluable aid in the construction of such programs; you can construct a framework consisting entirely of **PERFORM**s, with the routines following on in no particular order; for that matter, the routines themselves may consist of **PERFORM**s

234

for smaller routines! It also helps to think of a program as a succession of tests and processes (see 4.1, Classification by test and process). Such a structure can be quite clearly seen in the flow-chart for the Tabulation program, Fig. 4.4(c). The separation into tests, carried out by IFs, and processes, carried out by **PERFORM**s which are the consequents of the IFs, avoids the problems of change of sequence that arise from the nature of the COBOL **PERFORM**, and, to my mind, corresponds more closely to the basic nature of computer programs. However we must get back to practical programming.

4.7.2 The coding sheet

The standard coding sheet, on which the programmer writes his source program, is shown in Fig. 4.10. This sheet was designed for use with 80-column cards and you will invariably find that one card is punched for each line on which there is an entry. Each line is divided into *areas*:

Cols.

1-6	Sequence Number Area: otherwise Area L.
7	Continuation Area. Area C.
8-11	Area A.
12-72	Area B.
73-80	Area R.

The length of Area B and Area R may vary in different implementations; the arrangement above is the commonest. Area R is reserved for the programmer's own use, for identification or line numbers, etc., and is ignored by the compiler.

Headings for Divisions, Sections, and Paragraphs start in column 8 (actually, anywhere in Area A). Division and Section headings must have a line to themselves, and it is a good practice to keep paragraph headings on a line to themselves too, though it is permitted to start the first sentence on the same line as long as it starts in Area B, that is, in col. 12 or later. Sentences start in Area B and can be continued from one line to another merely by starting lines after the first in Area B—you can indent them if you like. On the whole, you will find it better to write one statement per line: it makes the program easier to follow and you don't have to repunch the cards if you want to

235

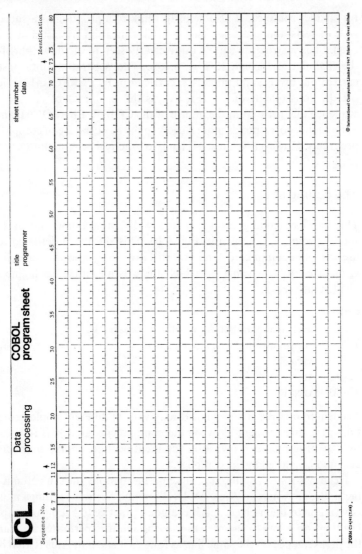

Fig. 4.10. The COBOL coding sheet

236

insert additional statements (putting in a paragraph name is a common amendment, when you find you want to jump to the middle of a previously continuous procedure). You should follow common sense, as I have tried to in this book: **IF**s, followed by a small routine, are the commonest cases of overflow from one line to another.

In the Data Division, you put the level indicators **FD** and **SD**, and the level numbers **01** and **77**, in Area A; the file-name, record-name, etc., begin in Area B. Other level numbers can follow the same pattern, or they can be indented any number of spaces to the right—there are plenty of examples in this book. Indentation does not affect the magnitude of a level number; it is purely for legibility.

Except in non-numeric literals (see below) blanks in a statement do not affect its meaning—a row of blanks is effectively the same as one (a single blank is sometimes mandatory; for example, before a parenthesis enclosing a subscript). You can have a whole line of blanks, to make the listing clearer by separating routines, data descriptions, etc., but such a line must have a sequence number. Because blanks don't count you can put **PIC**s and **FILLER**s, etc., at fixed places in the line in your source printout, which improves its appearance (see Fig. 2.6, Program BINGO). When you continue a sentence from one line to another, the compiler always assumes that there is a space between the last letter or digit on one line and the first letter or digit of the next, *unless* you put a hyphen in column 7, in which case these two characters are read as if there were no space between them (even if there are actually spaces). This is a source of confusion that is only necessary for one reason: when you have a *non-numeric literal* enclosed in quotes, every space in it on the form counts as an actual space. A non-numeric literal can be up to 120 characters long, and may thus spread over two or three lines. When it is necessary to continue from one line to another, put a hyphen in column 7 and a quote mark in column 12 (*not* at the end of the previous line); and put a quote at the end of the literal. Any blanks at the end of a line count in the literal; the continuation starts immediately after the quote on the continuation line.

Finally, the sequence number, which appears in columns 1–6 of every line. Implementors are left a good deal of freedom in the use of this (which they don't always pass on to the programmer!). Generally, you can either omit the sequence numbers altogether, or use them; if you do use them, there must be one on every card and they must be

237

in ascending order (the compiler will usually comment if they are out of order, but do nothing about it; no programmer can resist correcting the numbers, however). Most programmers follow some system in allocating numbers: for example,

numbers beginning 0 for Identification Division;
1 for Environment Division;
2 for Data Division, File Section;
3 for Data Division, Working-Storage section;
4 up to 9 for Procedure Division, with 9 reserved, perhaps, for Error Routines.

Your own installation may have standards; if not, the extent to which you standardise your numbering will depend on your use of standard routines, for example, routines which you can copy from one program to another by physically transferring or copying the cards. This sort of thing is left to your ingenuity. One word of advice, however: use the first three or four digit positions for your numbers, leaving positions 5 and 6 blank unless you really have to use them: for example,

417000 NEXT-STEP.
417100 MOVE SPACE TO NAMEPLACE.
417200 MOVE ZERO TO STREET-NUMBER.
417300 MOVE ADDRESS-RECORD TO OUTREC.
418000 WRITEIT.

and so on. If you have to insert another statement between **417100 and 417200**, say, call it **417110** or **417150**. If you use the last digit positions, you'll be surprised how often you want to put another statement between **417215** and **417216**!

4.7.3 Drafting the program

You will find that it is a waste of time to try to write your program straight away on to the coding sheets; you have to make so many amendments and insertions that it is impossible to keep up the standard of clarity and good writing that is essential if the source program is going to be punched correctly. Moreover, you may find yourself agreeing with one of the usual criticisms of COBOL, that is, that it is long-winded; the data name **SALARY-BEFORE-DE-DUCTIONS** is excellent in the finished program, for making the program clear to other people; it is an awful chore to write it in drafting. So you will probably find yourself inventing a COBOL shorthand for your own use, writing your first draft in terms such as

IF A = B M REC TO OUTREC GT Z

I don't think I need bother to explain this in detail!

Some attempts have been made to develop a standard COBOL shorthand, which could be punched as it stood and converted into full COBOL, expanding verbs and data-name abbreviations from a table, and perhaps doing simple checks at the same time.

.7.3.1 Checking

The beginner should not attempt to write complex programs; he may feel that he is wasting computer and punch time if he starts off with a 'trivial' program, but believe me not nearly as much as he will if he tries to write a program which he is not yet competent to write! Your first program, in particular, shouldn't be much more complex than program ALPHA, in Chapter 2: the important thing is to convince yourself that your instructions actually work, that they make the computer do what you want it to. The confidence that you are doing the right thing is an immense help—and you don't get it if you write a complex program that refuses to compile.

Where you can really save your own time and that of the data preparation and computer room people is in checking your program before sending it for punching (and, if your writing isn't too good, checking a proof print *after* punching). There must be *no* spelling mistakes, even in 'optional' words for example, **WRITE . . . AFTER ADVENCING 1 LINE** will be thrown out, even though **ADVAN-CING** is an optional word). Make sure that there are full stops where there should be, and not where they shouldn't:

IF A LESS THAN B PERFORM WRITEOUT
GO TO ENDIT.

means that you will not go to **ENDIT** if **A** is not less than **B**; if there

239

were a full stop after **WRITEOUT**, then you would go to **ENDIT** eventually whatever the result of the comparison of A and B.

> **JUMPOUT**
> **IF A LESS THAN B PERFORM WRITEOUT.**

will be rejected on compilation, since the paragraph name does not have a stop.

Check spaces and hyphens: **WORKING STORAGE** will not be accepted by the compiler, nor will **BERT(FRED)** (according to ANSI), where there is no space between the end of the data-name and the parenthesis at the left of the subscript (though some compilers will accept this). Add up the characters in record descriptions for printer output, and see that they add up to 120 or 132 or whatever it may be; otherwise the compiler will report a wrong record length. See that all your data-names, especially that ingenious little switch that you suddenly thought of to give you a **GO TO . . . DEPEND-ING ON . . .** are defined and described in the Data Division. Don't try to **WRITE** from Working-Storage areas, or **02** levels, or FDs; don't use reserved words as data-names or procedure-names ('**IF DATA EQUAL TO BLANK GO TO CONTROL**'). If you have defined a common numeral as a literal ('**77 ONE PIC 9 VALUE IS 1**') don't get carried away into writing **PERFORM ROUTINE FOUR TIMES**, unless you have defined **FOUR** in the Data Division.

A very valuable check is 'playing through', of which we have had several examples (the Sorting routine, in 4.2.5, Sequence-checking, 4.3.1, and Extracting Singles, 4.3.3). This is very useful in working out what is going to happen when you reach End-of-File, or with a complicated series of branches. One very common source of error is in the setting up of a loop, and the following section describes a 'loop-checking' table that will help to avoid mistakes.

4.7.4 Loop-checking

To carry out a procedure a specified number of times, the **PER-FORM . . . TIMES** is the simplest way. But this is not always convenient: a set of conditional statements in the **PERFORM**ed routine will need careful handling, with the use of the clumsy **EXIT** device (and remember that a **READ ... AT END ...** is a conditional statement); and your compiler may not have the **TIMES** option.

So in many cases, especially where you are only putting the routine at one point in the program, so that there is not much to be gained by using the **PERFORM** to save core space, it is just as easy to use the more elementary routine, in which we

Initialise the loop—for example, **MOVE 1 TO COUNTER.**

Process the data;

Increment the index or counter;

Test the counter to see if we have done the loop the required number of times—if not, return to the beginning; if yes, go to the next step.

For example, to carry out a **READ** 10 times, that is to, read 10 records:

MOVE 1 TO INDX.	—Initialise
START.	
READ INFILE AT END GO TO FINISH.	—Process
ADD 1 TO INDX.	—Increment
IF INDX NOT LESS THAN 11 GO	
TO START.	—Test and Branch
GO TO NEXT.	

But can you tell at once, by looking at this routine, that it will in fact carry out the process exactly 10 times? What would be the effect of testing for 10? Of incrementing *after* the Test? Of doing the Process last?

There are so many possible variations that such loops are one of the most frequent sources of error. Most people tend to adopt a standard form, but it's not always convenient, or logically possible, to stick to the same sequence in all cases. It seems worthwhile, therefore, to analyse this process in more detail so as to construct a form of table which will tell you at once whether your loop is valid, or how you should write the variables for one particular form of test.

The Initialising, of course, has to be done before anything else, and this can be done in Working-Storage, with a **VALUE**, though if you are going to use the routine more than once in the program you will have to use a **MOVE** in Procedure. After this, the Process, Increment, and Test can be carried out in six permutations:

241

1. Increment	Process	Test
2. Test	Increment	Process
3. Process	Test	Increment
4. Increment	Test	Process
5. Test	Process	Increment
6. Process	Increment	Test

The order in which these are done affects:

(*a*) the initial value to be given to the Index. In modes 1, 2, and 4, an increment is done before the process is carried out for the first time. If we are using the index as a *subscript* it must have value 1 (or at least the lowest actual value with which we want to start) on the first pass, so we initialise with zero. In the other cases, the process is done for the first time before the increment, so if we are using a subscript we must initialise with 1. If we are using the index merely as a counter, it doesn't matter whether we start with 0 or 1.

(*b*) the value of the index at which we jump out and go to the next process, that is, the value at which the loop is satisfied. If the process is to be carried out F times, then in some circumstances—where an increment is done between process and test—we shall jump out when the index is equal to $F + 1$; otherwise when it is equal to F. If Test comes after Process, we shall always do the loop at least once.

(*c*) the test itself is another variable. For any of the previous variables we can adopt at least some of the following forms:

IF COUNTER EQUAL TO (F or F + 1, etc.)
NOT EQUAL TO
GREATER THAN
NOT GREATER THAN
LESS THAN
NOT LESS THAN

(*d*) and, finally, the form of the action to be taken if the test is satisfied (the 'consequent') and if it is not.

..... **GO TO START. GO TO NEXT.**
or ..... **GO TO NEXT. GO TO START.**

where **START** is the beginning of the loop; so in the first case, if the answer to the test is **YES**, the loop is *not* satisfied and we make another pass; if the answer is **NO** the loop is satisfied and we go to the next process.

These variables give us a theoretical 240 forms for the loop. but not all of these are valid. Fig. 4.11 gives us a table of valid forms. It also allows for *decrementing*, where we start with the final value of the loop (**F**) and subtract 1.

Increments or decrements may be in steps of more than 1. The table works for these cases too as long as the number of times the loop is to be done is an exact multiple of the increment or decrement.

The table shows that the example given at the beginning of this section is in fact invalid. If we have **PROCESS INCREMENT TEST**, with Initial 1, and Final $F+1$ (11), then **NOT LESS THAN** requires **GO TO NEXT. GO TO START.**

Mode	Initial		Final	
Modify Process Test or Test Modify Process	0*	F	F	-
	1	F+1	F+1	F
	F*	1	-	1
Process Test Modify	0	F-1	F-1	-
	1*	F	F	-
	F*	1	-	1
Modify Test Process	0*	F+1	F+1	F
	1	F+2	F+2	F+1
	F	0	1	0
Test Process Modify or Process Modify Test	0	F	F	F-1
	1*	F+1	F+1	F
	F	0	1	0
	EQUAL TO	NOT LESS THAN	GREATER THAN	GO TO NEXT GO TO START
	NOT EQUAL TO	LESS THAN	NOT GREATER THAN	GO TO START GO TO NEXT

Fig. 4.11. The loop-checker

How to use the Table

'Modify' means either increment or decrement. Find which of the six permutations you are using, or want to use. Choose which of the three initial values (0 or 1, if incrementing; F, if decrementing) you want. If you are using the index as a subscript, only those initial values with an asterisk are valid.

The possible final values are shown in the three columns (' – ' means the form is invalid). The Test is shown at the foot of each column. If the Test is in the upper line (Equal to, Not Less than, Greater than) the Consequent to be used is **GO TO NEXT. GO TO START**. If it is in the lower line, the reverse is the case.

The table is not exhaustive. Some of the invalid forms can be got round by using a double test (**EQUAL TO OR NOT GREATER THAN**, etc.). It is possible to start loops with other values, particularly $F+1$, $F-1$, and so on. The table could be extended to include these, but this would make it too complicated.

4.7.5 Flow-charts and decision tables

Some people set great store by Flow-charts as an aid in planning and coding their programs, and for that reason we have used them liberally in this book. The beginner's programs should not be so complex as to require elaborate flow-charting, but there is no harm in drawing them. They are particularly useful as a check on the correctness of routines; if the routine is incorrectly written the flow-chart may have branches which end nowhere, or the two branches from a test going directly to the same process. A correct flow-chart *looks* better than an incorrect one; and polishing up your flow-chart so as to make it look more symmetrical and compact will often suggest ways of improving the routine. You only need two basic 'shapes', the diamond for decisions and the box for processes; you can, of course, add to these as you wish, but the two shapes with written captions are much more informative, and acceptable to management, than a string of esoteric symbols. You will often find that each box on a flow-chart corresponds to one COBOL sentence, which is why Systems Analysts often use COBOL as a specification language.

My own advice (though many would disagree) is: don't regard

flow-charts as compulsory. If you have got a clear idea what you want to do, you will quite often find that you can write the program and then *check* it with a flow-chart, if you want. If you have a long and difficult sequence of comparisons and decisions, you will find it best to draw up *decision tables* rather than flow charts. Decision tables are coming to be more and more popular with programmers (to the extent that proposals have been made for the direct conversion, by the computer, of decision tables to COBOL instructions); one reason is that you are not obliged to assume any particular sequence in which the tests are to be made, as you are with a flow-chart; and in a decision table the choices are presented in synoptic form, so that it is difficult to overlook any of the alternatives. You will probably find, too, that if the problem is laid out in the form of decision tables, discussion with the customer will be greatly simplified, because the decision tables may more nearly represent his way of thinking about the process than the artificially sequential method of the flow-chart.

4.7.6 Checking the completed program

The compiler itself analyses the program to see that it conforms to the formal rules for the language, as regards punctuation and 'syntax'; that the programmer has not used undefined data names, and so on. If it does find an error it will either make some 'reasonable' assumption and perhaps print out a reproof to the programmer, or it may ignore that statement, or it may stop the compilation, or both; in which case the cards, and a listing of the program and of the errors found by the compiler, will be returned to the programmer. Some programmers feel that this is a proper procedure; they don't waste their own valuable programming time by checking the program for formal errors; this is left to the computer, as all routine work should be.

When it is satisfied that the source program complies with the formal rules of the language, the compiler translates the source instructions into machine language, calls subroutines for incorporation into the program from a library tape (for example, input/output routines, mathematical functions, and any of the programmer's 'own' routines); assigns the absolute addresses of routines, indexes them against their mnemonic form, and puts them in program instructions (for example, after **GO TO**s); and it reserves and labels the data storage which the program requires.

4.7.6.1 Debugging

The object program is a translation into machine language of what the programmer actually asked for; before the program can be run operationally, on real data, the programmer must make sure that what he asked for, and got, is what he actually meant to ask for. It must be remembered that the source statements the programmer wrote are absolutely precise and specific in their meaning, within that implementation; there is no room for ambiguity or misinterpretation by the machine. The English words in COBOL are used much more precisely than the same words in conversation. The programmer can easily write a statement that would be correctly interpreted by an intelligent human, but is taken literally by the machine, by the use of a faculty which used to be known, unfairly, as its 'idiot resources'. As long as the statements do not violate the formal rules of the language, the compiler will accept them, and produce a program which incorporates them—in other words, if you tell the compiler to do something damned silly, it will do it, as long as it is legal (even if it is impossible it will do its best).

The programmer must therefore supply *test data* (a form of computerised play-through), covering, as far as possible, all the situations that the program is likely to cope with; and as far as possible the programmer should know what answer the computer should produce for this test data. Sometimes the presence of errors will be obvious, as for example when the computer produces no answer at all, but just sits there grinning, or pours out an unstoppable stream of gobbledegook; sometimes—much worse—the errors are such that they are not brought out by the test data, and only appear months later when the program is actually operational and is presented with data of a type not used in the testing stage: this may cast doubt, even, on all the work done up to that time. This is why an important program will be run 'in parallel' with the old program or manual system for weeks or months until it is thoroughly tested by comparison with the old system.

Such errors are known as *bugs*, and the detection and correction of

them is called debugging. In a difficult and complex program, debugging may take almost as long as writing the program itself. The
programmer may need to have 'dumps' of the store, that is, printouts,
more or less in machine language, of the contents of the store at
various points in the execution of the program which he can specify
in the program itself. There exist also 'diagnostic' machine routines to
help the programmer in his debugging, such as 'trace' programs, and
these are likely to become more powerful in future; we may even have
routines which will test a program without any data, that is, will
check that it is logically consistent and will not, for example, get into
a loop. It may be mentioned here also that COBOL provides facilities
for a 'restart', so that after some disaster, for example, a machine
breakdown or an unexpected fault in the program, we can return to
the *status quo* at a specified earlier point in the program, without
returning to the beginning and doing the whole job again.

The beginner's programs should not be so complex as to require
any elaborate diagnostic aids, nor so long-running as to require
restarts. He can use **DISPLAY**s at various points, to find the current
value of some index, for example; but such tricks, especially if
followed by **STOP**s, are likely to make him unpopular with operating
staff. The beginner should find that his errors are 'manifest', that is,
when he finds that the program doesn't run, a closer look at the
instructions and their actual meaning, perhaps a reference to the
COBOL manual issued by his manufacturer, should be sufficient to
pinpoint the errors.

4.7.7 Communicating with the computer

The **ACCEPT** and **DISPLAY** verbs (3.3.3) are useful in testing a
program, and can also simplify operational running by making it
possible to supply the computer with small amounts of information
which varies from time to time, perhaps with every run.

In testing, **DISPLAY** verbs can be used at strategic points to find
whether the current value of some variable is what it ought to be, for
example, to find whether a loop has been performed the specified
number of times. Such statements will be removed when the program
has been 'tested out' (an operational version of the program, omitting

247

such orders, will then be compiled). The use of such methods should be kept to a minimum.

In operational running, we might want to give the computer a latest-date to be used in a periodical updating run; a cumulative total brought forward from a previous run; a Hash Total supplied by the Data Preparation department or the customer, for comparison with the computer totals; the number of records to be read in for a particular run; and so on.

All of these types of information can, of course, be got in by reading a 'parameter' card, or, in the case of the cumulative total, storing the total for each run on a disc file and updating it after each run. All of such operations, however, require the operator to handle a pack of cards, to add a 'parameter' card, and to set up input devices which may not be used again by the program—operations quite out of proportion to the amount of information involved.

The **ACCEPT** statement is suitable for such small transfers of data. If I wish to read in a number of cards that varies with each run, I write in the program:

ACCEPT CARD-TOTAL.
PERFORM READEMIN CARD-TOTAL TIMES.

We can also change the processing sequence:

ACCEPT PROCEDURE-NUMBER.
GO TO ALPHA, OMEGA DEPENDING ON PROCEDURE-NUMBER.

Procedure-number, as put in, would be 1 or 2. You could use this method when there are alternative subroutines in the program, for example for metric and non-metric versions. The **ACCEPT** does not have to precede immediately the instruction in which it is used.

In some installations, you may be permitted or encouraged to insert a console message to the operator to indicate that your program has reached its proper end:

DISPLAY 'END OF BINGO. THANK YOU.'.

In other cases a **DISPLAY** can be used to give the operator the chance to take some action, generally in conjunction with a **STOP**:

IF INREC-TOTAL EQUAL TO ZERO DISPLAY 'NO RE-CORDS', STOP 25.

248

The operator will take the action specified by 'stop 25' in the instructions you have given him, for example, abandon the run and send the print-out, if any, and the 'log' entry from the console to you; or he may continue the run, which he does with non-COBOL action. If there is no **STOP** the program continues after printing the **DISPLAY** —it does not pause as it does after the **ACCEPT**.

4.7.8 If things go wrong

We have from time to time mentioned 'Error-routines', which you jump to, for example, if you get a **SIZE ERROR**. We will now consider briefly what such routines should be.

In the worst cases you will have to abandon the computer run. This may happen with a **SIZE ERROR**, for example; if the error occurs in computing some value which is to be used throughout the run, there is obviously no point in going on with it. All the subsequent results will be wrong. If it happens, however, in a program where you are operating on records independently of other records, for example, in a simple payroll program, it may be more economical to print out a **DISPLAY** on the typewriter reporting the **SIZE ERROR** and where it occurred, abandoning that record, and continuing with the run; the erring record will be corrected in a later run, or manually. Any cumulative results in the run will be wrong, of course. But if your program has been carefully tested and the input verified, a **SIZE ERROR** shouldn't happen, and if it does it's a sign there's something wrong; and in my view it casts doubt on the validity of the whole run. The routine should certainly include a **STOP**:

STOP 'SIZE ERROR IN RECNO' RECNO.

so that the operator can take some action.

In most other cases, if you put in a test and branch to an Error-routine, you will have foreseen that something can go wrong and you will know what to do. This will happen, for example, in Validation Runs, where you expect to find errors. You don't stop the run if you find one (if you find that the computer disagrees with a Hash Total, on the other hand, you probably would). If a record is found which does not agree with the validation rules, the whole record should be printed out. If you do this it is essential to include some sort of coding to indicate which type of error was the cause of the printout. For example, using the **PERSONNEL-RECORD** given as an example in Chapter 3, Fig. 3.1(*b*), we might get a printout:

SHUTTLWEORTH JOHN JAMES 31 OCT 1490 DM 2303

The customer will correct the spelling of **SHUTTLEWORTH** (not understanding that this is one error the computer *won't* spot) and put the record in again; and it will be thrown out again. Then he may see that **1490** is clearly wrong (**?1940**); put this right; and then find the record still rejected. Finally he may see that M and D, for Sex and Marital Status, have been reversed. At the third attempt the record will be accepted, unless indeed the computer has thrown it out because the Personnel Number is duplicated with another record.

Another lesson of this example is that if you find an error you should if possible continue to scan up to the end of the record. If the program had printed **ERROR DOB**, the **DOB** would have been corrected, but the invalid **D** under Sex would have caused the record to be thrown out again. Also if a mistake is found by a process which compares records, all of the affected records should be printed out.

However, fascinating though this subject is, it is taking us away from COBOL.

4.7.9 Documentation

Your own installation will almost certainly have quite elaborate rules about what is needed, in addition to the program itself, before it can be run, or at least run regularly. You will have to agree with the customer and with the data-preparation staff on how the data is to be presented and punched. You will have to agree with operations staff on frequency of running, speed of turn-round; you will have to tell them what the input files are called and what they are to call the output files, where they are to be stored and for how long; who is to receive the printouts; what the operator is to do if specific messages come up, indicating errors or various points in the program where he must take some action; he must be told what 'control cards', in addition to the simple data, will be required.

You may be required to issue a 'Program Description' or some such document, containing the above information and also a narrative account of the strategy and function of the program, with flow-charts. One object of this is to make it easier for someone else to modify your program, if necessary, when you have moved on to the better job you will certainly be qualified for if you have read this far. In fact, a smallish, not very important program won't get modified by someone else: the new programmer will almost certainly prefer to rewrite rather than try to reproduce the idiotic logic of the original programmer. Here, of course, your narrative will help. But you may want to modify the program yourself, and it is easy to forget what the various data-names stood for, in a few months. So you should include a 'glossary' of data-names, even if you have used what appear to be self-explanatory forms in your final version of the program.

There is a COBOL verb **NOTE**, which is called a compiler directing verb (the compiler ignores everything in the sentence after **NOTE**, unless **NOTE** is the first word after the paragraph name, in which case it ignores the whole paragraph; the **NOTE** is printed out in the source program listing). The **NOTE** is supposed to be a free-flow (that is, unformatted) explanation of the coding in the paragraph or section or section or sentence to which it refers:

NOTE: THIS PARAGRAPH COMPARES THE VALUE OF INCOME IN THE INPUT RECORDS WITH THE ITEM 'ALLOWABLE-INCOME' IN WORKING-STORAGE. IF INCOME IS EQUAL OR GREATER A BRANCH IS MADE TO SURTAX-ROUTINE.....

If you have a good narrative, I don't think these **NOTE**s are of much value. You will generally find that the opening paragraphs of a program are conscientiously sprinkled with **NOTE**s, but they fade out after the middle of the program!

NOTE and the text that goes with it is written in Area B. It can contain any characters which can be punched or printed in your installation.

To sum up: documentation is a bore, but it takes so little time in comparison with the program itself, and it pays off in so many ways, that you will never regret it.

4.8 Conclusion

You should by now have a good practical working knowledge of how to write programs in general. You will still have to rely on your own computer people for help in writing the COBOL and non-COBOL statements necessary to get your programs to run on a particular computer; but as far as the specification of the data and procedures go, you should be able to manage on your own.

You may like, at this stage, to see how the COBOL you have learnt fits in with the rest of COBOL.

4.8.1 The ANSI modules of COBOL

ANSI COBOL defines eight modules, each of which has two levels, except Table Handling which has three. They are:

The **NUCLEUS**, which 'provides a basic language capability for the internal processing of data within the basic structure of the four divisions of a program'. You now have at least a nodding acquaintance with all the elements of Nucleus Level 1, though there are a good many subtleties which I have omitted for reasons I explained in the introduction. The features not mentioned at all are:

In the Environment Division, the **SPECIAL-NAMES** paragraph, which provides a means of relating implementor-names to specified mnemonic-names—this provides for such things as console switches which can be set to control the program; a way of specifying the **CURRENCY-SIGN** (£, $, etc.); and a facility, for continental users, to specify that the comma is to be used for the decimal point.

In the Data Division, the **SYNCHRONISED** clause, which provides a way of aligning numerical items with word boundaries in the machine so as to provide optimum processing speed.

In the Procedure Division, the Class Condition, which tests whether an operand is alphabetic or numeric; the **ALTER** statement, which modifies the sequence of operations (in my view, it has no advantage over **GO TO . , DEPENDING ON . .**); **ENTER** makes it possible to insert chunks of another language in a COBOL program: **ENTER PLAN . . .** and when you want to return to COBOL, **ENTER COBOL.** Those who have knowledge of another language will have no difficulty with it; those who haven't will have no use for it.

252

EXAMINE is a complicated verb which replaces or counts the occurrence of a given character in a data item. It works rather like the Space-Count program (Chapter 3, Example 5) but is a good deal less flexible.

The **TABLE HANDLING** module 'provides a capability for defining tables of contiguous data items and accessing an item relative to its position in the table'. In Level 1 there is an Indexing facility which is an alternative to subscripting.

The **SEQUENTIAL ACCESS** module includes, in the Environment Division, entries for **MULTIPLE REEL** or **UNIT** and **FILE LIMITS** in the File-Control Section, and **RERUN** and **SAME AREA** in **I-O–CONTROL**. None of these can or needs to be handled by a beginner. In the Procedure Division I have omitted discussion of the functions of the **OPEN** and **CLOSE**: the simple description is enough. In the **WRITE** statement I have not mentioned **WRITE . . . BEFORE . .** as an alternative to **WRITE . . . AFTER . . .**; you can work out for yourself the effect of this! Nor have I considered the instructions for handling mass storage files in sequential mode.

The **SORT** module and the **RANDOM ACCESS** module have briefly described, in sufficient detail I hope to enable you to use them according to the requirements of your own configuration.

The remaining modules are:

REPORT WRITER, which 'provides the facility for producing reports by specifying the physical appearance of the report rather than requiring specification of the detailed procedures necessary to produce that report'. A lot of the procedures used as illustrations in Chapter 4 will be found in Report Writer. It will be familiar to you if you have had anything to do with 'Report Generator' programs, or even the good old-fashioned tabulator.

SEGMENTATION enables you to specify object program overlay requirements, that is, if your program is too large to fit into core you can call segments of it in from tape or disc as they are required, and to 'overlay' parts of the program not being used, to be 'overlaid' in their turn.

LIBRARY has one verb, **COPY**. It enables you to copy source language statements from a library at compile time; they will be included in your program, at the point indicated by **COPY**, exactly as if they had been in the main program. Do not confuse this with **ENTER**, which allows the more sophisticated practice of including portions of programs written in another language, particularly Assembly language, in order to improve the efficiency of the program. **LIBRARY** merely incorporates well-used routines to save you the trouble of writing them again.

The essential minimum COBOL is Level 1 of Nucleus, Table Handling, and Sequential Access. Higher versions of COBOL can be formed by various combinations of modules and levels (it has been calculated that 2916 combinations are possible). It has been proposed in America to define a Federal standard COBOL, in three levels:

Level 1. The minimum defined above, plus Random Access 1 and Segmentation 1. This illustrates the way in which Random Access has increased in importance even since the ANSI report was published.

Level 2. Nucleus Level 2, Table Handling level 2, Random Access 2, Sort 1, Segmentation 2.

Level 3. The highest possible level of all modules.

As stated at the beginning, this book conforms by and large to the minimum COBOL, namely Level 1 of Nucleus, Table Handling, and Sequential Access. A few features of higher levels have been included: commas and semicolons have been freely used; the Sort and Two-Dimensional Tables have been introduced. You will almost certainly find that your compiler omits some of the features in this book, but on the other hand includes elements from higher levels. Every manufacturer, not unnaturally, tries to implement COBOL in the way that will make his machine behave, in COBOL, with maximum efficiency; there are still considerable ambiguities and room for different interpretations in the ANSI specifications; and his compiler may, in any case, have been written before the ANSI standard was published. In spite of all this, COBOL has achieved an admirable degree of standardisation, if we take into account the fact that it is almost certainly the most widely used programming language. The divergences are meat and drink to the experts, but the beginner will have little trouble with them. In Appendix 1 you will find a short account of the history of COBOL, and of the way it has developed and is still developing—for COBOL is not static. The beginner need have no fear, however, that the COBOL he has learnt will become obsolete. Any changes that are likely to take place, in addition to those aimed at improving standardisation and clarity of definition, will be aimed mainly at the extension of COBOL into the spheres of Communications Processing, debugging, operating system interaction (permitting the dynamic allocation of store and peripherals), data file management, Floating Point facilities (for mathematical work), default options (which will reduce the programmer's work because if he doesn't specify some feature the compiler will supply a 'standard' value), a standard shorthand and syntax checker, and a Decision Table interpreter.

4.8.2 A last word of advice

If you haven't written any programs yet, then if you do keep them *simple*; this will give you confidence and help you much more than struggling with a complicated and difficult program will. You will find a lot of gaps to be filled in—for example, the rules for **MOVE**ing and comparing fields of different modes and sizes—but tackle these as you come to them: don't try to learn the rules from the manual, because you may never need them. If you don't intend to write programs, then I hope this book will at least have been of interest for its own sake—it must have been, if you have got this far—and that what you have read will help you to understand the limitations and potential of your computer and its programmers.

Appendix 1

The history, development and standardisation of COBOL

COBOL began with a meeting on 8 April 1959, at the University of Pennsylvania, of a small group of computer people representing users, manufacturers, and universities. They decided that it was feasible to develop specifications for a problem-oriented, but machine-independent, common language for business problems, and asked the US Department of Defence, as one of the agencies principally interested in such a language, to sponsor the first meeting to organise the project.

Later in the year the task was assigned to committees reporting to CODASYL(Conference on Data Systems Languages), a voluntary independent group of users and manufacturers. Various existing languages for commercial data processing were studied. From September a small group of six people were at work on the draft specification; it was then that the name COBOL was adopted. The draft specification was distributed on 17 December 1959. To us, nowadays, such speed seems almost unbelievable. Their work bore fruit in the publication of an official report by the Government Printing Office in April 1960, entitled *COBOL—Report to Conference on Data Processing Systems Language, Including Initial Specifications for a Common Business Oriented Language (COBOL) for Programming Electronic Digital Computers*. The language described in the Report has since become known as COBOL-60.

It was recognised that the publication of a specification, to be implemented by manufacturers, was not the end of the story. Committees were set up by CODASYL with the object of maintaining, improving, and extending the language. Various versions of the language (COBOL 61, COBOL 61 Extended, etc.) were brought out. The latest is COBOL 65, but the *CODASYL COBOL Journal of Development* has been established to publish official specifications and changes.

CODASYL is responsible for the maintenance of COBOL and the adoption of developments. The design of a Standard COBOL is in

256

the hands of the American National Standards Institute (ANSI), which is a voluntary and privately supported body and is the US member of the International Standardisation Organisation (ISO). This body has had since 1960 a US Standards Committee on Computers and Information Processing, called X3, sponsored by BEMA (Business Equipment Manufacturers Association). In 1962 it set up a 'Task Group', X3.4.4, for Processor Documentation and COBOL. It decided to define a standard which would be a subset of CODASYL COBOL; the result of its labours was the publication in August 1968 of *USASI* X3.23 – 1968: *Standard COBOL*, which is taken as standard COBOL for the purposes of this book. The 1968 standard includes all modifications to COBOL 65 accepted by CODASYL up to 1 January 1967.

The main authority for COBOL in CODASYL is now the Programming Language Subcommittee. It is possible that this committee may accept clarifications and extensions that cause the existing ANSI Standard to become inconsistent with the COBOL set forth in CODASYL's *COBOL Journal of Development*.

Appendix 2

Reserved words in ANSI COBOL

The following is the complete ANSI list

ACCEPT
ACCESS
ACTUAL
ADD
ADDRESS
ADVANCING
AFTER
ALL
ALPHABETIC
ALTER
ALTERNATE
AND
ARE
AREA, AREAS
ASCENDING
ASSIGN
AT
AUTHOR
BEFORE
BEGINNING
BLANK
BLOCK
BY
CF
CH
CHARACTERS
CLOCK-UNITS
CLOSE
COBOL
CODE
COLUMN
COMMA
COMP
COMPUTATIONAL
COMPUTER
CONFIGURATION
CONTAINS
CONTROL, CONTROLS

COPY
CORR
CORRESPONDING
CURRENCY
DATA
DATE-COMPILED
DATE-WRITTEN
DE
DECIMAL-POINT
DECLARATIVES
DEPENDING
DESCENDING
DETAIL
DISPLAY
DIVIDE
DIVISION
DOWN
ELSE
END
ENDING
ENTER
ENVIRONMENT
EQUAL
ERROR
EVERY
EXAMINE
EXIT
FD
FILE-CONTROL
FILE-LIMIT,-S
FILLER
FINAL
FIRST
FOOTING
FOR
FROM
GENERATE
GIVING

GO
GREATER
GROUP
HEADING
HIGH-VALUE,-S
I-O
I-O-CONTROL
IDENTIFICATION
IF
IN
INDEX,-ED
INDICATE
INITIATE
INPUT
INPUT-OUTPUT
INSTALLATION
INTO
INVALID
IS
JUST
JUSTIFIED
KEY,-S
LABEL
LAST
LEADING
LEFT
LESS
LIMIT,-S
LINE,-S
LINE-COUNTER
LOOK
LOW-VALUE,-S
MEMORY
MODE
MODULES
MOVE
MULTIPLE
MULTIPLY
NEGATIVE
NEXT
NO
NOT
NOTE
NUMBER
NUMERIC
OBJECT-COMPUTER

OCCURS
OF
OFF
OMITTED
ON
OPEN
OPTIONAL
OR
OUTPUT
PAGE
PAGE-COUNTER
PERFORM
PF
PH
PIC
PICTURE
PLUS
POSITION
POSITIVE
PROCEDURE
PROCEED
PROCESSING
PROGRAM-ID
QUOTE,-S
RANDOM
RD
READ
RECORD,-S
REDEFINES
REEL
RELEASE
REMARKS
RENAMES
REPLACE
REPORT,-S
REPORTING
RERUN
RESERVE
RESET
RETURN
REVERSED
REWIND
RF
RH
RIGHT
ROUNDED

RUN
SAME
SD
SEARCH
SECTION
SECURITY
SEEK
SEGMENT-LIMIT
SELECT
SENTENCE
SEQUENTIAL
SET
SIGN
SIZE
SORT
SOURCE
SOURCE-COMPUTER
SPACE,-S
SPECIAL-NAMES
STANDARD
STATUS
STOP
SUBTRACT
SUM
SYNC

SYNCHRONIZED
TALLY,-ING
TAPE
TERMINATE
THAN
THROUGH, THRU
TIMES
TO
TYPE
UNIT
UNTIL
UP
UPON
USAGE
USE
USING
VALUE,-S
VARYING
WHEN
WITH
WORDS
WORKING-STORAGE
WRITE
ZERO,-S,-ES

Index